Luso-American Literatures and Cultures Today

Spring 2019

Tagus Press
Center for Portuguese Studies and Culture
University of Massachusetts Dartmouth
Portuguese Literary & Cultural Studies (PLCS) 32

EDITORS
Mario Pereira, Executive Editor
Anna M. Klobucka, Co-Editor
Isabel P. B. Fêo Rodrigues, Co-Editor

EDITORIAL BOARD
Ana Paula Ferreira (University of Minnesota)
Cristiana Bastos (Universidade de Lisboa)
Fernando Arenas (University of Michigan)

ADVISORY BOARD
Vítor Manuel de Aguiar e Silva (Universidade do Minho)
Gonzalo Aguilar (Universidad de Buenos Aires)
Luiz Felipe de Alencastro (Université Paris–Sorbonne)
Maria Aparecida Ferreira de Andrade Salgueiro
    (Universidade do Estado do Rio de Janeiro)
Vincenzo Arsillo (Università di Venezia)
Dário Borim (University of Massachusetts Dartmouth)
Flávio Carneiro (Universidade do Estado do Rio de Janeiro)
Bruno Carvalho (Princeton University)
Alda Costa (Universidade Eduardo Mondlane)
Patricio Ferrari (Rutgers University–Newark)
Memory Holloway (University of Massachusetts Dartmouth)
Kenneth David Jackson (Yale University)
Johannes Kretschmer (Universidade Federal Fluminense)
Christopher Larkosh (University of Massachusetts Dartmouth)
Alexander Luz (Universidade Federal Rural do Rio de Janeiro)
Nataniel Ngomane (Universidade Eduardo Mondlane)

Horst Nitschack (Universidad de Chile)
Marcus Vinicius Nogueira Soares (Universidade do Estado do Rio de Janeiro)
Carlinda Fragale Pate Nuñez (Universidade do Estado do Rio de Janeiro)
Rita Olivieri-Godet (Université Rennes II)
Carmen Villarino Pardo (Universidad de Santiago de Compostela)
Rodrigo Petrônio (Poet, Essayist—FAAP— Fundação Armando Álvares Penteado)
Isabel Pires de Lima (Universidade do Porto)
Jerónimo Pizarro (Universidad de los Andes)
Andrea Portolomeos (Universidade Federal de Lavras–MG)
Valdir Prigol (Universidade Federal da Fronteira Sul)
Roberto Acizelo Quelha de Sousa (Universidade do Estado do Rio de Janeiro)
Sonia Netto Salomão Sapienza (Università di Roma)
Nelson Schapochinik (Universidade de São Paulo)
Kathleen Sheldon (University of California Los Angeles)
Boaventura de Sousa Santos (Universidade de Coimbra)
Carlos Mendes de Sousa (Universidade do Minho)
Maria de Sousa Tavares (Universidade de Macau)
Alva Martínez Teixeiro (Universidade de Lisboa)
José Leonardo Tonus (Université Paris–Sorbonne)
Sandra Guardini Teixeira Vasconcelos (Universidade de São Paulo)
Jobst Welge (Stockholms Universitet)
Valquíria Wey (Universidad Nacional Autônoma do México)
Regina Zilberman (Pontifícia Universidade Católica do Rio Grande do Sul)

EDITORIAL ASSISTANT
Maggie L. N. Felisberto (University of Massachusetts Dartmouth)

PREVIOUS ISSUES

Fronteiras/Borders (PLCS 1)
    Edited by Victor J. Mendes, Paulo de Medeiros, and José N. Ornelas
Lídia Jorge in other words / por outras palavras (PLCS 2)
    Edited by Cláudia Pazos Alonso
Pessoa's Alberto Caeiro (PLCS 3)
    Edited by Victor J. Mendes
2001 Brazil: A Revisionary History of Brazilian Literature and Culture (PLCS 4/5)
    Edited by João Cezar de Castro Rocha
On Saramago (PLCS 6)
    Edited by Anna Klobucka
A Repertoire of Contemporary Portuguese Poetry (PLCS 7)
    Edited by Victor K. Mendes
Cape Verde: Language, Literature & Music (PLCS 8)
    Edited by Ana Mafalda Leite
Post-Imperial Camões (PLCS 9)
    Edited by João R. Figueiredo
Reevaluating Mozambique (PLCS 10)
    Edited by Phillip Rothwell
Vitorino Nemésio and the Azores (PLCS 11)
    Edited by Francisco Cota Fagundes
The Other Nineteenth Century (PLCS 12)
    Edited by Kathryn M. Sanchez
The Author as Plagiarist—The Case of Machado de Assis (PLCS 13/14)
    Edited by João Cezar de Castro Rocha
Remembering Angola (PLCS 15/16)
    Edited by Phillip Rothwell
Parts of Asia (PLCS 17/18)
    Edited by Cristiana Bastos
Facts and Fictions of António Lobo Antunes (PLCS 19/20)
    Edited by Victor K. Mendes
Garrett's Travels Revisited (PLCS 21/22)
    Edited by Victor K. Mendes and Valéria M. Souza
Economies of Relation: Money and Personalism in the Lusophone World (PLCS 23/24)
    Edited by Roger Sansi
Lusofonia and Its Futures (PLCS 25)
    Edited by João Cezar de Castro Rocha
Literary Histories in Portuguese (PLCS 26)
    Edited by João Cezar de Castro Rocha
The South Atlantic, Past and Present (PLCS 27)
    Edited by Luiz Felipe de Alencastro
Fernando Pessoa as English Reader and Writer (PLCS 28)
    Edited by Patricio Ferrari & Jerónimo Pizarro
The Eighteenth Century (PLCS 29)
    Edited by Bruno Carvalho
Transnational Africas: Visual, Material and Sonic Cultures of Lusophone Africa (PLCS 30/31)
    Edited by Christopher Larkosh, Mario Pereira & Memory Holloway

Portuguese Literary & Cultural Studies (PLCS) is an interdisciplinary, peer-reviewed hybrid online and print journal that publishes original research related to the literatures and cultures of the diverse communities of the Portuguese-speaking world from a broad range of academic, critical and theoretical approaches. PLCS is published semi-annually by Tagus Press in the Center for Portuguese Studies and Culture at the University of Massachusetts Dartmouth.

Manuscript Policy

Portuguese Literary & Cultural Studies welcomes submission of original and unpublished manuscripts in English or Portuguese appropriate to the goals of the journal. Manuscripts should be between 6,000–8,500 words in length and must be accompanied by an abstract. Manuscripts should be in accordance with the *MLA Style Manual and Guide to Scholarly Publishing* (latest version) or *The Chicago Manual of Style* (latest version) with parenthetical documentation and a list of works cited. The author is responsible for the accuracy of all quotations, titles, names, and dates. Manuscripts should be double-spaced throughout. All of the information must be in the same language (e.g., abstract, body of the article, bio-blurb). Updated guidelines are available at https://ojs.lib.umassd.edu/index.php/plcs/index. PLCS encourages submission of manuscripts in the form of a single attached MS Word document. Please send submissions to Mario Pereira, Executive Editor, at mpereira6@umassd.edu.

Portuguese Literary & Cultural Studies 32

Luso-American Literatures and Cultures Today

Edited by Christopher Larkosh
with Emanuel da Silva,
Maggie L.N. Felisberto and Jo-Anne S. Ferreira

Tagus Press
UMass Dartmouth
Dartmouth, Massachusetts

Portuguese Literary and Cultural Studies 32
Center for Portuguese Studies and Culture/Tagus Press
University of Massachusetts Dartmouth
© 2019 The University of Massachusetts Dartmouth
All rights reserved
Manufactured in the United States of America
Designed by Richard Hendel
Cover design & typesetting by Inês Sena

For all inquiries, please contact:
Center for Portuguese Studies and Culture/ Tagus Press
University of Massachusetts Dartmouth
285 Old Westport Road
North Dartmouth MA 02747–2300
Tel. 508–999–8255
Fax 508–999–9272
www.portstudies.umassd.edu
Tagus Press is the publishing arm of the
Center for Portuguese Studies and Culture at
the University of Massachusetts Dartmouth.
Center Director: Victor K. Mendes

Cover Image: As malassadeiras, photo by Christopher Larkosh.
Rhode Island and Massachusetts, Spring 2018.

ISSN: 1521-804X
ISBN: 978-1-933227-88-7 (pbk.: alk. paper)
ISBN: 978-1-933227-XX-X (Ebook)

Library of Congress Control Number: 2019940357

5 4 3 2 1

Contents

Luso-American Literatures and Cultures Today

Introduction: "Say It Right":
　On Luso-American Literatures and Cultures Today　1
　CHRISTOPHER LARKOSH

Voicing the Community, or a Voice for the Community:
　Katherine Vaz, a Portuguese American Writer　26
　CARMEN RAMOS VILLAR

Trans-Atlantic Imbalances:
　Indexicality, Translingual Signs, and Power in the Portuguese
　"Global Nation"　50
　DANIEL F. SILVA

Being Portuguese in Montreal: Cultural and Traditional
　Practices as Markers of the Community's Identity　75
　FABIO SCETTI

Angolamania: Affective Bonds with Angola in the Music
　of the Cabo Verdean Diaspora　95
　BENJAMIN LEGG

Judeotropicalism[1]: Jewish Transculturations in the Lusophone New World　115
　BONNIE S. WASSERMAN

Box Art, Food Science, and Portuguese Protestants:
　An Interview with Katherine Vaz　134
　MAGGIE L. N. FELISBERTO

Ten Questions for Jarita Davis　144
　CHRISTOPHER LARKOSH

Poetry & Fiction

Three Poems 153
> BOBBY MARTINEZ

Four Poems 158
> MILLICENT BORGES ACCARDI

The Teacher 165
> ANTÓNIO LADEIRA

Five Poems 173
> IRENE MARQUES

An Imagined Encounter 179
> ANGELA FERREIRA

Forum

Descolonizando os Estudos Luso-Afro-Brasileiros:
Uns passos concretos 187
> CHRISTOPHER LARKOSH

Realidade dos alunos negros na universidade brasileira 188
> DAMARES BARBOSA

Racismo: Incitação ao Discurso e Economia do Conhecimento em Certas Geografias da Diáspora Africana 193
> PATRICIA SCHOR

Afro-descendência, nova categoria politica e novo espaço do activismo anti-racista negro? 201
> MAMADOU BA

Precarity in and through Black Bodies:
A Response from a Transnational Perspective 206
> SELINA MAKANA

Review

Maggie L. N. Felisberto on The Work of Millicent Borges Accardi 213

Luso-American Literatures and Cultures Today

CHRISTOPHER LARKOSH

Introduction: "Say It Right": On Luso-American Literatures and Cultures Today

> From my hands I could give you something that I made
> From my mouth I could sing you another brick that I laid
> From my body I could show you a place God knows (only God knows)
> You should know this space is holy
> Do you really wanna go? (Two, three, four...)
> —Nelly Furtado, "Say It Right"

On Listening to Nelly Furtado on WJFD 97.3 FM (And Thinking Seriously About Lusodiasporic Cultural Explorations)

One of the most enduring characteristics of Portuguese-American life, particularly here in southeastern New England, has been that of having a broad selection of local Portuguese-language media to choose from: local cable television networks like The Portuguese Channel, bilingual newspapers like O Jornal or The Portuguese Times, or the growing number of examples of internet media, from participating in bilingual exchanges on social media to watching locally-made amateur videos on YouTube.

Despite the ever-expanding access to a wide range of Portuguese-language books, cultural materials and media in diaspora communities, it may seem somewhat behind the times to admit that perhaps most important among these media offerings for me and many other Portuguese speakers in my region remains an analog local radio station, WJFD 97.3 FM in New Bedford, with its powerful 50,000-watt signal that can reach the majority of Portuguese speakers in the region, from the North Shore of Boston to the outer Cape and Islands to much of Worcester County and the eastern edges of Connecticut. Its eclectic mix of Portuguese-language programming combines news from RTP Antena[1] Açores with community programming from interviews to call-in shows, Portuguese soccer matches, advertising in Portuguese and Cabo Verdean Creole for local businesses, and, as always, a wide range of music from the Portuguese-speaking world and beyond. In fact, sometimes when asked how I would define the borders of the part of southeastern New England that I call home, I have often responded by saying it is anywhere that I can turn on my car radio and listen to WJFD. Like so many others in this region, Portuguese-English bilingualism is as American as hot dogs and apple pie, or as the by now all-American Portuguese feast would counter, linguiça and malassadas; after all, our local Lusodiasporic cultures would no doubt be unrecognizable for so many of us if they did not maintain this continually alternating kind of cultural multiplicity.

So while it is not all that common that a song popular in the mainstream commercial media is also played on WJFD, there have been notable moments of overlap and crossover. For me at least, none is more emblematic in this way than the international hit song "Say It Right" by the Portuguese-Canadian singer Nelly Furtado, a song played so frequently on the air around the same time that I was hired to teach Portuguese-American literature and culture at UMass Dartmouth in 2007 that it came to symbolize that moment of translating myself, professionally and literally, back into Portuguese once again.

This recognition of Nelly Furtado as a virtually all-encompassing cultural icon should come as no surprise for teachers of Portuguese in North America, whether to heritage students or others, given that she is so often cited as somehow representative of the twenty-first century Lusophone diaspora, whether it is in Portuguese language textbooks as just one among numerous other well-known cultural figures, or in exhibits in museums alongside personalities of other ethnic backgrounds to underscore the cultural diversity of North American societies. I recall seeing a two-dimensional poster board cut out of Nelly Furtado in a provincial history museum in Victoria, British Columbia, the city where she grew up (even if such references as an exemplary representative of her community seldom engage with her music or other forms of creativity directly, much less in-depth). She is, of course, also celebrated on the Azorean island of São Miguel where, as she herself maintains, all of her lineage can be traced back centuries not only in the Azores, but also in mainland Portugal, where she was honored with the Order of Prince Henry the Navigator for her service to Portuguese culture in the diaspora (Blayer & Pacheco 2015).

What is encouraging, if not outright ironic, about this official embrace of Nelly Furtado as a recurrent representative example of ethnic identity (even if it may well be an overly simplistic understanding of cultural identity as largely ethnically determined, one that she has clearly never been exclusively committed to) is that not only is she far from being a traditional folkloric or fado singer, much less a emblematic cultural navigator or explorer, she also does not make a particular point of singing in Portuguese (although she has done so on occasion, be it the refrain to the Euro 2004 anthem "Força," or her own version of the song "Sozinho" by the Brazilian MPB icon Caetano Veloso). Furtado has always explored a wide range of musical genres and collaborated with a wide range of artists, all while collapsing the often arbitrary cultural distinctions between them: from other featured North American pop icons like Timbaland and Justin Timberlake to their Latin counterparts like Colombian pop sensation Juanes ("Fotografía," 2009) and the Mexican La Mala Rodríguez ("Bajo otra luz," 2010). Even in her own songs and solo videos, she has incorporated Mexican "Día de los Muertos" imagery into her visual aesthetic ("Waiting for the Night," 2013).

It is in this way that Nelly Furtado, both as pop cultural fugure and real-life artist, can be seen as continuing to rebel against any number of definitions, especially in terms of ethnic category or musical genre, unless, of course, if it is in the broadest terms possible, such as that of world music, as she collaborates with figures from a number of different musical styles and ethnic backgrounds, apparently more concerned with breaking the limits of musical categories than observing or obeying them. After what is now practically a two-decade career in the international spotlight, the words from her first single "Like a Bird"—the one through which her fans came to know her and for which she was awarded a Grammy—still ring true to some extent, ones so familiar at this point that they probably need no repeated quotation here: "I'm like a bird, I only fly away. I don't know where my home is. I don't know where my soul is." Or one might even ask whether this affirmation of cultural homelessness or continual migration is not in fact a kind of home in and of itself. Yes, Lusodiasporic cultures, regardless of what we call them, have always been something like this: somewhere along a line of flight, a set of uncertain places in/between, but no less a place that one can still inhabit, even without knowing exactly where we are at any given moment, or even who "you," "I" or "we" are in any certain and immutable terms.

This is not to say that Nelly Furtado's contemporary approach to music, her artistic persona, or 'sex appeal' are as appreciated in more conservative sectors of the Portuguese-American cultural landscape as they have been by other audiences. One cannot deny the potentially controversial move of performing a song with a title or lyric like those of the song "Promiscuous," no matter how ironically the lyrics and its message might be interpreted, especially in the cultural context of a still firmly entrenched traditional culture of gender norms, one in which many Portuguese-American women to this day still don't have the option of dating more than one guy (or gal, for that matter) without the very real possibility of being shamed by their families and friends.

Much of this resilience to adversity that Furtado sings of, however, is far from being merely some sort of self-absorbed response to the demands and vicissitudes of her own international stardom or reception from increasingly conservative mainstream audiences. To interpret a song like "The Spirit Indestructible" (2012), it might be important to be aware, whether as a listener or as a critic, that it was inspired by her visits to small and remote villages in Africa and contact with the realities of everyday human life there. To be fair, that is something that a good number of Western music critics, to say nothing of academic specialists in African cultures—Portuguese or North American, Lusophone or otherwise—have not taken as much time and effort to incorporate into their own lived experience as Nelly Furtado has.

While her work as an artist, musician, lyricist and performer may currently be subject to the volatility of a consumer market in a prolonged state of disruption caused largely by new reproduction and distribution technologies, her most recent album *The Ride*, released in March 2017, apparently sold only 1,814 copies in the first few days after it was released in the US. Such numbers are always relative, however; I imagine that most of my academic and literary counterparts would be overjoyed to sell 1,814 copies of one of their books over the course of their entire careers. Admittedly, it does not help matters when artistic vision and commitments are deemed less important than bottom-line sales and profit considerations, especially by massive media outlets like iHeart Radio (not coincidentally, the same sort of corporate conglomerate that, with the help of federal communications deregulation, threatens the range and long-term survival of local independent radio stations like WJFD).

The short promotional film that Furtado made to publicize the release of "The Ride" seems to point out at least two things: 1) how committed she is to being true to her own artistic vision, while 2) how relatively uninterested she appears to be in using the usual teasers to promote or sell herself to her potential audience in traditional ways. Instead, just to give one example, she recurs to black-and-white, *cinéma vérité*-style filmed conversations with other women, in which she expresses what artistic freedom means to her, not by speaking directly into a camera or being interviewed in the glossy, commercial way so favored by the entertainment industry and its promotion teams. In this overwhelming context of promotional conformity, one of the most moving tracks on the album, "Phoenix," still seems to speak to the idea that it is not only artists who play with fire; moreover, as they pass through it, they may find themselves rebuilding themselves emotionally, not once, but continually. In the end, this commitment to creativity just might end up bringing new life to an increasingly unforgiving environment, not just for the artist herself, but for all those in need of inspiration in community, or who simply need a sign of life in others to remain true to their own creative vision as well.

Ultimately, what some of us, even those of us who claim to focus on such things, may not have been sensitive enough to acknowledge, is that both her music and the messages it divulges, both in the more immediate community and beyond, are not just those of some superficial pop star, but at least for those who have taken the time and effort to listen and interpret them, from that critical space both beyond the limits of authorial intentionality and still within the range of possibility and good faith, they invariably become something new, if not something entirely different.

From this renewed critical perspective, they are those of an uncompromising and authentic musical and mixed-media artist, whose songs consistently challenge conventional norms and the notions of cultural propriety, something that in and of itself could well be considered the most critical of engagements with community:

> It is clear and documented that the current problems facing our youth with regards to education are ideological and systemic. There are also socio-economic barriers. However, I believe that there is an old guard in our culture that we need to intentionally and consciously shake up.
>
> As a youth, I was lucky to adopt a personal identity that I was "pan-ethnic", that made me feel connected to many other first-generation peers beyond the Portuguese community alone. This saved me, as I never felt like I was only Portuguese, or only Canadian. I felt like I was part of a new and improved identity that belonged to the broader world, and this was key for me in finding my own voice.
>
> Growing up, I visited my own Catholic Church community, but I was also open-minded about exploring other religions, identities and cultures, including Buddhism, Hinduism, Presbyterianism, Spiritualism, Taoism, Sufism, and beyond. I refused to believe that being Portuguese just meant being Catholic, or that being Portuguese just meant being heterosexual or that being Portuguese just meant belonging to a "traditional family" or a "traditional lifestyle."

> Throughout my life, I have chosen not to pigeonhole myself into the boxes and labels of my Portuguese-Canadian culture. Let's remember that a stifled Portuguese culture was imported to Canada and left to ferment at a time when Portugal itself was undergoing revolution and real change.
>
> Overall, let's admit that our Portuguese culture sometimes still prescribes to the old-world fear of being outcast for being different. Our culture does not always honour individuality. Our culture still suffers from extreme gender bias. All of these ills can create a poverty of the mind for young people that is excruciatingly difficult to overcome.
>
> We need to push past generalizations about our culture for the sake of our youth. We should not be limited by religion, gender, sexuality, race, or lifestyle. Our doors need to be wide open for opportunity. Inflexible viewpoints on how to be a "real Portuguese" will only limit us in our achievements. We should focus on what makes us unique and revel in what I believe is our true nature - unbridled creativity, adventure, passion and inventiveness! These are the ingredients of a truly potent and rich sense of identity - not an identity limited by the categories of antiquity. (Furtado, in Blayer & Pacheco 2015).

Who could the author of these ideas on cultural identity possibly be? Are they of an academic specialist in migration and ethnic history with an advanced degree, a tenured university professor of literature, or a renowned novelist or literary/cultural critic? No, these too are the words of Nelly Furtado, offered to her transnational diasporic listeners after revisiting Portugal and receiving yet another honor from her country of ancestral origin.

So ultimately, who really is the most far reaching, audible and immediately identifiable (if not firmly entrenched and canonical) among Lusodiasporic voices today, whether on the radio or elsewhere? With so many of the arbitrary distinctions between high and low culture swept away long ago (this age of authoritarian reconsolidation notwithstanding), and with even our own Portuguese language megastation WJFD undergoing its own set of recent challenges to its geographic limits of transmission,[1] these may be the years that we look back on as those of an intensity, brilliance, originality and diversity impossible to repeat or return to, much like the ones invoked in Nelly Furtado's 2001 hit "On the Radio (Remember the Days)"?

It might quite possibly be only then, in a future that looks back on this present, albeit one already transformed into a irrevocably lost past, that we will be fully able to hear Furtado's musical lyrics as literary as any other literature, to say nothing of her cultural viewpoints, just as incisive and necessary as those of our most sophisticated cultural theorists. Hopefully we as a community will one day arrive at a more appreciative place from which to view her multifaceted contributions, with not just her globally broadcast visual and sonic image, but also the thoughts behind them, deemed as worthy of consideration as those of any other philosopher or transcultural explorer of the Lusophone diaspora.

Ultimately, all that remains for us as Luso-American cultural workers is to incorporate these words into our research and writing, and then perhaps, like Furtado herself, to encourage others to be true to one's own cultural vision; that, in the end, is what it might mean, more than anything else, to "say it right," if not necessarily to "say it all."

Our Disparate (Yet Confluent) Luso-Diasporic Moments

So what does it really mean for us, as scholars in contemporary Luso-American literary and cultural studies, to back up Furtado's lead vocal, and with our own voices, also "say it right"? What we propose in this issue is to offer a variety of possible answers to that question, not with a presumably unified vision of culture led by a set of well-known voices, much less by relying on the same cultural models, approaches and methodologies that others have turned to in order to identify and interpret in any definitive or all-encompassing way, or to determine what is considered truly significant for one and all in what remains an admittedly diverse set of diasporic cultural communities.

Whether in southeastern New England, a quickly expanding global metropolis like Toronto, a Caribbean island nation like Trinidad and Tobago, or elsewhere in this far-flung Lusodiasporic archipelago (the San Joaquin Valley of California, the Big Island of Hawai'i?), living between Portuguese, Cabo Verdean and indigenous or other locally represented cultures remains an indisputable fact of life, with its transnational implications ever more complicated, especially when juxtaposed alongside other European immigrant and indigenous cultural traditions; the particularities of North Atlantic archipelagos, as well as Brazilian, Cabo Verdean and other African diaspora communities; cultural elements from Spain, Latin America and the Caribbean where European languages are spoken alongside Papiamentu and other Creole languages to further complicate the picture. One need only reference the longstanding presence of Cabo Verdeans alongside Azoreans and Madeirans, or the more recent arrival of Spanish-speaking and Mayan-language Central Americans who have joined the Portuguese on Acushnet Avenue in the North End of New Bedford, to find nearby examples of this ever-expanding transnational context.

One might find countless other instances in the culturally diverse cities of Western Europe, East Asia, or southern Africa, where Lusophone cultural heritage is cut and configured differently according to the enduring presence of indigenous and African cultures, as well as the continual flux of contemporary postcolonial transmigrations and other demographic shifts. It is, however, against this comparative global and transnational backdrop that understanding cultural identity becomes increasingly possible and necessary, in order to gauge the depth of potential intercultural communication as this increasingly interconnected environment for literary and cultural production continues to develop.

Any number of authors might point us in the direction of this Lusodiasporic perspective that has never been, and can never be, anything other than fundamentally transnational: whether from established canonical voices, to lesser-known or more obscure historical, literary and cultural figures. Here in southeastern New England, one by-now recognized example of this perspective can be found in the work of Portuguese-American poet and novelist Frank X. Gaspar, whose work seems to be in continual search of ways to escape the ethnic *cul-de-sac*, even as he probes its most intimate depths. In his novel *Leaving Pico*, this cultural counterpoint might be best personified by the gay men from New York City who come to his still largely Portuguese-American Provincetown to spend the summer together, and in so doing, leave behind used books that eventually come to assist in providing his Portuguese-American characters with alternatives to the more traditional or culturally specific ways of understanding their own cultural identity, above all those that rely on continued identification with Portuguese maritime explorers from the so-called Age of Discoveries.

Nonetheless, such historical identifications naturally have their limits: not only in the amount of understanding they can impart on the historical realities of cultural encounter between Portuguese explorers and other peoples and communities in the Early Modern World, but also in the limits of the relevance of such navigational exploits and imagined discoveries of usually already inhabited lands to our own present-day understandings of cultural identification, as we attempt to navigate a much more complex set of transnational reference points, to say nothing of the always possible yet often unexpected discoveries of others we might encounter (and perhaps even come to identify with?) along the way.

Perhaps we find those moments in Gaspar's collections of poetry like *A Field Guide to the Heavens* and *Night of a Thousand Blossoms*, where the cultural commonplaces, his "paper routes," are juxtaposed alongside his travel experiences in East Asia during the Vietnam War, his readings of poetry and prose outside the Portuguese, US and Western canons, and his contemplation of constellations, the stars above and their lines of imaginary connection, both to each other and to us, one that might even lift us up and give us greater meaning in the process (Larkosh 2011).[2]

Other points of departure, however, may offer equally illustrative examples; one that stands out from recent literary production is the Portuguese-Canadian author Erika de Vasconcelos, whose two well-known novels also deftly and provocatively combine Portuguese cultural elements in English with those from other cultures and languages. Her best-known book, *My Darling Dead Ones*, was so successful that it was later translated into Portuguese; it not only revisits the memories of women from the main character Fiona's family who are gone but not forgotten, but also integrates poetic voices in French from her childhood in Montreal, thus creating one of the most concrete and practical incorporations, however unintentional and uncommon, of Canada's official French-English bilingualism into that Portuguese-Canadian literature written primarily in English. Like most if not all Anglophone Canadian literature, it departs from the assumption that the language it uses to articulate a tradition or identity is somehow common or representative of all those within that national grouping, but the fact that French speakers using their own official language can also claim to be Canadian and thus be writing Canadian literature even when it cannot be considered part of the same literary tradition as that written in English, might make those distinction of identity and community that separate Portuguese-American, Portuguese-Canadian and Portuguese-Caribbean literature seem minimal in comparison.

For my part, I remember that after reading the novel, I found these pages fascinating, and ended up asking de Vasconcelos about them at an academic conference. Apparently she didn't find my curious question all that pertinent to her work, probably because it was the kind of question many academics like me are prone to have, one that focuses on a particular detail, sees meaning in it, an important point of concentration that might contribute to a broader discussion. But then again, this is often the kind of comment or question that authors can come to resent, as it means that the reader has read and understands something about the work that was not necessarily understood by the author in the same way, and thus something that may not be intended to be understood a certain way. Who knows why my curious questions from a U. S. American about how she expressed being Canadian through this particular use of language seemed almost out of place. Then again, why should it matter or not that the reading a novel by another reader might allow the novel to mean something different, something new, something more?

Such considerations are important for those who continue to read and see things in the works of others, and in the work of de Vasconcelos, I too continue to reread and see new things. Her second novel from 2001, *Between the Stillness and the Grove*, incorporates an even more complex transnational premise, that of an Armenian immigrant in Portugal in the early 90s, the years following the end of Soviet Communism and the Nagorno-Karabakh War, and provokes even more curious questions about Lusodiasporic writing as fundamentally and immutably transnational writing. While this transnational connection between Portugal, Canada and Armenia may at first glance be considered a rarity, might it not be in fact de Vasconcelos' own lived perspective on language and cultural transit between Montreal, Toronto and Lisbon that makes such transnational narratives not only possible, but natural, basic, obvious, even unavoidable? Maybe that is why my question to her on the transnational elements in her writing seemed so uninteresting to her. And if that is the case, perhaps it was within the realm of reason not to give it much thought, much less offer a response to it.

And yet, against the complex and varied fabric of narrative and transnational reference that de Vasconcelos has undoubtedly succeeded in weaving in this novel, how to reconcile the fact that in recent years she has reportedly set aside her literary aspirations to more practical ambitions as a Toronto real estate agent? Here a whole new set of irrepressible, curious, if not overtly impertinent questions arise: What led de Vasconcelos to make such a definitive break with the literary world? Was it just a simple question of sales, or of promotion and marketing? Was some sort of formal statistical analysis done—in the downtown office of a Toronto publisher, no doubt—conclusively showing that, say, her work was considered to be too Portuguese for mainstream audiences, or not Portuguese enough for Portuguese-Canadian audiences? At any rate, this real (e)state of things, at least as we perceive it, continues to intervene in culture, in ways increasingly difficult to grasp. Even if one might wish only success to the influential agents and brokers of our cultural reality, success is always predicated on a shifting set of terms and conditions, and there might well be nothing about this pragmatic recognition of the role of material necessities in the making of what we call success that could be said to make more sense, above all in today's economic and political context.

The vicissitudes of acceptance and artistic freedom, security and precarity, exemplary and not-so-exemplary behavior both within and outside the community, are far from being common and recurrent themes in Luso-American literatures and cultures alone; one need only compare these first two books by de Vasconcelos to those of her Portuguese-Canadian counterpart Anthony De Sa to recognize how the second novel is all too often the repository of what is suppressed or elided in favor of the closer-to-home themes of the semi-autobiographical memoir that brings their work to the attention of their ethnic community. While de Sa's first book from 2008, the collection of short stories titled *Barnacle Love*, appears overall to take a more traditionally nostalgic approach to Toronto's Little Portugal neighborhood, his 2013 novel *Kicking the Sky*, based on his short story "Shoeshine Boy," included in *Barnacle Love*, seems to expand upon its themes of sex and murder, religion and corruption that have also preoccupied other ethnic communities, above all in the riskier moments of their migratory journey, perhaps as inescapably so as those many of us consider to be more familiar (B. Davis, 2013).

Moreover, what authors, academics and cultural agents experience today as economic precarity, lack of recognition, pushing the envelope, or all of the above, cannot but allow for comparison with historical and contemporary figures from a wide range of literary traditions. One that comes to mind, especially as we continue to construct this transnational Lusodiasporic perspective on literature and culture, is the Luso-Trinidadian author Alfred Mendes, whose first two novels from the mid-1930s, *Pitch Lake* and *Black Fauns*, established him as one of the most recognized West Indian authors of his generation. At this point, however, what may prove to be even more transformational than a rereading of his best known work on its own is the renewed cultural and historical context to it provided by literary scholar Michèle Levy, who has edited and finally published his autobiography as well as three collections of his short stories and more, many of which approach the topic of mixed-race relationships between people in one of the most ethnically diverse societies in the Americas, if not the world—to be fair, with a dedication to speaking of race and racial difference that many contemporary Lusodiasporic authors still have not developed to the same degree.

In her introduction, Levy provides valuable biographical information not only in order to understand the lesser-known collected works of short fiction in connection to the numerous causes for his precarious existence as a writer, but to also showcase the longstanding friendship that Mendes had with other Trinidadian cultural figures; not just Albert Gomes, the editor of the journal *The Beacon* where Mendes published many of his short stories in the 1930s, but most notably his intellectual dialogue with the man considered to be the West Indian intellectual *par excellence*: the Afro-Trinidadian novelist, historian and social critic C. L. R. James, author of *The Black Jacobins*, the classic history of the Haitian Revolution; *Beyond a Boundary*, perhaps the definitive book on cricket, social stratification and racism; and the equally influential *History of Pan-African Revolt*, the book that, especially when its updated editions and reprints are taken into account, seals his reputation as a leading figure in the Black and pan-African movements of the mid-twentieth century.

Seen in the shadow of this more prolific and influential intellectual contemporary, one can only wonder what Mendes' literary legacy would be if he had found a way to balance more equitably his undeniable literary gifts with the material demands placed upon him; even so, Levy's critical contribution of reintroducing and publishing both his autobiography and collected short stories does much to reposition Mendes as a significant point of reference on the kind of expanded Lusodiasporic literary map we are charting here, and leads us to ask about the kinds of conversations this expanded comparative approach to literary studies could resume at this point with other ethnic literatures, and not just those of European origin, but perhaps more importantly with African-American literature, Asian-American, and US Latina/o/x literatures: especially on the precarity that continues to characterize our literary and cultural lives, as well as the enduring importance of questions such as ethnic identity, racialization and class consciousness in movements for political, social and cultural change.

Our Current Issue

It is out of this increasingly interconnected transnational and global context that this latest issue of PLCS, with its topic of Luso-American Literatures and Cultures Today, now emerges. After so much has been published in the field of Luso-American literature and culture at Tagus Press, especially in the Portuguese in the Americas series, I am happy to be able to edit the first issue of PLCS—an internationally recognized academic journal based at a public university situated at the center of one of North America's largest Portuguese-speaking communities—dedicated to Portuguese-American and other Lusodiasporic literatures and cultures.

And now that the time has finally come for such an issue, it is a transnational approach that prevails, drawing on materials not only from communities of Portuguese origin in our local region or elsewhere in the US, but also the cultural production of Cabo Verdean or Brazilian migrant communities who often came to live alongside them, as well as those Portuguese communities who settled in Canada and the Caribbean.

Our clearly stated objective was that this was to be an issue on newness, diversity and difference, on those marginalized and unexpected elements hidden both within and just outside of that which might already appear conventional, normative and familiar. Despite the fact that the field all-too-often remains dominated by the usual interpretations of familiar themes (e.g., family, arrival, the old neighborhood) from we might call the hard core of Portuguese-American writing—i. e., autobiographical memoirs all written by Portuguese-Americans, most of them men—we were still able to attract submissions that highlight the new directions featured here.

So it is at times: what might be considered the most immediate of our cultural concerns, whether in the sense of being local, evident, or urgent, are all-too-often precisely those that established modes of academic research and scholarship has often ended up either neglecting, or even ignoring altogether. But, as this issue demonstrates, there is room for change.[3]

The idea of a transnational approach to Luso-American culture that encompasses not only the US and Canada but also the Caribbean was developed largely during a lecture visit I made while I was serving as Director of Tagus Press in January of 2017, after a Trinidadian friend of mine now working in the Cayman Islands, Steve Ali, provided me with contacts and suggested that I get in touch with University of the West Indies senior lecturer and linguist Jo-Anne Ferreira. I did, and she invited me to give a talk there on contemporary Goan women's literature in English. I donated some of our publications to their university library on behalf of our press and university, and mentioned that I was about to edit an issue on PLCS on Luso-American Literatures and Cultures Today. When asked by PLCS Co-Editor Mario Pereira to invite outside guest editors, Jo-Anne, with her seminal study on the Portuguese in Trinidad and Tobago about to go into reprinting, was a natural choice.

I wanted to choose someone from Canada as well, someone who not only knew the scene, but also was able to synthesize critically what was new and dynamic in Portuguese-Canadian cultures and bring it into a productive conversation with what is going on here south of the border. I remembered Emanuel da Silva from conferences in Toronto, then a recent PhD working at the cutting-edge Ontario Institute for Studies in Education, and asked him to participate as well. Unfortunately, however, tragic personal circumstances in his family ultimately came to limit his eventual involvement in the project. This loss experienced by a colleague, far greater than the mere loss of an article or any co-editor's participation in an academic journal, served to remind us nonetheless that what is most important in these projects is not always our level of academic achievement or professional engagement, intellectual brilliance or practical commitment, but our deceptively simple capacity to affirm our own all-too-human vulnerability and fragility in the company of others. Luckily I was also able to count on my capable collaborator Maggie Felisberto, a PhD candidate in Luso-Afro-Brazilian Studies and Theory at UMass Dartmouth, editorial assistant at Tagus Press, and a Luso-American author in her own right. Her work in the final stages of this project, especially in the sections for reviews and short fiction, has done much to provide an even more diverse and inclusive perspective to our topic. It is with this fundamental sense of compassion, grounded in the spirit of our own shared humanity and community across cultural, ethnic and political borders, that we present this issue of PLCS 32.

The issue's contents were chosen with the main criterion in mind of how they provoke a discussion on the current challenges to Luso-American literatures and cultures. As a fitting lead article to this issue, Carmen Ramos Villar not only provides an incisive study and analysis of the work of one of Portuguese-American Literature's best-known authors, the novelist and nonfiction writer Katherine Vaz, but also offers a renewed and more comprehensive narrative of both literary and critical activity in this ever-emergent literary discipline. Ramos Villar departs from an extensive overview of current anthologies and existing research to consider some of this literary tradition's most salient new directions as it continues to develop in nuance and complexity, characteristics that are articulated most visibly in Vaz's most recent fiction.

In contrast, Daniel Silva takes a more theoretical approach by discussing the recurring questions of global Lusodiasporic cultural subjectivity by way of the concept of the translingual sign; he engages an impressively multifaceted and theoretically complex methodological model, one that combines a wide range of intellectual approaches, from linguistics and literary cultural theory to points of reference from twentieth-century intellectual history that include points as disparate as Gramscian political theory, Russian formalism, Lacanian psychoanalysis, and perhaps most importantly, examples of material culture such as Espírito Santo festivals and ceramic statuettes of the Galo de Barcelos found in homes and public spaces throughout the Portuguese speaking world.

Naturally, sociological concerns still come into play here; Fabio Scetti's article on the Portuguese community in Montreal explores both its historical origins and current cultural manifestations such as popular festivals and personal testimonies of cultural identity, set within concentric or overlapping political, cultural and linguistic contexts: the officially French-speaking political entity called Quebec that enjoys an exceptional, perhaps even exemplary degree of cultural autonomy in comparison with other Canadian provinces and within the broader context of an officially bilingual and multicultural Canada, and one whose points of reference are relevant far beyond any single ethnic enclave, as other recent research on multidirectionality in Quebec literature and culture has shown (Larkosh 2017).

Clearly, reaching out beyond the boundaries of any one ethnic community is essential to this volume if it to be considered to be providing a new methodological paradigm. Ben Legg's innovative study of transcultural affinities between the Cabo Verdean diaspora of southeastern New England and recent trends from the vibrant Angolan music scene encourage a reconsideration of how cultural identities can never be imagined as static objects, but rather are subject to influx from directions that may come to challenge the very foundations of our understanding of cultural and ethnic identity. Furthermore, Legg's scholarly expertise combined with a deep familiarity of local iterations of a broad range of Lusophone cultures, despite his putative cultural status as an ethnic outsider to Luso-American identity, however broadly we may come to imagine it, ultimately compel us to revisit fundamental questions on the terms of Lusodiasporic cultural belonging in North America and beyond, be it local or transnational.

In the final analysis, literary and cultural critique at its best should always be an in-depth interrogation of a culture's myths of origin and belonging, not an unquestioning validation of them. Bonnie Wasserman's broad-ranging study of Portuguese Jewish presence in the New World is an emblematic example of this kind of destabilizing critique, upending the conventional and totalizing myths of origin away from official narratives of exploration and colonization under the signs and symbols of Roman Catholicism in order to restore a Luso-American historical narrative that has, in fact, always been subject to divergent understandings of belonging, belief, and cultural survival.

Also included in the volume is a forum discussion by recent participants in special events at UMass Dartmouth on the possibilities of decolonizing the field of Luso-Afro-Brazilian Studies, confronting anti-black racism, and recognizing the important role of students of color in the intellectual life of the public university. There are also two interviews with contemporary authors, the aforementioned Katherine Vaz and the emerging Cabo Verdean American poet and activist Jarita Davis. Poetry from Bobby Martinez, a Californian queer poet of Luso, Latino and Native American descent, is juxtaposed with poems from Portuguese American Millicent Borges Accardi, someone also recognized for her work in promoting community among contemporary Portuguese American authors. In addition, two authors also known for their work in academic settings contribute their creative work, which not surprisingly engages the challenges of teaching in the current confluence of often troubling political and institutional trends. Antonio's Ladeira's short story "O professor" from his recent collection *Os monociclistas* is a throught-provoking consideration of the effects of the Internet on literary creativity: when it is translated into English by a group of Portuguese-English translation students under the supervision of their teacher, it takes on yet another layer of meaning. Luso-Canadian poet and Toronto resident Irene Marques rounds out our selection with her unique perspective on living between literatures, languages and cultures.

To complete the volume is a short prose piece from a new voice in Luso-Canadian culture, Angela Ferreira, perhaps precisely the kind of work that tends to evade the often imperfect academic attempts at comprehensive categorization discussed earlier. This text is an experiment in semi-fictional narrative and stream of consciousness, one that incorporates both fictional imagination and actual lived experience as its narrator returns once again to the traditional neighborhood of Luso-Canadian culture in East Vancouver centered around Commercial Drive. In this ethnic neighborhood supposedly in decline, there are still possibilities for unexpected encounters, a possibility that hopefully also extends to all the other spaces that we still inhabit, imagine ourselves belonging to, however complicated that belonging may be, and yes, to the places we still call home.

Some Final Thoughts on Luso-American Literatures and Cultures (And Other Stories We Are Part Of)

And so, as we put the final touches on this latest issue of PLCS, another summer begins. In the local region of southeastern New England, that means the unavoidable start of the still varied and vibrant Portuguese feast season, one that still stretches across from East Providence (pictured on our cover) and Oak Bluffs on Martha's Vineyard, to Frank Gaspar's Provincetown and virtually everywhere in between (from my home in East Providence, I have already heard the festivities from at least two feasts going on nearby, and it is only the end of May). Like the broadcast range of WJFD, wherever there is a festa within earshot, there is also a palpable example of this culture both living on and reinventing itself in new and unexpected ways at the same time (Larkosh 2008). In spite of any sudden changes or unforeseen disruptions, this culture is one that so many of us remain a part of and emotionally and personally invested in, especially when such cultural shifts make access to cultural activity more immediate and convenient, or the conventional terms of identity and belonging, which were always relatively fluid to begin with, even more inclusive.

As mentioned earlier, there has never been a shortage of traditional male role models around which to shape conventional constructs of Portuguese-American cultural identity; while that of the Portuguese navigator, explorer and discoverer still retains a powerful symbolic hold over many cultural historians as they attempt to provide a suitable historical backdrop for contemporary cultural activity, there are a few more examples from more recent sets of events that one would hope we could discuss before arriving at any definitive conclusions as to the usefulness or relevance of the explorational model of Lusodiasporic cultural identity.

One of the most elaborate examples of this, if one not entirely grounded in proven historical fact, was the narrative of Dighton Rock promoted by the late Dr. Manuel Luciano da Silva, a medical doctor turned community historian, who claimed that a rock in the Taunton River appeared to have a set of inscriptions on it, including the date 1511, which proved the arrival of the Portuguese explorer Miguel Corte-Real on these shores long before the arrival of other Europeans (da Silva 1971/1974).[4]

While the controversy over the origin of the inscriptions has died down over the years, the historical debates it provoked still serve a purpose in realigning the discussion alongside a series of other questions. First, does the Corte-Real foundational narrative or any other narrative of this kind ever need to be fully verifiable in order for so many of "The Portuguese Around Us" to believe it to be so? Beyond whether the evidence of Portuguese here over 500 years ago is true or not, are these explorational narratives, whether real or imagined, really the most important historical and cultural facts on which we base our sense of self? And if so, why do they still matter to us so much?

In the absence of the good Doctor, beloved by so many in the local community, and now departed (and perhaps with him, his amazingly resilient historical thesis), it might now be time to take a serious look elsewhere for alternative models, perhaps back once again to our radio station to think of Edmund Dinis, the founder of WJFD, a man who, years before his decades-long foray into Portuguese-language broadcasting, also held public office as a US District Attorney. On the national stage, he is famous not so much for his radio station, but for the national incident that occurred one summer in the late 1960s during his period of service, one that culminated in his role as prosecutor for the Chappaquiddick trial. For many of us, the cast of characters in this historical event central to US political culture is not just a list to be found in a historical archive, but those names recurrent in our own memories and lived experience: to complete the picture, I often think of Leslie Leland, the local pharmacist in Vineyard Haven, who was not only the lead juror for the Chappaquiddick trial, but who was also the man behind the counter whenever I bought a magazine or filled a prescription at Leslie's Drugstore. In this region, one need not be a Kennedy to be recognized as an identifiable figure in a continually developing local or national portrait, as most if not all of us find an individual entry in the archive somewhere on some forgotten page of a local newspaper or academic journal, and thus perhaps become, at least to some extent, a cultural protagonist in our own right in some time and place, however limited.

And to those who question the academic relevance of any of these minute, perhaps trivial, cultural phenomena, historical remnants, or personal anecdotes, I say: as one of the few ever hired specifically to research and teach the literature and culture of the local Portuguese-American community where I both grew up and am currently situated, and to place it in a transnational and global context, I would consider myself not only entitled, but actually obligated to examine this dispersed collection of cultural activity and historical detail in what I consider to be its proper context: i.e., alongside other forms of literary narrative, both literary, journalistic, cinematic, and yes, personal. And if they are to be subjected to a sustained and rigorous critique, perhaps conventional canons, traditional research methodologies, the styles of academic writing they endorse, and the identifiable politics of strategic quotation they reproduce could also be given the same degree of critical attention, in the recurrent critical interest of making it new, or as our title suggests, today. Hopefully this responsibility to culture, in all of its variegated forms of transit and connection, will not be lost on anyone here.

So of course, this inescapable lens of personal reality, that of each and any one of us, extends naturally, perhaps inescapably, to interpretations of mass media and popular culture in the here and now. I think of two boys from among the countless Portuguese-Americans who lived alongside me as a child on Martha's Vineyard, Chris Rebello and Jay Mello. They were chosen by Hollywood director Stephen Spielberg to play the sons of Sheriff Brody in the summer blockbuster *Jaws*, to this day one of the highest grossing Hollywood films of all time. Each summer I am taken back to that film, more or less involuntarily, as it is replayed on screens and on television, no matter whether I am back on the Island or wherever else I might happen to be in the world, even when teaching or researching something others might consider completely unrelated (Larkosh 2015).

Once again I find myself before these two faces once so familiar from my childhood now up on the screen again, sitting at a kitchen table in a seaside house on East Chop chosen as their home for the film. Or, perhaps more disturbingly, in the pivotal scene of a shark attack, with Chris' frightened expression visible at the surface as he treads water off State Beach, the shark circling him invisibly underwater, and then, miraculously, sparing him once again. This image is now over forty years old, and even now, with Chris Rebello himself having passed away years ago, already an adult with a child of his own, yet still at an age far too young to die as abruptly as he did, it is still difficult to separate these fictional characters from the very real local people chosen to play them.

And so, what of the frightened face of a young Portuguese-American boy in the water, as a by-now legendary Hollywood shark endlessly threatens to devour him? This recurrent iconic image, preserved forever in celluloid, is perhaps as emblematic an image for where we are today, in some inescapably recurrent way, as much as any other we might identify from our own vantage point as we look out over the rich and varied panorama of contemporary Luso-American diasporic identity today in its constant struggle to the death with a mainstream mass media culture that seems destined to devour it. After all, each of us will invariably return to our own undeniably symbolic images and stories like this one, even if they are not yet critically recognized as such, but in which the image we insist on identifying with is always endangered to some extent, at risk, yet still treading water, escaping death for now, even if their fate remains to die, suddenly and inexplicably, on another day in real life years later.

But then again, this is a fact that perhaps only either a diehard fan or a local could ever begin to know existed, much less see the sadly ironic cultural significance in. Perhaps that is one reason why cultural critics and literary theorists are here: not only to remember and write down such obscure details, but to try to interpret their overarching significance for myself and anyone else in this community who wishes to listen in and respond, much like a weekend radio call-in show broadcast from across the Sound in another language. Yes, it may be late, the show almost over, but at least for now, we are still here, and the lines are still open.

And as this endless and repeating New England summer wears on, it will also no doubt be difficult to ignore, say, how Cabo Verdean Independence Day celebrations come only a day after the Fourth of July, thus underscoring the ways in which there are always things happening on the day after any cultural celebration that extend its field of signification and add yet another dimension to it. Such is the case of recent Cabo Verdean-American literary activity as well, perhaps most notably in the work of another cultural neighbor, also from across the water if you will: the Falmouth-based poet and prose writer Jarita Davis.

While her poems from the 2016 collection *Return Flights* focused on her exploration of Cabo Verdean culture, both in southeastern Massachusetts and back in Cabo Verde, a recent short prose piece takes us on a markedly different tack. Titled, perhaps somewhat ironically, "Creating a Positive Self Image," Davis opts to reference here not the members of her local Cabo Verdean family or extended community, or related elements of Cabo Verdean language or culture she rediscovers in a voyage home, but of all things, a series of black characters from US television shows:

> not some monkey eating bananas in public not waiting on the corner like a prostitute not leaning out the window shouting like in the projects not poking out those liver lips til they're thick enough to chop off & fry up for dinner not rollerskating in the house like Tootie—not on the linoleum!! not brushing up your eyebrows all thick and bushy to look tough or somethin not a thousand braids sticking up all over your head, runnin around like a little pickaniggy, not my child, not nappy headed like your cousin Felicia if you stay under that dryer & leave those rollers alone til I say so not all that wild hair in your face so the boys hardly get a good look atcha not Vanessa Williams' fake light eyes that look like somebody just pucked right in em not with your head always stuck in some book ruining your eyes til you have to wear bottle thick glasses & no boy will marry you not Sanford & Son not Good Times not What's Happening not What's Happening Now (J. Davis 2019)

Here the models for cultural identity are not positive ones to be emulated and followed, but ones considered best avoided: among the identifiable references to anyone familiar with the television of the last thirty to forty years is to the character Tootie, played by the actress Kim Fields on the 1980s TV series *The Facts of Life*. She was the youngest and only black character living in Mrs. Garrett's otherwise all-white boarding house, and as we see here, she was usually characterized on the basis of her misbehavior. Not just for those in the United States, but also for so many people living and consuming culture on the edges of the US empire, whether the random fragments and racialized characters of US television shows, films and music, no matter where we lived in the last days of the twentieth century. These were also unavoidable "facts of life," whether as part of mainstream mass media, or now as part of Cabo Verdean-American cultural critique, on the unavoidable simplifications of race and its impact on one's sense of cultural belonging and yes, one's "positive self image." As Davis so deftly points out, our literary and cultural traditions have not always produced models for creating this kind of self-image to the same degree for everyone, and in such cases where racism is still clearly an issue, a healthy dose of sarcasm, satire or even anger may well be in order.

But once again, why are we here really, and speaking of Luso-American literatures and cultures today, no less? Is it to make us all feel better in a difficult cultural and political moment, to stroke each other's fragile egos and self-esteem, and tell each other that everything is okay, with me, you and other minor characters, as we all attempt to reaffirm, in our own ways and often against all odds, the value of the commonalities we are still said to share? Perhaps, especially if what is at stake here is an ethnic culture or set of cultures characterized not only by shows of community and affinity, but also one beset with grudges and animosities of equally long standing.

As I conclude, however, I cannot help but think of two perhaps diametrically opposed contemporary cultural figures. First, there is the internet comic commonly known as Jeffrey Popsick, whose series of prank YouTube videos featuring his "Portuguese Grandmother," set in a 'casa portuguesa' somewhere in metropolitan Toronto, seem to represent the most uproarious, unapologetically irreverent, and even nihilistic potential, both in our present and future interactions with previous generations, language and traditions, as well as our own all-too-often insufficiently ironized sense of cultural identity.

And at the other end of the spectrum, there is the university psychology professor Laurie Santos, a Portuguese-American from New Bedford, whose semester-long course on happiness is the most popular in the history of the Ivy League college where she teaches, receiving rave reviews from the overworked, stressed-out aspirants of a future transnational elite, who at some point will also have had to ask their own questions about what success really means.

In the end, is there anyone or anything in this minor culture of limited reach and resources that can "say it right, say it all"? That is, what not only can help us calm our cynicism, sarcasm and hopelessness in the present moment, but also learn from and teach others, perhaps even in an emotionally sincere and earnest way, what it might mean to be truly happy? Or might it still have something more to do with not taking ourselves too seriously, being able to laugh at ourselves at least somewhat self-effacingly and honestly, perhaps even being able to take a joke that is clearly on us? Most likely we need a bit of both, both in our own lives and in our literature and culture, in order for them to be considered of a richness and complexity we can both be proud of and find affirming, character faults and all.

Whichever you choose, I do hope you enjoy your issues, including the one you find before you here today.

NOTES

1. I recently visited the current owner of WJFD 97.3 FM, Henry Arruda, down in their studios in the South End of New Bedford. He had wanted to speak to me because of something I had said to him and longtime radio host Dionísio Garcia after the Ana Moura concert in Boston a few weeks before. I had told him how important WJFD was in giving me a way to listen to spoken Portuguese in my teens and early 20s, as well as learning about Portuguese popular music. When I arrived, we discussed what I might be able to do to help WJFD protect its broadcasting range in southeastern Massachusetts from encroachment by applications on its edges by mainstream commercial stations, usually owned by large conglomerates with immense political pull at the Federal Communications Commission in Washington. Even as this kind of community outreach remains an important part of my work in Luso-American cultures, this is a much more personal issue for me. I dedicate this introduction to the local communities that have welcomed me and so many others over the years, but also to WJFD and to many more years of uninterrupted broadcasting free from interference, be it from other transmissions or from other entities unaware of its importance and value to Portuguese speakers in the region.

2. As for what Gaspar is doing at the moment, in connection to our current topic of Luso-American Literatures and Cultures Today, I guess that I, as his current literary editor at Tagus Press, can perhaps answer that question better than anyone apart from Frank himself. As I complete this issue of PLCS 32, he is out in southern California working on a final draft of a new book of poetry and accompanying prose fiction titled *The Poems of Renata Ferreira*, to be published in the Portuguese of the Americas Series of Tagus Press.

3. Many thanks as well to my local fellow travelers and collaborators at Tagus Press Mario Pereira and Maggie Felisberto for their unflagging dedication and hard work, my MA students Matt de Matos and Orlando Ramos for the courage and willingness to take their work in Luso-American cultural studies to an advanced level with me, and colleagues Bonnie Wasserman and Ben Legg for their expert insights from the always certain cultural interstices of Luso-American community and identity.

4. The edition that I refer to here is the Portuguese edition of 1974, published in Porto three years after Dr. da Silva published the original English edition in 1971. I had the chance to meet Dr. da Silva in May of 2004 at the Dighton Rock Museum that explains his theory, years before I had even begun work as a professor of Portuguese language and literature. Even then, however, it appears that Dr. da Silva already had plans for me and my research, long before I had any clear idea of what my professional involvement in this culture would turn out to be—that is, at least if the dedication he wrote in the copy of his book he gave to me is any indication: "Ao Dr. Christopher Larkosh. Como lembrança da sua visita ao Museu da Pedra de Dighton, ofereço com sinceros votos para que venha a escrever em inglês a odisséia dos Portugueses na Nova Inglaterra desde o tempo dos Corte-Reais. Com o grande abraço do autor, Manuel Luciano da Silva, 14 de Maio de 2004." No wonder that so many of us still struggle with letting go of these perhaps overly ambitious historical assignments in Luso-American literary and cultural studies, even today.

WORKS CITED

Bettencourt, Jeffrey (aka Jeffrey Popsick). "Portuguese Grandmother."
    https://www.youtube.com/watch?v=wa-fAFu6_6E
Blayer, Irene (and Luis Pacheco). "I Never Felt Like I was Only Portuguese, Or Only
    Canadian" Nelly Furtado. RTP Açores website (Blogue Comunidades), October 12,
    2015. Web. http://www.rtp.pt/acores/comunidades/i-never-felt-like-i-was-only-
    portuguese-or-only-canadian-nelly-furtado_48353
Davis, Barrie. "Anthony de Sa's first novel walks down the dark end of the street."
    The Globe and Mail, 20 September 2013. Web. (Updated 11 May 2018). https://www.
    theglobeandmail.com/arts/books-and-media/book-reviews/anthony-de-sas-first-
    novel-walks-down-the-dark-end-of-the-street/article14443557/
Davis, Jarita. *Return Flights*. Dartmouth, MA: Tagus Press, 2016.
———. "Creating a Positive Self Image. In Larkosh, Christopher and Oona Patrick,
    eds. *Behind the Stars, More Stars: The Tagus/Disquiet Collection of Luso-American Writing*.
    Dartmouth, MA: Tagus Press/UMass Press, 2019.
Ferreira, Jo-Anne S. *The Portuguese of Trinidad & Tobago: Portrait of an Ethnic Minority*.
    Second Revised Ed. Kingston: UWI Press, 2018.
Gaspar, Frank. *A Field Guide to the Heavens*. Madison: U of Wisconsin P, 1999.

———. *Night of a Thousand Blossoms*. Farmington, ME: Alice James Books, 2004.

———. *Leaving Pico*. Hanover and London: Hardscrabble Books/UPNE, 1999.

———. *The Poems of Renata Ferreira*. Dartmouth, MA: Tagus/UMass Press, 2019. (forthcoming).

Hevesi, Dennis. "Edmund Dinis, Prosecutor in Chappaquiddick Case, Dies at 85." *New York Times*, March 20, 2010.

James, C. L. R. *The Black Jacobins*. Knopf Doubleday, 1989.

———. *Beyond a Boundary*. (50th Anniversary Edition). Durham/London: Duke University Press, 2013.

———. *History of Pan-African Revolt*. Oakland, CA: PM Press, 2012.

Larkosh, Christopher. "Espírito Santo: Uma festa transatlântica." *AndarILHAgem* (Nº 4). Ponta Delgada: Governo dos Açores, 2008.

———. "Portuguese Past, Still Imperfect: Revisiting Asia in Luso-Diasporic Writing." In Jarnagin, Laura, ed. *The Making of the Luso-Asian World, Volume I: Intricacies of Engagement*. Singapore: ISEAS, 2011, 259-272.

———. "Submarine: Germany Resurfacing in the Contemporary Brazilian Novel." In Finger, A., G. Kathöfer, and C. Larkosh, eds. *Kulturconfusão: On German-Brazilian Interculturalities*. Berlin: De Gruyter, 2015, 247-266.

———. "The Worlds of Québec: On Post-Bilingualism, Multidirectionality, and Other Critical Detours." In Gilmour, Rachel and Tamar Steinitz, eds. *Multilingual Currents in Literature, Translation and Culture*. London/New York: Routledge, 2017, 34-54.

Mendes, Alfred H. *The Man Who Ran Away, and Other Stories of Trinidad in the 1920s and 1930s*. Edited with an introduction by Michèle Levy. Kingston: UWI Press, 2006.

———. *The Autobiography of Alfred Mendes 1897-1991*. Edited by Michèle Levy. Kingston: UWI Press, 2002.

———. *Selected Writings of Alfred H. Mendes*. Edited by Michèle Levy. Kingston: UWI Press, 2013.

———. *Alfred H. Mendes: Short Stories, Articles and Letters*. Edited by Michèle Levy. Kingston: UWI Press, 2016.

De Sa, Anthony. *Barnacle Love*. Toronto: Penguin Random House Canada, 2008.

———. *Kicking the Sky*. Toronto: Doubleday Canada, 2013.

Santos, Laurie. "The Science of Well-Being." Web. https://www.youtube.com/watch?v=5RsiB8V4vxo

Da Silva, Manuel Luciano. *Os pioneiros portuguesese a Pedra de Dighton*. Porto: Brasília Editora, 1974.

Spielberg, Stephen (dir.) *Jaws*. Universal Pictures, 1975. With Roy Schneider, Richard Dreyfuss, Lorraine Gary, Robert Shaw, Chris Rebello and Jay Mello.

Taylor, Trey. "Nelly Furtado's New Album 'The Ride' Sold Only 1,814 Copies in the U.S." iHeart Radio (Canadian website). http://www.iheartradio.ca/news/nelly-furtado-s-new-album-the-ride-sold-only-1-814-copies-in-u-s-1.2536723

de Vasconcelos, Erika. *My Darling Dead Ones*. Toronto: Vintage Canada, 1999.

———. *Between the Stillness and the Grove*. Toronto: Vintage Canada, 2001.

CHRISTOPHER LARKOSH was born in Oak Bluffs on the Island of Martha's Vineyard, Massachusetts, where he also spent most of his early childhood, never far from the local Portuguese-American Club just down the street on Vineyard Avenue. He is currently Associate Professor of Portuguese at UMass Dartmouth. He has published and lectured around the world in a number of global languages, not only in relation to Portuguese-speaking, colonial and diasporic cultures, but also others including Quebec, Argentina, Italy, France, Germany, Turkey, South and East Asia, as well as on the transnational, transcultural and gendered interactions between them. He served a two-year term as Director of Tagus Press from 2015 to 2017, and continues to serve as literary editor for its Portuguese in the Americas series. He also currently serves on the Editorial Board of the internationally recognized Montréal-based translation journal *Meta*. He is the editor of *Re-Engendering Translation: Transcultural Practice, Gender/Sexuality and the Politics of Alterity* (London/New York: St. Jerome/Routledge, 2011) and has co-edited two additional volumes in transcultural studies, one entitled *Writing Spaces*, compiled in collaboration with colleagues in Taiwan (Kaohsiung: NSYSU Press, 2013), and another entitled *KulturConfusão: German-Brazilian Interculturalities* (Berlin: De Gruyter, 2015).

CARMEN RAMOS VILLAR

Voicing the Community, or a Voice for the Community: Katherine Vaz, a Portuguese American Writer

ABSTRACT: This essay traces the debate about Portuguese American literature, the role that anthologies of Portuguese American literature play in defining this literary category, and then examines Katherine Vaz as a case study. In so doing, the essay considers how Portuguese American writers like Vaz contribute to the shaping of Portuguese American literature, the challenges Portuguese American literature faces, and how the community can help to shape the future of this literary category.

KEYWORDS: community, anthologies, Portuguese American literature debate, Katherine Vaz, literary categorisation.

RESUMO: O presente ensaio examina o debate sobre a literatura luso-americana, o papel das antologias na criação de uma definição da categoria de literatura luso-americana, e o caso específico da autora Katherine Vaz. Ao assim fazer, o ensaio considera o papel de escritores luso-americanos como Katherine Vaz na delineação da categoria de literatura luso-americana, os desafios que a literatura luso-americana encara, e como a comunidade pode ajudar no futuro de esta categoria literária.

PALAVRAS-CHAVE: comunidade, antologias, debate sobre a literatura Luso Americana, Katherine Vaz, categorização literária.

This essay will begin by examining the debate about whether Portuguese American literature exists. It will set this debate within the development of community-based initiatives that have placed value on the Portuguese American community before examining the role that the anthologies of Portuguese American writing have in providing a definition of what constitutes Portuguese American literature. The essay will then examine the author Katherine Vaz as a case study of an author seeking a place within the American mainstream, the

Portuguese American mainstream, and also perhaps wanting to make a claim to the Portuguese literary field. The essay argues that Vaz's prominence arises from her self-conscious position as a transnational writer and as a transnational cultural broker. The essay concludes by considering the role that writers like Vaz have in shaping Portuguese American literature as a literary category, the challenges Portuguese American literature faces, and how the community can help to shape the future of this literary category.

The Portuguese American literature debate

In 1979, Nancy Baden wrote an article that asked whether Portuguese American literature existed. Baden's article emerged from a series of events that discussed the role of the Portuguese American writer and the existence of a Portuguese American literature. In her article, Baden argued that Portuguese writers who lived in the US like José Rodrigues Miguéis, Alfred Lewis, Onésimo Teotónio Almeida and Lawrence Oliver were examples of immigrant literature, rather than Portuguese American literature, in the sense that these writers either depicted the experience of emigration or maintained a strong connection with Portugal and, therefore, remained "entrenched in the Portuguese mainstream" (23). Baden's observations about Onésimo Teotónio Almeida's work suggest that the Portuguese American writer needs to both write for the ethnic group, "articulating their needs, aspirations and frustrations to the broader American public" (21), and to place the ethnic experience itself as a central theme within his or her work. At the time, Baden's conclusion was that Portuguese American literature did not yet exist, but that it was starting to take its first steps; "[w]hat exists is a young immigrant literature, the product of two successive waves of immigration" (27). Baden then went on to state that "[t]he term 'Portuguese-American literature' is useful to describe the works of writers who are neither Portuguese nor American in the usual sense and thus will undoubtedly be used for the sake of convenience" (28). Baden was alluding to the fact that Portuguese American literature was not yet a category, but that it had the potential to bring together Portuguese immigrant writers in the United States who describe their emigration experience to an American and Portuguese audience.

Baden's statement that Portuguese American literature was a convenient label raises questions regarding where to place writers who write from the emigration setting. In many ways, Onésimo Teotónio Almeida's 2005 article considers this question of placement, and constitutes the next step in tracing the development of Portuguese American literature. Almeida's article draws upon his extensive publications in which he defends Azorean literature as a distinct category within Portuguese literature, arguing that Azorean literature is composed of writers in the Azores and the United States. By including Azorean writers in the United States in his definition of Azorean literature, Almeida highlights the artificial borders created when examining who belongs to a literary canon. He begins his examination of Portuguese American literature by briefly mentioning previous contributions to the debate over whether Portuguese American literature exists, citing Francis Rogers, Nancy T. Baden and Leo Pap, before making the following comment:

> [A]re we in the presence of a specific literature? My answer is two-fold. From a literary perspective, I argue no, it does not, for a very simple reason – literature is written in a particular language. Beyond this, however, from a sociological viewpoint I say yes, Portuguese-American literature does indeed exist. (735)

The sociological basis Almeida mentions derives from his argument that an author writes in the language in which s/he feels more comfortable in order to depict the reality in which the writer finds himself or herself in. To this end, Almeida speaks of a fluid and inclusive Portuguese American bilingual community that the Portuguese American writer addresses, which comprises

> three major, overlapping groups: Portuguese-speakers, English-speakers and bilinguals. An important bond connects them all: they identify themselves as belonging to an ethnic group distinct from the mainstream of American and Canadian societies. They have created community structures including radio and television stations, newspapers, magazines, associations of all types and yet function simultaneously at another level as members of the mainstream societies that received them, even while existing as a society unto itself. Writers emerging in their midst produce books that reflect the world they inhabit. (735)

For Almeida, then, Portuguese American literature is the product of a hybrid reality that depicts the community of the author (737). In Almeida's view, Portuguese American literature is not an ethnic literature, per se, but a literature that dialogues with the literary and cultural traditions of both Portugal and the United States and that, in sociological terms, speaks to the Portuguese

American community regardless of the language in which it is written. In this way, Almeida opens up categorisation in literature to a multiplicity of belonging; the writer can belong to many literary categories and, at the same time (in sociological terms), contribute to shaping Portuguese American literature as a category in itself.

The debate over the existence of a Portuguese American literature was next taken up by Reinaldo Silva three years later, in a book entitled *Representations of the Portuguese in American Literature*. Here, Silva observes that Portuguese American literature has moved beyond its embryonic state. Silva sees Portuguese American literature as a literature of English expression that discusses ethnic interests, meaning that writers

> explore what it means to be a Portuguese living at the margins of American society, [...] [finding] different ways to express their experiences; some employ the Portuguese language, while others use both Portuguese and English, and still others write exclusively in English. This reflects a gradual, steady movement towards a truly ethnic fiction in the English language in America. (2008: 156)

The impulse to write, in Silva's analysis, is to correct the image of the Portuguese migrant within the American mainstream, and writing is seen as a way of exploring the author's heritage. For Silva, authors like Thomas Braga, Frank X. Gaspar, Julian Silva, Katherine Vaz, José Rodrigues Miguéis, Jorge de Sena and Charles Reis Felix

> exhibit a common sense of puzzlement, fascination, and frustration in response to the culture of their adopted country. Furthermore, these writers provide an in-depth account of Portuguese people, their ways and culture – not just a glimpse at surface customs [...] [to convey] what it means to be Portuguese-American. (157, see also 2009: 25)

Silva's definition of Portuguese American literature aligns itself with Baden's perception of ethnic literature, particularly when he comments that "[a]n ethnic literature emerges when second- and third-generation writers succeed in retrieving their ancestors' roots so as to learn more about where they come from" (205). In a later study, Silva agrees with Baden when he concludes that the "great [Portuguese] American novel [...] is yet to be written" (2009: 104). As can be seen, Silva places the definition of Portuguese American literature not just on ethnic grounds, but also on an American readership that receives (consumes?)

the written texts that are produced in English (2009: 169). For Silva, Portuguese American literature will exist when it is recognised as a literary category in its own right, beyond the ethnic literature label.

The next person to contribute to the Portuguese American literature debate, Christopher Larkosh, suggests that

> Portuguese American literature examines the presence of pockets of Portuguese culture in the US through a perspective in which the Portuguese American author shows the resonances of Portuguese cultural references in his or her writing. Larkosh sees Portuguese American literature as multilocal, through the connections made between Portuguese cultural and literary references within the specific setting of the Portuguese American community. Larkosh takes up the idea of the "ethnic garden" presented by Silva in his 2005 article, and develops it to see how Portuguese American authors rework cultural references, particularly Portuguese literary references, to depict the Portuguese American reality in their works. The multilocality of Portuguese American literature, however, re-presents the Portuguese heritage of the Portuguese American in a renewed way. Larkosh describes this as an "ex-centric" process in which cultural resonances are found, but also renewed and reworked (2013, 43-45) so that Portuguese-American literature thus combines literary myth and ethnic memory in a potent New World vision for reconfiguring the present terms of ethnic identity and imagining one's "place in the world," both in the Americas and in the greater Portuguese-speaking diaspora, one that stretches across the world to this day. (49)

For Larkosh, then, Portuguese American literature is a field that shapes itself at the junction between cultures and literary traditions. As such, it builds upon Almeida's comments about the porous nature of literary categorisations.

The most recent scholar to comment on the Portuguese American debate has been Vamberto Freitas, who observes that recognition of Portuguese American literature, as a field, will happen gradually, with an author having his or her work recognised by the mainstream, and by being joined by other authors "to be accepted and appreciated one by one, and through literary works that will stand first as great aesthetic performances. Content, theme and referential geographies will then impose themselves on other serious readers of literature" (293).

Freitas sees the existence of Portuguese American literature as a *fait accompli*, as being in the process of growth, but he calls attention to the need for Portuguese

American literature to receive sustained academic attention in order to achieve visibility, to call attention to the quality and quantity, so that, incrementally, the conditions are created for the literary field to be recognised (see Borges Accardi: 289-290). For Freitas, Portuguese American literature exists, but the field needs the gradual combination of being cemented academically and of being recognised for its quality by the mainstream (both in Portugal and in the United States).

It could be stated that the debate over whether Portuguese American literature exists is evolving towards a consensus. The consensus seems to be that Portuguese American literature depicts the concerns of the Portuguese American community, and that it speaks *about*, and *to*, that community. Here, it is pertinent to examine António Ladeira's comments on Portuguese American literature, particularly his statement that a literary field "starts as a community's dream, but it needs to be willed into existence" (20). Back in 1979, Baden observed that the Portuguese American community was not homogeneous, and that the (then) more recent wave of emigrants "had a generally higher level of education and display[ed] a real sense of being Portuguese. Their political ideas often clash[ed] with the more conservative views of established residents" (17). Ladeira makes it clear that the long list of authors who comprise Portuguese American literature is the result of many initiatives that have converged to form it: social, cultural, political, and academic initiatives. The beginning of this rapprochement between immigrant waves and between different Portuguese-speaking migrant communities might have been the result of bilingual education programs of the early 1980s, which, according to Almeida "advocat[ed] that migrants should be taught in their native language as they learned English, through text books that connected these students to their own worlds" (733). It is also, as Ladeira points out, the result of university programs, of publications that analyse the Portuguese American community and, I would add, the work of community associations like the Casa da Saudade, in New Bedford, MA, which provide a first point of contact to study and place value on the community, the visibility gained by initiatives like "Kale Soup for the Soul," a cooperative comprised of new Portuguese American writers who read their work at conferences and symposiums, and by the Disquiet literary program, and the work by Tagus Press, from UMass Dartmouth, in publishing and promoting Portuguese American writers. The development of the Portuguese American literature debate could be seen as accompanying the need to provide a voice of representation for the Portuguese American community. What, then, is the role of the anthologies of Portuguese American literature?

The role of anthologies in the Portuguese American literature debate

The role of anthologies in canon formation should not be underestimated within the Portuguese American literature debate outlined above. Anthologies of Portuguese American writing provide an initial step towards establishing the categorisation of Portuguese American literature.[1] The publication of anthologies like *Luso-American Literature: Writing by Portuguese-Speaking Authors in North America* (2011), edited by Robert Henry Moser and Antonio Luciano de Andrade Tosta, *The Gávea-Brown Book of Portuguese American Poetry* (2013), edited by Alice Clemente and George Monteiro, and the *Writers of the Portuguese Diaspora in the United States and Canada: An Anthology* (2015), edited by Luis Gonçalves and Carlo Matos, show just how many authors comprise, or could be said to belong to, Portuguese American literature. As the essay will now explore, the introductions to each anthology take it as read that Portuguese American literature exists.

Moser and Tosta published the first Portuguese American literature anthology. In their introduction, the definition of Portuguese American literature was opened up to authors who explored their experience of living in the United States and who were identified, or identified themselves, as having a connection to the Portuguese-speaking world. In the words of the editors, the anthology

> functions as a literary ethnoscape of cultural encounters, of hyphenated experiences, within an "imagined world" located somewhere between North American society and the Lusophone diasporas, than as a written expression of a single, cohesive group struggling to address, for example, the repression of its communal history (2011: xxviii).

The anthology sees Portuguese American literature beyond the label of ethnic literature, in that the writers chosen examine both the cohabitation of different Portuguese-speaking communities within the same space in the United States and how the writers dialogue with the emigration setting. The definition of what constitutes a Portuguese American writer in this anthology is more complex. It is not an ethnic writer looking at his or her place in the United States. It is constituted in terms of the transcultural dialogue between cultures; how the culture and history of their Lusophone origins interact with the myriad Portuguese cultural spaces within the United States, and also with the wider multicultural setting within the United States.

Alice Clemente and George Monteiro's anthology is perhaps simpler in its definition of what constitutes a Portuguese American writer, limiting it to "poets of Portuguese ancestry who acknowledge their roots as a component to one degree or another of their artistic consciousness" (2013: 16). The emphasis here is on the writers' exploration of the relationship between cultures.

Gonçalves and Matos' anthology continues in the same vein as Clemente and Monteiro's anthology. Indeed, the prologue, written by George Monteiro, states that the anthology aims to explore "the genuine literature produced in our shared space by Portuguese emigrants and their descendants" (2015: 13). What is interesting about Gonçalves and Matos' anthology is that it was organised entirely by the writers themselves, calling on contributions from those who identified themselves as being Portuguese Americans and Portuguese Canadians.

The three anthologies examined above present Portuguese American literature as a transcultural exchange of ideas between the cultures that comprise the Portuguese-speaking world in the United States. Although the three anthologies take it as read that Portuguese American literature exists, the definition of the Portuguese American writer is different. Moser and Tosta's definition is based on how the authors examined dialogue with an emigration setting where different Portuguese-speaking communities cohabit. This is quite close to the consensus reached by the critics examined in the previous section, which saw Portuguese American literature as depicting the concerns of the Portuguese American community. The anthologies also echo the consensus reached by critics examining the debate on Portuguese American literature: Portuguese American authors speak *to* a Portuguese American community and *about* that Portuguese American community. However, Moser and Tosta expand this perception to a more multilocal dialogue that extends beyond the Portugal/US dichotomy, particularly in their inclusion of writers from other places of the Portuguese-speaking world. In this way, the anthologies present the Portuguese American writer as someone whose Portuguese heritage (in the widest sense) influences the writing produced. This more inclusive approach opens up the possibility for a definition of Portuguese American literature as a porous category in dialogue with multiple cultures and literary traditions. It is here that the essay turns to the work of Katherine Vaz in order to examine how she seeks a position within different literary categories.

Katherine Vaz, the Portuguese American writer

To date, Katherine Vaz has published two novels and three collections of short stories. The novels are *Saudade* (1994), published by St Martin's Press, and *Mariana* (1997), published by Flamingo. The collections of short stories are *Fado & Other*

Stories (1997), published by the University of Pittsburgh Press, *Our Lady of the Artichokes* (2008), published by the University of Nebraska Press, and *The Love Life of an Assistant Animator & Other Stories* (2017), published by Tailwinds Press. With the exception of *Mariana*, which is set in Portugal, her works depict Portuguese American communities, and the lives of their Portuguese American main characters. In this way, Vaz's work fits the definition of the function of Portuguese American literature as outlined above. Vaz's writing style could be described as fragmented, creating fleeting impressions of a character, or his or her emotions, and this is reflected in how the plot is constructed. The result is a story that is told haltingly, almost in stages, not so much like a prose poem, but as a self-conscious experiment in form and on the limits of prose.[2]

Vaz's first novel, *Saudade*, is a story of revenge that spirals out of control and sees Clara, a Portuguese immigrant child from the Azores to California, take ever more desperate measures against Father Eiras, a priest who acts as Clara's guardian after the death of her parents and who Clara believes has cheated her out of her family's inheritance in California. Clara is no ordinary child; she has been unable to hear since birth, and does not speak, communicating instead through a made-up language involving sugar, until her mother dies. It is worth quoting the passage explaining the moment of her mother's death in full, to get a sense of Vaz's writing style and to see how Vaz brings her Portuguese ethnicity into her writing:

> In Portuguese death, the soul flies away as a moth, white as a snowflake. It first perches on the lips, then hovers and ascends. Conceição, trying to inhale the beating wings, fought so hard to swallow them that she spent her final hour kissing the empty air. Clara awoke to feel her mother's hand groping, desperately searching for her child's hand so that her work could be done with the two of them bound, but as Clara turned to reach for her, the moth paused, touched its wings together, and then abandoned its station. Clara was frantic – she had not held her mother's hand in time! She had seen the mouth in spasms but had not kissed it properly! Her mother had gone on ahead – not anywhere – without her! [...] She found her voice.
> Mouth a jagged black world.
> She released a sound enormous and sharp-edged.
> Her cry burst out so unnaturally past tissue that been determined to stay inviolate that her ears were startled into turning a violent red, and she slapped

her face, trying to put out the flames that had risen to its surface. Her cries came out in long streams and drove birds from the trees. [...] It was the bellowing protest Clara had refused to give at birth like everyone else. (47)

The notion of a Portuguese death presented here is a shorthand strategy to present Portuguese culture in a particular way. Reframing death within a Portuguese experience, with its call to the emotions evoked at the pain felt in the moment of death, enables Vaz to self-consciously tap into the taste for the ethnic in her American readership at the time *Saudade* was published.

It is no coincidence that, just before the publication of *Saudade*, Vaz hinted at how she was to be interpreted by the reader when she provided her working definition of Magical Realism:

> magical realism is very much the attempt to find what is the fantastic or sublime in everyday things and it's also about finding out what's ordinary within wonderful or sublime things. [...] In my case, what I'm doing is using the senses primarily to uncover what those are and to create new worlds and new perceptions according to what the senses dictate. (LA Times: 21/01/1992)

Vaz had a clear strategy in highlighting how to be read; she was tapping into the tail end of a taste for Magical Realism during the 1980s, through Chicano literature, and the interest and appetite for the ethnic experience in the US.[3] When *Saudade* was published in 1994, Vaz offered an ethnic experience with a difference; the Portuguese ethnic experience, couched within the wider umbrella of the Hispanic ethnic experience in the US. This is a view echoed by Reinaldo Silva, who commented that *Saudade* "aims at capturing the ways and mentality of Portuguese characters transplanted to American soil" (2005: 196). The appeal of Vaz, as a writer, is that this is an ethnic experience that is different, yet familiar to the US reader; it brings forth a feel of the Old World and its weight of heritage, of rites and cultural beliefs. In his analysis of Vaz and Frank X. Gaspar, Larkosh commented that both authors "invoke the land – and the seascapes of their ancestral Azores as a point of departure for other discoveries further west, [whereby] this common trajectory becomes a conduit for the transatlantic passage" (2013, 49). The Old World becomes a place of origins, where certain myths and imaginings can be inscribed (as in the made-up notion of a Portuguese death), enriching the portrayal of the ethnic experience in the New World setting so that, in the words of Thomas Keneally's blurb on the cover to *Saudade*, in the "beautifully textured narration, you encounter a previously un-encountered, gorgeously enriched America, and characters with real blood in their veins."

For the Portuguese reader, there is a similar effect of the familiar yet different. According to Vamberto Freitas, this is a narrative "de desafios a todos os níveis, recorrendo desde a primeira página a um realismo mágico que o catolicismo português e as suas crenças facilitam tanto para a libertação como para o amesquinhamento das personagens" (2010: 63). Teresa Cid develops this in her analysis of *Saudade*, seeing Vaz's novel as an expansion of the conquest narratives, and as an intervention that raises the power of women's agency, which is forgotten in these narratives (257). Cid goes on to analyse the main character, Clara, as a metaphor for Portugal's perverse following of a goal in history, highlighting that Vaz writes "improbable stories about improbable events, feeding upon a history of improbabilities: the Portuguese achievements in navigation, or the incredible existence of the Azores islands themselves" (258). Larkosh sees the novel as a world of fantasy that stretches between the Azores and the US, connecting Portuguese traditions with American lived experience (2013, 49). Vaz, therefore, reframes Portuguese culture from within the Portuguese American experience (see Cid; Coutinho Mendes), turning herself into a cultural broker who presents a Portuguese American ethnic experience that is approachable, but that still maintains the right balance of the exotic and the familiar both to a US reader immersed in the discourses of the US melting pot and of the portrayal of the ethnic experience in the US, and to the Portuguese reader immersed in the discourse of Portugal as a nation with global communities. In other words, through *Saudade*, Vaz provides a perspective that renews both national discourses while being distinctive enough to be recognisably different to each discourse. In this way, Vaz echoes Portuguese American literature's multilocal approach outlined by Larkosh as well as the dialogue between cultures that the three anthologies of Portuguese American literature point to in the Portuguese American writer.

The familiar yet distinct Portuguese American experience depicted by Vaz is found in the way the characters undergo a journey of adaptation, of negotiating two cultures. For instance, in *Saudade*, Clara emigrates to California immediately after her mother's death. Under the wing of her Portuguese American neighbours, Clara adapts to her new life in the US and undergoes two parallel journeys: the magical and the real. The magical journey sees her becoming aware of, and entering, a different plane of perception, where she converses with her dead uncle and almost kills herself just by using her willpower. The real sees her intentionally seduce Father Eiras and, as a consequence, become pregnant. Her child is born with an open wound in his chest and dies shortly thereafter. The end of the novel sees Clara walking away from a loving relationship with a widowed man. In a sense, what we are shown in *Saudade* is the folly of youth taken to an extreme. It is also a story that is dressed up as the experience of an immigrant in the US; the child Clara bears, and her subsequent grief following his death, could be read symbolically as the pain inherent in adapting to the emigration setting. As Reinaldo Silva comments,

> Vaz's narrative captures hybrid, hyphenated realities in blending Portuguese and American realities. In other words, *Saudade* wonderfully conveys what happens when the values, culture, and literature of an Old World country come into contact with those of the New World (2008: 198).

Or, in the words of Vamberto Freitas, the novel is "um constante chamamento tanto à mítica de uma comunidade de origem fechada e depois precariamente aberta no seu novo mundo californiano como a uma história ora universalizada ora reduzida às isoladas comunidades de ilhas atlânticas" (2010: 62-63). *Saudade* calls upon a universal experience of the pain inherent to emigration and to "melting" into the American pot, yet it is different enough to pass as ethnic through the inclusion of references to Portuguese culture. It is also, for Portuguese readers, an evocation of a reality that calls upon the imagining of the lived experience, of the trials and tribulations of the Portuguese abroad. Although Vaz's novel conforms to the definitions of Portuguese American literature explored above, it does so in a particular way, as will be explored below.

Vaz, the cultural translator

As was briefly mentioned, in her writing, Vaz exoticises the Portuguese and their culture, creating a surreal and distinctive world that is somehow plausible. In so doing, Vaz positions herself as a cultural broker between the exotic and the familiar for Portuguese and American readers. The made-up notion of a Portuguese death examined earlier could be seen in this way, but there are other examples interspersed in her text. For instance, in *Saudade*, Vaz starts her chapters with a section in italics so as to explain a legend or story from the Azores. In Chapter 7, for example, a *fado* is explained in the following terms:

Fados, the songs of fate, wail in the cafés of the Azores and all of Lusitania, including the homes of the Portuguese in California. The lyrics approximate the timbres of grief: disjointed, in the cadence of actual moans and pleadings, and the music weaves them into a net that can catch whatever listener's soul cast towards it.

> Two lines from a fado
> Navegar é preciso
> Viver não é preciso
> This has two meanings:
> To navigate is necessary
> To live is not necessary
> Or:
> To navigate is precise
> To live is not precise
> A widow in the town of Lodi, California, wrote a fado (233)

In explaining Fado, Vaz becomes a translator not just of the meaning behind Portuguese words, but also of Portuguese culture for the US reader. For the Portuguese reader, it is an unusual look at Portuguese culture that, according to Teresa Cid, produces a distancing effect that enables a renewed interpretation of Portuguese culture (261), and, in the process, gives "added clarity to the way this present-day woman writer is dealing with the voices of a predominantly male canon, both American and Portuguese" (257). However, what Vaz fails to point out in her explanation is that the *fado* she quotes is in fact two lines taken from a poem by Fernando Pessoa.[4]

It is useful to examine Vaz's role as a cultural translator in light of João Leal's discussion of the evolution of the concept of *saudade* within Portugal. Leal traces *saudade*, as a concept, from its emergence in the late nineteenth century as a way to provide a unique typology or "trope for speaking about being Portuguese" (269), to its adoption by Portuguese ethnologists, and later the Portuguese State, to describe the Portuguese character as undefinable, yet anchored in "key moments of Portuguese history, [on] what made Portugal great" (274). Leal examines the evolution of the concept of *saudade* to its current use within the Portuguese national discourse, as a trope, as a way of thinking about the nation and its people. Crucially, Leal also examines how the concept of *saudade* was embraced within the Portuguese American communities, describing it as an invented tradition whereby the "process of ethnicisation turned *saudade* from a rather bizarre 'invention' of a Portuguese poet who strongly disliked cosmopolitanism into a widespread device for travellers, emigrants and cosmopolitans alike [...] to deal with the issues of home and dislocation" (2000: 281). Leal also comments that the concept of *saudade* has developed a "particular version of portugueseness" (282). For Leal, *fado*, as a musical style, plays a strong role in the definition of Portugueseness, having transformed itself from the music of the lower classes in Lisbon to being embraced by the elites and becoming recognised as one of the national songs. Fado, however, has a troubled history. During the Estado Novo regime, *fado* was used to promote a populist ultranationalism. Manuela Cook notes the social function of *fado* as an instrument of social control against social unrest directed towards the Estado Novo and as a way of promoting pride in all things Portuguese (22). In the words of Manuel Halpern, "o Estado Novo serviu-se do fado para hastear a sua bandeira. Muitas vezes criou-se uma coincidência entre o que se cantava no fado e o espírito salazarista" (119). Both Halpern and Cook highlight the fact that *fado* singing was promoted both at home and abroad during the Estado Novo, particularly through the famous *fado* singer Amália Rodrigues. After the April Revolution in 1974, a Revolution which put Portugal on its path to democracy and ended the Estado Novo regime, the popularity of *fado* declined in Portugal due to its association with the Estado Novo past, in a conscious strategy to move away from certain cultural aspects that had been embraced by the Estado Novo (Halpern: 70). However, as Leal points out, *fado*'s popularity did not wane within the Portuguese American communities; it was actually promoted by certain official organisms in what he terms the *market of saudade*, becoming a vehicle for the promotion of *saudade* both at home, in Portugal, and abroad. Within the Portuguese American context, Leal observes that both the concept of *saudade* and *fado* songs were part of

> a celebration of personal memories of emigrants: it was sung by folk singers at formal gatherings and celebrations of Azorean migrants taking place in the USA; it was used to baptise the new market that Azorean emigrants provided to Portuguese and American products, the so-called *market of saudade*; it was enthusiastically evoked by cultural and political leaders of Azorean-American communities at the Congresses of Azorean emigrants organised and sponsored since 1976 by the Azorean Regional Government. Finally, it was also celebrated by Luso-American writers, novelists and poets closely linked to

the Azorean-American community. [...] Although writing in English for an American audience, this new wave of Azorean-American writers keeps on celebrating *saudade* as a privileged trope for the evocation of Portuguese texts, as the case of Katherine Vaz suggests (280).

If we take Leal's words into account, Vaz depicts the way the Portuguese American community has continued to embrace *fado* and its function as the tangible embodiment of the concept of *saudade*, even if these two specific markers of Portuguese identity have been rejected, and then rediscovered and embraced once more within Portugal in recent years. This, as Leal observes, results in the Portuguese American community being an example of long distance nationalism; the construction of a more vigorous concept of home within the emigrant setting (281). What Vaz is reproducing in her novel *Saudade*, and within her other works, therefore, is how the Azorean Americans view themselves and how they relate themselves to Portugal and its cultural heritage. In so doing, Vaz could be seen to align herself with the view that Portuguese American literature dialogues between cultures and heritages explored earlier in this essay. But is there something more at play here?

Vaz as Self-Conscious Transnational Cultural Informant

Frequently calling upon Portuguese writers like Camões or Pessoa, or including Portuguese legends and stories, such as the creation of the Lagoa das Sete Cidades in *Saudade*, or describing how the ukulele arrived in Hawaii in *Fado & Other Stories*, enables Vaz to give her texts ethnic authenticity. It also operates on another level; in seemingly explaining an aspect of Portuguese culture and cultural heritage, culture becomes a commodity that is called upon in Vaz's quest to define and cement her role as a transnational cultural informant. This role becomes increasingly evident in her 1997 novel, *Mariana*, which depicts the life of Mariana de Alcoforado. Mariana de Alcoforado was a Portuguese nun whose love letters to a French lieutenant during Portugal's war of independence from Spain were published in the seventeenth century, and circulated widely, although their authenticity has been a source of academic debate. In the postscript at the end of the novel, Vaz outlines the debate regarding the authenticity of Mariana de Alcoforado's letters, and frames her own fictionalised portrayal of this Portuguese nun in the following terms:

> Bad enough that her letters should be taken from her. Unforgivable that anyone should attempt to brush her spirit aside. My conviction is that her life and

authorship should be returned to her. Though the translation of the love letters is mine, the sentiments are Mariana's. I have fleshed out her story based upon my research in the original Portuguese sources. This novel relies on true events, including some that may seem uncanny. (324)

As can be seen, Vaz presents herself as a cultural informant who has not only done research, but who also sees herself as having a duty to redress a wrong, even an oversight. After all, as Vaz comments, "[w]hy, then, is [Mariana de Alcoforado] virtually unknown in Great Britain and the United States of America?" (323) If we are to believe Vaz's postscript, Mariana's story is also unknown in Portugal. There, Vaz suggests that her visit to the convent in Beja put her in contact with Leonel Borrela, the caretaker who allowed her to visit the convent, even though it was closed, so as to share his passion for Mariana de Alcoforado with someone. Vaz, thus, becomes the accidental discoverer of something that is not as valued as it should be, positioning herself as a cultural informant with a conscience; she introduces readers to the story of Mariana de Alcoforado so that her story is recovered and appreciated beyond the few scholars who are aware of it. For the Portuguese reader, Mariana's story is extended beyond the letters to encompass the whole of Mariana's life. The reader, thus, benefits from a chance encounter and becomes informed about a feature of Portuguese history and culture, which Vaz seemingly "rescues."

Vaz's claim of "rescuing" is only for the benefit of a reader not familiar with the controversial publication of *Novas cartas portuguesas* in Portugal in 1972, which saw a revival of the interest in the letters of this Portuguese nun, particularly within the field of Portuguese Studies. As such, Vaz's stance could be seen as an example of Portuguese American long-distance nationalism that Leal pointed to earlier, and the slight disconnect of this long-distance nationalism with cultural debates within Portugal. In adopting this role of "rescuer", Vaz is seemingly unaware of the international importance of *Novas cartas portuguesas* during the 1970s and beyond, or the academic attention the text has received over the past 40 years. I would argue, however, that Vaz consciously chooses to sidestep acknowledging this attention so as to prevent destabilising her image as cultural informant with a conscience. An interview with Vaz published by the Portuguese newspaper *Diário de Notícias* in June 1998, conducted by Maria Teresa Horta (*Mariana* was first published in 1997), would suggest that Vaz would have been briefed on the importance of *Novas cartas portuguesas* prior to her publicity tour in Portugal. Vaz's review of the English translation of *Novas cartas portuguesas* in 2001 highlights the controversy of the original publication and her own fascination with Mariana de Alcoforado. This review article highlights the translated text as an example of feminine resistance to oppression, and by mentioning her own fictional recreation of Mariana de Alcoforado, Vaz appeals to readers to read her own interpretation of the life of Mariana de Alcoforado in similar terms: "I wrote a novel in which I interpreted Mariana's life, and the television host in Portugal who wanted to interview me was *none other than* Maria Teresa Horta, delighted that another woman in another country had also found this splendid nun an inspiration" (81, my emphasis). Whether Vaz is aware of the international and academic importance that *Novas cartas portuguesas* has received or not, the fact is that Vaz consciously positions herself as an authoritative informant of Portuguese culture to the reader.

All of this demonstrates that Vaz is a writer who is not afraid to trade with her ethnicity, or her role as a woman writer, in order to be known, published, recognised, asked to comment on aspects of Portuguese culture, and so on. She, therefore, is happy to become a marketable good, a brand, a representative voice, or spokeswoman for the Portuguese and the Portuguese American experience. This fuels her (justifiable) pride in being the first Portuguese American to have her work recorded in the Library of Congress, in being one of the two writers in the list of top Luso American figures, or in teaching creative writing through the Disquiet literary program.[5] In seeking to represent the Portuguese American experience, and also to translate, or become an ambassador, for Portuguese culture, Vaz could be seen to fashion herself as a transnational writer. Such fashioning takes advantage of any opportunity given to raise her status as a writer.

Here, it is useful to trace Vaz' career within the backdrop of Portuguese American initiatives. Her publications in English coincided with a period of Portuguese American community initiatives that Ladeira and Almeida referred to. These began with the study of Portuguese American communities in university programs[6], and with the educational initiatives to service the local Portuguese American community.[7] In other words, Vaz emerged at a time when she could be used as a source of pride within the Portuguese American community that was seeking a voice of representation.

When the Portuguese translation of *Saudade* was published in 1999, and the Portuguese translation of *Mariana* came out in 2002, Vaz's reception in Portugal had already been framed within the literature produced by Azorean descendants in the US, but it has also moved steadily towards representing the Portuguese American community to Portuguese readers by those who examine her within academia. This is not so strange when one connects all the dots; the Azorean emigrants are mostly concentrated in New England, where the university programs looking at the Portuguese American experience started, and where respected scholars of Azorean literature work.[8] At the turn of the millennium, Vaz was embraced in Portugal by the *Suplemento Açoriano de Cultura*, which published two critical articles on her novels in December 1997 and October 1999, penned by Adelaide Batista, interpreting her work as a bridge between cultures (1999). In the interview between Vaz and Maria Teresa Horta for the Portuguese newspaper *Diário de Notícias* in June 1998 mentioned above, Vaz again reinforces the idea of being a cultural ambassador for Portugal in the US, moving herself beyond the Azorean label to cement a certain self-fashioning strategy as a transnational cultural broker. Vaz's participation in the Disquiet program also consolidates her role as transnational cultural ambassador.[9] Current scholarly work on Vaz frames her writing as Portuguese American and as part of the Azorean emigrant community in the US. It would seem, therefore, that Vaz's work places her as an author with movable categorisations, and as a writer who serves different aims for representation.

The reality is perhaps more complex; Vaz emerged as an outsider from the Portuguese American literary and cultural field. As mentioned above, her rise to fame was within the interest for the ethnic experience in the United States. However, her Portuguese ethnicity, and her conscious use of that ethnicity, meant that she was quickly adopted to answer the needs of the Portuguese American community to gain visibility in the US literary and cultural mainstream. The fact that her works were published by mainstream publishers, rather than the Portuguese American publishers (as is the case for Charles Reis Felix, Julian Silva, Darrell Karstin, Brian Sousa, or, to an extent, Alfred Lewis and Sam Pereira, for example) helped the Portuguese American community to gain more visibility.[10] Her work was quickly adopted by different audiences to answer the specific needs of those audiences who saw her as a writer who wrote about the ethnic experience, but from the Portuguese perspective (American mainstream), as a writer depicting a familiar, yet different reality (Portugal), and/or as a writer depicting the experience of emigration and adaptation and talking about the difficulties faced in both (the Portuguese American community). As a result, the reception of her work suited particular agendas. Thus, Vaz became visible, and enabled a visibility for Portuguese American culture that built upon the Portuguese American community-based initiatives examined above.

Concluding remarks

In what may be seen as an obvious statement to make, care needs to be taken when the aspirations of a community to nurture its cultural heritage combine with the aspirations of the individual author who arises from the community in question. In Vaz's case, this is an author who is carefully constructing, nurturing, and even promoting, specific versions of Portuguese, American, and Portuguese American communities, and what it means to be a part of these, to raise her profile as a writer. The danger inherent in this lies in thinking uncritically about the wider context in which the author emerges from, and in examining the work of authors such as Vaz as examples of long distance nationalism, as this implies that authors such as Vaz can be absorbed within a wider global discourse of the Portuguese as a nation made up of many overseas communities, or even as ethnic literature in the countries in which these authors write, and not as part of a literary category in its own right. Or does it?

Vaz's self-fashioning, reinvention, and malleability as a writer within different contexts raises possibilities about the malleability and movable categorisation that can be found in the figure of the Portuguese American writer, and the role these Portuguese American authors play in different settings. Vaz exemplifies the case of an author who not only seeks to speak from the Portuguese American community, but also uses that community as a starting point through which to make herself a marketable good to different audiences so as to have her work read, even published. Using Portuguese American ethnicity as a marketable good to produce visibility, however, is a double-edged sword. On the one hand, we have the commodification of Portuguese American culture for the mainstream, both in Portugal and in the US, and the concomitant risk of reducing this culture to a cliché of difference, as an example of ethnic literature, even a curiosity held up for recreation and meaningless consumption. On the other hand, as Ladeira comments, "[j]udging by what happened in the most successful ethnic literatures, producing several widely visible authors, with powerful mainstream appeal, might just diminish – paradoxically – the need for having (and obsessively protecting) such an ethnically defined field in the first place" (14).[11] This observation perhaps explains Reinaldo Silva's comment that, although both Vaz and Gaspar have taken the first steps towards writing a truly ethnic Portuguese American fiction within the US context, both authors have written about the localised ethnic community from which they originate (2009: 104). However, is there such thing as ethnic literature?

In his study about how language politics in the US have shaped literary cultures and the notional formation of an US discourse of belonging, Joshua Miller (2011) points out that the debate regarding ethnicities, and their place in US society, has repeatedly emerged in the US in response to what he terms as Anglophone primacy. For Miller, Anglophone primacy results in the homogenisation of the US literature category in specific and narrow terms that push works that are not written in English to the category of ethnic literature. Miller's study suggests that the category of ethnic literature is a construction that responds to wider drives for assimilation within a US society based on Anglophone primacy. To support this argument, Miller's study highlights how, despite continuous efforts in legislation, there is no single official language in the US. With this in mind, and extending Miller's argument, we could affirm that there is a multiplicity of literatures written by different groups that forms a whole, regardless of the language in which it is written, and the cultural heritage it draws upon. This sounds slightly familiar, particularly considering Moser and Tosta's more inclusive definition of the Portuguese American writer in terms of a relationship with the author's Portuguese linguistic and cultural heritage, regardless of where they come from in the Portuguese-speaking world. It also echoes the observations about how literary categories are porous, and how writers that could be said to belong to Portuguese American literature can also belong to other literary categories. In the same way that a writer should not be restricted to a single literary category, this same writer can also serve the needs of a particular literary category. For Portuguese American literature, belonging to that literary category means exploring the negotiation of different cultures and traditions, the examination of the interactions of the Portuguese community (and communities) within US society, and even the exploration of the writers' Portuguese heritage in the widest sense. As Vaz's case exemplifies, the Portuguese American writer can move between categorisations and serve different aims. In other words, Portuguese American literature can be defined as a porous literary category whose authors simultaneously belong to other literary categories, but who also address the specific parameters for inclusion within the Portuguese American literary label. Such an approach is not without its problems, but it is a productive start towards forming a recognised literary category that is more inclusive and representative of the reality of the Portuguese American community on the ground. Crucially, a more inclusive approach to the definition of Portuguese American literature can aid, and be aided, by community-led initiatives already present within the US that promote pride in being Portuguese American in the widest sense of the word. It requires, however, that differences are set aside in order to work together for a common project.

Ultimately, as Vamberto Freitas points out, we are talking about an incremental, gradual process. Any visibility, community-led initiative, even academic attention, of the Portuguese American community is desirable in order to encourage future generations to have pride in their heritage, and to write about the community to which they belong. This creates the conditions for the appearance of more works that could be seen as belonging to the Portuguese American literary canon, even if they are seen as belonging to ethnic literature. Taking into account the list of authors found in the anthologies and the authors published by Tagus Press, to give two examples, Portuguese American literature is a healthy field well on its way to moving beyond being an example of ethnic writing, but it needs the support (in the widest definition of the word) of the Portuguese American community (in the widest sense) to get there.

NOTES

1. Elsewhere, I have written about the role of anthologies and canon formation, in the context of Azorean literature (see Ramos Villar 2007). Vamberto Freitas has also commented on how anthologies help to build a picture of how big a canon is (2012: 296).

2. Her most recent publication, *The Love Life of an Assistant Animator & Other Stories*, also includes montages of photographs, perhaps asking the reader to make connections between the image and the text.

3. A possible reason for this is that her first editor was Bob Wyatt, García Márquez's North American editor (LA Times, 21/02/1992). Around the time when Vaz began to publish her work, US readers had seen the publication of Glória Anzaldúa's *Borderlands/La Frontera* (1987), Sandra Cisneros' *Woman Hollering Creek and Other Stories* (1991), and Júlia Álvarez's *How the García Girls Lost Their Accents* (1991), along with the publication of Laura Esquivel's *Como agua para chocolate* (1989), which was quickly turned into the blockbuster film (1992).

4. I wish to express my gratitude to Cláudia Pazos Alonso for highlighting this.

5. See her biographical details in her author's webpage (http://katherinevaz.com/bio/longer-bio/).

6. For instance, university programs offered at Brown (since 1980s), UMass Amherst (from 1990s), and UMass Dartmouth (since the mid 2000s, also home of Tagus Press).

7. To name two examples, please see the work undertaken by the Casa da Saudade in New Bedford (which is near Brown, UMass Amherst, and UMass Dartmouth), and the J. A. Freitas Library in California.

8. Just to name two, we have Onésimo Teotónio Almeida and Francisco Cota Fagundes, who are very active within both Azorean and Portuguese academic circles.

9. According to its website, the Disquiet International Literary Program is "run by a group of North American writers with ties to Portugal [...] to deepen mutual understanding among writers from North America and writers from Portugal." For more information on the Disquiet Program, see http://disquietinternational.org/who-we-are/.

10. Anecdotally, I am told that, in the 1980s, there had been efforts by the Portuguese embassy in the US to promote prominent public figures in the US who had Portuguese heritage. This is part of the reason why Danielle Steel, whose mother was Portuguese, could possibly be included in the list of Portuguese American writers, or why the actor Tom Hanks forms part of the list of important Portuguese American figures. Such lists could be seen as forming part of a wider move for Portuguese American visibility within the US by providing inspirational examples so as to aid the Portuguese American community's aim in promoting cultural initiatives.

11. In his introduction to a volume on Portuguese American literature, António Ladeira (2013) poses a series of provocative questions about the double bind of producing and promoting Portuguese American literature on ethnic grounds.

WORKS CITED

Printed sources:

Almeida, Onésimo Teotónio. "Portuguese-American Literature: Some Thoughts and Questions." *Hispania* 88.4 (2005): 733-738.

Baden, Nancy T. "Portuguese-American Literature: Does it Exist? The Interface of Thoery and Reality in a Developing Literature" MELUS 6.2 (1979): 15-31.

Batista, Adelaide, "Língua/Linguagens ou uma ética de sobrevivência em *Saudade* de Katherine Vaz." *Suplemento Açoriano de Cultura* N. 99 (28 Outubro de 1999): 1-4.

———. "Língua/Linguagens ou uma ética de sobrevivência em *Saudade*, de Katherine Vaz." *La Lusofonie – voies/voix océaniques*. Université Libre de Bruxelles: Edições Lidel, 2000: 320-329.

Borges Accardi, Millicent. "An Interview with Vamberto Freitas." *BorderCrossings: leituras transatlânticas* 3. Ponta Delgada: Publiçor, 2012: 287-306.

Cid, Teresa. "Katherine Vaz, Rethinking the Portuguese Diaspora." *Feminine Identities*. edited by Luísa Maria Flora, Teresa F. A. Alves and Teresa Cid, Lisbon: Edições Colibrí, 2013: 250-269.

Clemente, Alice, and George Monteiro. Eds. *The Gávea-Brown Book of Portuguese American Poetry*. Providence, Rhode Island: Gávea-Brown Publishers, 2013.

Cook, Manuela. "The Woman in Portuguese Fado-Singing." *International Journal of Iberian Studies* 16.1 (2003): 19-32.

Coutinho Mendes, Ana Paula. "Ficções de luso-descendentes e identidades híbridas."' *Cadernos de literatura comparada* 8/9. Porto: Instituto de Literatura Comparada Margarida Losa, 2003: 27-49.

———. "Portugal imaginado por escritores luso-descendentes." *Revista da Faculdade de Letras – Línguas e Literaturas* XXI (2004): 185-197.

Freitas, Vamberto. "Da obra de Nancy T Baden: literature luso-americana e algo mais." *Imaginários luso-americanos e Açorianos: do outro lado do espelho*. Ponta Delgada: Edições da Macaronésia, 2010: 17-33

———. "Outras narrativas americanas." *BorderCrossings: leituras transatlânticas*. Ponta Delgada: Publiçor, 2012: 245-248.

Gonçalves, Luis, and Carlo Matos. Eds. *Writers of the Portuguese Diaspora in the United States and Canada: An Anthology*. Roosevelt, New Jersey: Boavista Press, 2015.

Halpern, Manuel. *O futuro da saudade: o novo fado e os novos fadistas*. Lisbon: Dom Quixote, 2004.

Horta, Maria Teresa. 'Katherine Vaz apresenta "Mariana."' *Diário de Notícias*, 29 Junho 1998.

Ladeira, António. "Invisible no More. Introduction: a Few Perplexities and Perspectives on Portuguese-American Literature." *Gávea-Brown* XXXIV-XXXV (2013): 7-22.

Larkosh, Christopher. "'Ex-Centric' Lusophonias. On Remembered Language and its Possible Futures in Portuguese American Culture' *Lusofonia and its Futures. Portuguese Literary and Cultural Studies* 25 (2013): 42-65.

Leal, João. "The Making of *Saudade*: National Identity and Ethnic Psychology in Portugal." *Roots and Rituals: The Construction of Ethnic Identities*. Edited by Tom Decker, John Helsloot and Carla Witjers, Amsterdam: Het Spinhuis, 2000: 267-287.

Miller, Joshua. *Accented America: The Cultural Politics of Multilingual Modernism*. Oxford: Oxford University Press, 2011.

Moser, Robert Henry, and Antonio Luciano de Andrade Tosta. Eds. *Luso-American Literature: Writing by Portuguese-Speaking Authors in North America*. New Brunswick, New Jersey: Rutgers University Press, 2011.

Ramos Villar, Carmen. "Anthologies and Azorean Literature: The Construction of an Azorean Identity." *Reading Iberia: Theory/History/Identity*. edited by Helena Buffery, Stuart Davies and Kirsty Hooper, Bern: Peter Lang, 2007: 141-158.

Silva, Reinaldo Francisco. "The Ethnic Garden in Portuguese-American Writing." *Journal of American Culture* 28.2 (2005): 191-200.

———. *Representations of the Portuguese in American Literature*. Dartmouth, MA: Center for Portuguese Studies and Culture, University of Massachusetts Dartmouth, 2008.

———. *Portuguese American Literature*. Penrith: Humanities E-Books / LLP, 2009.

Vaz, Katherine. *Saudade*. New York: St Martin's Press, 1994.

———. *Fado & other Stories*. Pittsburg, PA: University of Pittsburgh Press, 1997.
———. *Mariana*. London: Flamingo, 1998.
———. *The Love Life of an Assistant Animator & Other Stories*. New York: Tailwinds Press, 2017.

Web sources:
The Disquiet website: http://disquietinternational.org/who-we-are/ (last consulted 15/03/2018)
Katherine Vaz's website: http://katherinevaz.com/bio/longer-bio/ (last consulted 15/03/2018)

CARMEN RAMOS VILLAR is a Senior Lecturer in Hispanic Studies in the School of Languages and Cultures at the University of Sheffield. Her doctoral thesis (2004) examined the theme of emigration in Portuguese literature, concentrating on the works produced by writers from the Azores islands and from the Azorean-American community. Her research interests centre on Azorean literature, and on Portuguese American literature. She is currently looking at how autobiographical writings, and biographical studies, portray the Portuguese migrant in the United States.

DANIEL F. SILVA

Trans-Atlantic Imbalances:
Indexicality, Translingual Signs, and Power in the Portuguese "Global Nation"

ABSTRACT: Following the dissolution of the Portuguese Estado Novo regime and subsequent crumbling of the nation's overseas colonial empire, the Portuguese state, media outlets, and many cultural elites fomented a narrative of a diasporic Portuguese "global nation," looking to bring together the former imperial metropolis with the many Portuguese emigrant communities abroad. This essay will interrogate how marginalizing notions of center and periphery within this "global nation" play out in the realm of language. This marginalization along the lines of speech is carried out by dominant discourses surrounding "normative" and "orderly" linguistic practices and concomitant national identities that pervade and construct the global nation, including mass media and Portuguese-language education in emigrant communities. In this regard, what follows will examine the discrepancies in cultural value ascribed to lexical loans performed by metropolitan speakers in comparison to those of Portuguese emigrants abroad.

KEYWORDS: Luso-American, Portuguese Migration, Portuguese Language, Portuguese National Identity, Power, Ideology

RESUMO: Após a dissolução do Estado Novo português e a subsequente queda do império ultramarino, o estado português, meios de comunicação portugueses, e membros das elites culturais abraçaram e promoveram uma nova narrativa nacional posicionando Portugal, agora pós-imperial, como uma "nação global," interpelando, assim, as numerosas comunidades de emigrantes portugueses radicadas no estrangeiro a participarem nesta reinvenção nacional, embora de uma posição liminal em termos de poder, privilégio, e prestígio social. Deste modo, o ensaio que se segue procura analisar alguns dos discursos marginalizantes, sobretudo, no domínio linguístico, que, por sua vez, produzem uma paradoxal presença simbólica e exclusão cultural no que diz respeito às comunidades no estrangeiro, designando práticas linguísticas "normativas" e "ordeiras" versus "ilegítimas" e "disordeiras" através de meios de comunicação e instituições escolares transnacionais.

Esta análise desenvolver-se-á em torno de uma comparação a nível de empréstimos lexicais entre falantes da metrópole e aqueles das comunidades portuguesas no estrangeiro.

PALAVRAS-CHAVE: Identidade Luso-Americana, Emigração Portuguesa, Língua Portuguesa, Identidade Nacional Portuguesa, Poder, Ideologia

Introduction

A 1977 editorial in the Portuguese newspaper *Diário de Notícias* proposed a rethinking of how Portuguese post-imperial national and cultural identity was to take on global specificities following the fall of the Estado Novo and the subsequent official dissolution of Portugal's imperial project: "O destino de Portugal nunca esteve como agora, tão intimamente ligado à capacidade do Estado para coordenar o intercâmbio cultural entre os portugueses do continente, das ilhas e das comunidades de emigrantes em países europeus ou americanos" (cited in Lourenço 118). In her exploration of the Portuguese State's fomentation of a "global nation" (54), Bela Feldman-Bianco outlines the objectives behind the creation of the Secretariat of Portuguese Communities after the Carnation Revolution: "a) strengthening the persistence of Portuguese language and culture in the world; and b) economic, social and cultural cooperation among Portuguese communities abroad as well as among those communities and the different regions of Portugal" (56).

Such a Portuguese "global nation" began to take shape through state initiatives, such as the access to citizenship for certain Portuguese descendents born abroad and the creation of the Instituto Camões, and Fundação Luso-Americana para o Desenvolvimento, which have played a vital role in the opening of community schools for Portuguese language and education in Portuguese enclaves abroad, as laid out in the first clause of the Secretariat of Portuguese Communities' mission statement. To these, we can add media initiatives from state and private television networks, such as RTP's *Contacto* and SIC's *Alô Portugal* or +351. Across such initiatives—state-driven or through private companies—one finds a primary focus on disseminating the Portuguese language as the core of the global nation. Sónia Ferreira underscores the presence of the Secretariat's mission in Portuguese media outlets geared toward Portuguese emigrant communities:

> a língua e a cultura popular adquirem particular destaque na configuração de identidade portuguesa na diáspora, através do consumo de conteúdos mediáticos. Estes, quer seja como informação, entretenimento ou divulgação, ancoram-se numa suposta portugalidade pela língua [...] a questão que assume contornos mais expressivos é, sem dúvida, a que remete para a utilização da língua nacional." (341)

The Secretariat's mission statement, moreover, reads like a rehashing of the old Estado Novo nationalist/imperialist slogan "Portugal não é um país pequeno." The mantra was often accompanied by a map superimposing Portugal's colonies over the rest of Europe. The goal was to demonstrate that, along with its colonies, or "overseas provinces," Portugal was comparable in size to Europe. The comparison with Europe continued to be relevant with the integration of Portugal into the European community and the nation's insistent claims of global impact and historical clout. In a similar vein, the death of empire is assuaged by another form of expansion now centered on emigrant communities and individuals with cultural and/or biographical ties to Portugal. As with other expansionist projects, one finds here an assimilationist mission which is also the means through which the global nation will be formed; that is, "creating" Portugueseness.

It is in this sense that one finds the pedagogical and subjectivizing role of the Secretariat—not only teaching about Portugal, but how to perform Portuguese identity, a message sent from center (metropolis) to margin (emigrant communities abroad). This ideologically disseminated Portugueseness is further complicated by the nation's transition from fascist imperial state to post-imperial democracy and insertion into late capitalist modes of production and consumption. In addition to symbolic and imperially nostalgic objectives, teaching Portugueseness and thus giving meaning to any ancestral connection an emigrant may have to Portugal, incurs significant revenue for both the State and metropolitan businesses through frequent travels to Portugal, investment in Portuguese financial institutions, or the purchase of real estate there. As the first objective underscores, a key instrument and criteria for the performance of Portugueseness concerns language. It is in the linguistic realm, therefore, that we can observe the formulations of center and margin in the "global nation." What follows proposes an examination of how such notions play out in terms of linguistic production, looking specifically at the use of non-Portuguese words by speakers in both the metropolis and emigrant communities.

I have opted to refer to such words as translingual signs because of their ambivalent categorization across geographic sites within the global nation. The borders between different products of contact between languages, such as code-switching, loanwords, and nonce borrowing, have been an object of debate among scholars in different branches of linguistics. Shana Poplack, for instance, defines code-switching as "the alternation of two languages within a single discourse, sentence or constituent" ("Sometimes" 583). A central component of code-switching, Poplack further argues in reference to the transition from Spanish to English among bilingual Puerto Rican subjects in New York City, is the preservation of (in this case) English phonological patterns (583). This is in contrast to English terms adapted to Puerto Rican Spanish patterns which Poplack attributes to monolingual Spanish discourse. A code-switch must, according to Poplack's criteria, avoid either phonological, morphological, or syntactic integration into the base language—Spanish in the case of Poplack's study, or Portuguese in the cases explored in this paper.

Some of the results of language contact considered here would, instead, be considered nonce borrowing, as in the case of an utterance further analyzed below from Lídia Jorge's novel *O Cais das Merendas*: "Aquele encontro não tinha nada a ver com as merendas, mas com os *parties*" (17). As Poplack explains, "the nonce loan tends to involve lone lexical items, generally major-class words, and to assume the morphological, syntactic, and often, phonological identity of the recipient language" ("Code-switching" 3). An example of "Portinglês" from Luso-American poet José Brites to be examined below offers a further complicated instance of nonce borrowing: "Na América, são vaqueixas" (337). Here, the nonce loan from the English "vacation," undergoes a profound morpho-phonological adaptation into Portuguese, as indicated by the change in the final syllable from "vacation" to "vaqueixas;" arguably reflective of the Portuguese equivalent "férias" existing solely in the plural.

Nonce borrowing also differs from loanwords in that the latter are, due to widespread use, conventionally accepted into the recipient language and, therefore, more likely to be understood by most speakers of the recipient language. Like other, less official nonce loans, conventional loanwords have also undergone morphological, phonological, and syntactic integration into the everyday practice of monolingualism. As the larger excerpt from *O Cais das Merendas* will suggest, the nonce *parties* in Portuguese is understood by the novel's main characters mainly through context clues. This liminal comprehension of Portugal's new bourgeois consumer vocabulary underscores the protagonists' (reconfigured) marginality within post-Estado Novo Portugal. The novel also marks a moment in the transition of some nonce loans into conventional loanwords, such as *hotel*.

What I wish to explore below has less to do with the different categories of inter-lingual contact than with the repercussions in terms of social power and privilege for using the results of this contact within the Portuguese diaspora. As this paper will explore below, the use of translingual signs among Portuguese emigrants comes into conflict with that of metropolitan speakers, and with the prerogatives of the Portuguese State to disseminate the official language, which is imposed "on the whole population as the only legitimate language" (Bourdieu 45). As I will consider below, part of reproducing the legitimacy of the official language implies establishing and consistently articulating a system of norms that regulates linguistic practices.

These norms ultimately reproduce notions of center and margin between different geographic and socioeconomic partitions of the Portuguese global nation in terms of "legitimate" and "illegitimate" speech. This divide can be seen precisely in the permitted lexical borrowing of metropolitan speakers and the delegitimization of the same phenomena among emigrant communities. One stark example of this inequity concerns a term for shopping mall used by metropolitan Portuguese speakers versus the term commonly used by Portuguese-Americans. In standardized Portuguese (in Portugal and the Lusophone world), the term *shopping* has successfully undergone the transition into conventional loanword, whereas the term *mall* used by Portuguese and other Lusophone emigrants in the United States in Portuguese utterances continues to be invalidated.

Drawing on the work of linguistic anthropologist Jane Hill (1999), in a different sociolinguistic context, the underlying argument that shall guide my paper posits that the transnational public space of the Portuguese global nation is constructed through (1) the persistent surveillance of othered (and therefore marginal) members of the global nation for linguistic disorder, such as "incorrect" lexical borrowing; and (2) the invisibility and/or conventional acceptance of almost identical signs in the speech of metropolitan speakers for which language mixing is "required for the expression of a highly valued type of colloquial persona" (Hill 680). The designation of lexical borrowing among Portuguese emigrants abroad as disordered speech (as in the case of *mall* versus *shopping*) reproduces, in other words, the cultural and socioeconomic liminality of such speakers within the global nation. This marginalization along the lines of speech is carried out by the dominant discourses surrounding language and national identities that pervade and construct the global nation, including mass media and Portuguese-language education in emigrant communities.

Language, Ideology, and the *Luso-* Subject

To begin, we can think of the Portuguese state initiatives mentioned above as examples of transcontinental nationalism; a form of transnationalism that would suggest an interaction or movement across nation-spaces. Although there is a transnational component at work here, by creating Portugueseness across borders, it is a national consciousness that is institutionally and culturally (through media) disseminated across states. In terms of engendering consciousness, it is helpful to think of these initiatives as looking to interpellate, drawing on Louis Althusser (1972), a *luso-* subject—referring to the nationalist adjective anteceding that which designates the host country (i.e. Luso-American, Luso-Trinidadian, etc). The *luso-* subject, existing across different national/ideological spaces, is culturally formed in relation to the metropolitan Portuguese subject. In this sense, the Portuguese global nation, as an imperially nostalgic endeavor of national expansion, also very much recreates imperial notions of center and periphery, notably in linguistic realms. Such notions of otherness are themselves evident within the metropolis along the lines of urban/rural, southern and northern regions, class, race, gender, sexuality, age, and (dis)ability.

The aforementioned interpellation functions as "a hailing" (Althusser) that names and places the subject within the realm of ideology, where nationalism, as well as relations of power, exist. Interpellation into the Portuguese global nation does not negate the subject's interpellation into other fields of meaning. Rather, several interpellations take place simultaneously, and it is how different interpellations interact with one another that will inform how the subject resides in the larger social world. In other words, it is the relationship between the *luso-* subject's different and overlapping interpellations—into birth country, production, race, gender, sexuality, etc. —that will inform their place in the global nation. The Portuguese global nation is not, then, its own discursive field, it exists within a larger global plane of meaning formed by historical movements of capital, bodies, and ideas. The relationship between the *luso-* subject and the metropolitan hegemonic constructions of Portugueseness is thus born from these dimensions and concomitant interpellations.

The shaping of global Portugueseness emanating from metropolitan cultural initiatives reproduces the centrality/hegemony of the metropolis while establishing the liminality of Portugueseness in communities abroad. One of the ways through which this simultaneous hegemony and liminality is manifested and reproduced can be found in language, or in this case, in the interaction of languages. We can, in other words, pinpoint modes of othering in linguistic production, as well as the geographic and socioeconomic underpinnings of these, through the use of lexical borrowing in relation to standard Portuguese language, and adjacently, standard Portugueseness. As Marxist linguist Valentin Voloshinov (1973) underscores, language and ideology (such as that of Portuguese global nationalism located within late capitalism) cannot be separated, as the former is the medium of the latter. More recently, the fields of sociolinguistics, linguistic anthropology, and semiotics have grappled, in different ways, with the connections between speech, language, and the construction of social meaning within which power and privilege are embedded and reproduced. In a similar vein to Voloshinov, Pierre Bourdieu demands that we treat language as "an instrument of action and power" (37) while arguing that linguistic exchanges "are also relations of symbolic power in which the power relations between speakers or their respective groups are actualized" (37).

Notably, in the subfield of linguistic variation—studying phonetic, lexical, morphological, and/or syntactic phenomena—which concerns us here, scholars such as Penelope Eckert have theorized that such variation and variables:

> are not precise or fixed but rather constitute a field of potential meanings – an *indexical field*, or constellation of ideologically related meanings [...] Thus variation constitutes an indexical system that embeds ideology in language and that is in turn part and parcel of the construction of ideology. (454)

Lexical borrowing as a form of variation leads us to a larger consideration of the indexical field of Portuguese language use. Other examples of the concept of variation include particular varieties that are more or less identifiable, such as Rio de Janeiro Portuguese. Each variety may be made up of variables—speech practices that vary from those of other identifiable varieties—such as the pronunciation of /r/ in Rio de Janeiro. Studying the indexical field of Portuguese language use will, of course, carry implications not only for the Portuguese global nation, but for *Lusofonia* as well—designating the nations whose official language is Portuguese as well as diasporic Portuguese-speaking communities around the world. Examining the indexical field of *Lusofonia* can serve as a useful tool for unpacking the imperial and exploitative legacies contained in the imagined collective and expressed through the politics of power surrounding variation in Portuguese. Such an undertaking is relevant not only to scholars working in different branches of linguistics, but also to those interested in questions pertaining to ideology and power, such as myself.[1]

Discrepancies in Lexical Borrowing

Lídia Jorge's *O Cais das Merendas* (1982) brings to light the geographic and socioeconomic underpinnings of hegemonic Portugueseness in the wake of Portugal's imperial demise—a time of cultural renegotiation regarding the imperial past and the possibility of integrating into Europe. The novel's protagonists, a group of Algarvian peasants, are confronted with the new everyday language of modern Portugueseness and international bourgeois consumption after leaving agricultural labor for employment at a trendy oceanfront tourist resort, the Hotel Alguergue, in the southern Portuguese region. The group, as metonymic representatives of pre-Carnation Revolution rural life, undergoes the erasure of past signifiers in favor of those pertinent to, and indicative of, a modernized post-imperial present guided by the development of the tourist industry that inserts Portugal into late capitalism's network of bourgeois consumption. In her reading of the novel, Helen Kaufman argues that the "hotel symbolizes 'modern' European culture that invades the Algarve and is expected to change the region. Although the Algarvians seek assimilation and seem, at least in theory, ready to join the modern world's progress, they find themselves alienated and lost" (172).

As the narrator reflects on a particular gathering during the tourist off-season in which the group of protagonists attempts to appropriate the lexicon of their "modern" consumers:

> aquele encontro não poderia continuar a ser merenda. Porque merenda, como disse, sempre lembraria o tempo das ceifas, por exemplo, quando a dor de macaco tanto apertava o rim [...] Lembrava a era do trabalho sem hora, de sol a sol, o calor [...] Era preciso esquecer tudo isso... Aquele encontro não tinha nada a ver com as merendas, mas com os *parties*. (16-17)

The representation of everyday life of the Estado Novo era, embodied by the protagonists, is undergirded by imagery of rural peasantry and/or small land ownership; evoking a subject that resides temporally and spatially outside of the speech that marks the present. In this sense, time and space in relation to labor, specifically rural/resort and pre-/post-Revolution dichotomies are conveyed in the novel via the relationship between characters and dominant modes of production and consumption. Through this lens, the aforementioned temporal and spatial dichotomies come to stand for developed versus undeveloped. Subsequently, in the idiom of hegemony, culturally normalizing and standardizing the dominant, the subjects emanating from the nation's rural areas are thus categorized through the frame of underdevelopment and backwardness. The other side of this frame is that of the global marketplace within which Portugal is now placed; its coastal areas now existing as a commodity to be consumed largely by an emerging national bourgeoisie and an existing international one.

In an approach similar to that of Pierre Bourdieu, Lídia Jorge connects the subject's existence within capital to modes of linguistic production. In the wake of the Estado Novo's fall, both of these have taken new directions. The protagonists move from rural subsistence-based production to the hospitality industry's production of tourist experiences. In being exposed to a new mode of production in terms of labor, they also confront a new mode of linguistic production, one to which they consider assimilating, yet from which they are largely barred. The linguistic production they encounter corresponds to the performance of a new (read post-Estado Novo), bourgeois Portugueseness that deploys the lexicon of international consumption, namely from English vocabulary. The word *estalagem*, for example, is replaced with *hotel*, leaving the narrator to observe: "bastaria o novo nome dado à coisa para a coisa se transformar" (55). The narrator connects this new reality of labor, language, and consumption to a geographic space now to be considered "a verdadeira Europa" (34). *Hotel* thus becomes a lexical prestige variant evoked in the performance of contemporary bourgeois notions of Europeanness. The aforementioned term *shopping* for shopping mall, instead of *centro comercial*, has arguably also entered conventional Portuguese language through its indexicality of post-Estado Novo bourgeois consumer culture. Meanwhile, the use of *mall* among Portuguese-American emigrants indexes, within the global nation, working-class migratory consumption, a subaltern subject-position in relation to the metropolitan middle-class.

The lexical borrowing in Jorge's novel now becomes part of the language of contemporary European Portugueseness, which simultaneously comes to linguistically embody the center of the Portuguese global nation. Access to this lexicon is, moreover, limited to existent bourgeois circles previously possessing particular cultural capital, including those subjects that were able to access the signifying process of Portuguese nationhood—intellectuals, politicians, journalists, business magnates—through a variety of media. The privileged role in the realm of capital and production translates, in other words, into a prominent place in fields of cultural production, and is therefore reflected in linguistic production.

The *luso-* subject that is to be interpellated while residing abroad in Portuguese emigrant communities targeted by state-driven and private cultural initiatives occupies a place within labor and production that is similar to that of the hotel laborers in Jorge's novel. The Portuguese diaspora has largely been propelled by economic marginalization at home and subsequent occupation of unskilled labor in countries such as the United States (Klimt and Holton 2009), Canada (Klimt 2009; da Silva 2014), Germany (Klimt 2009), Trinidad and Tobago (Almeida 2004), Brazil (Rowland 2004), France (Leandro 1995; Cordeiro 1997; Carvalheiro 2014), among many others. One can thus observe a similar sociocultural dynamic between metropolitan elites and Portuguese émigré populations that we also see in Jorge's novel between elites and laborers. Additionally, the majority of Portuguese waves of emigration occurred prior to 1974, and was composed primarily of members of the rural working class, thus becoming inserted into the global flow of capital and migrant labor. As such, many Portuguese emigrants/*luso-* subjects, of multiple generations in some cases, are interpellated into a marginality of the diasporic nation, as they would have been had they resided in the metropolis; with language once again playing a prominent role.

As a result of contact with other languages throughout the Portuguese diaspora, many writers of the diaspora have incorporated code-switching and lexical borrowing into their literary works as part of emigrant experiences they look to convey. In exploring the relationship of Luso-American writers to Portugueseness and the Portuguese language, Christopher Larkosh describes their cases as "ex-centric Lusofonias"—"referring to that off-center space, mental flight, or exploration of geographical horizons, diasporic cultures, or other presumably marginal spaces, all of them hospitable to poetic imagination and intellectual discourse" (43–44). We can read further into and expand Larkosh's term to consider also how the center and margins of *Lusofonia* and the Portuguese global nation are constructed in terms of race, place, gender, sexuality, class, (dis)ability, age, religion, and most crucially for our study, linguistic production; and how these play out for *luso-* writers. The work of some Luso-American writers in

Portuguese has overtly named this marginality in linguistic production. This is the case with José Brites's poem "Emigrês e Portinglês"—the first term referring to Luso-American scholar and writer Eduardo Mayone Dias's coining of the term for lexical borrowing from the host nation's language(s) into Portuguese spoken by Portuguese (Dias 1989). Both terms, furthermore, seem to name a variety of Portuguese spoken in different sites of the Portuguese diaspora.

The tension between emigrant communities and metropolitan constructions of normative linguistic production is at the heart of Brites's poem.

> A palavra é magia
> e sua ausência, a morte.
> Dos peitos, a alegria.
> A sonora é a mais forte.
> A escrita é o documento
> que sempre há-de comprovar
> qu' na história em cada momento
> se soube comunicar.
> Mas dos linguistas as queixas:
> "Se foram nossas esp'ranças!
> Na América, são vaqueixas...
> e na França são vacanças....
> Porque diabo o Mayone
> que dizem ser português
> anda armado em camone
> com isso do emigrês?!"
>
> Nós dizemos a tais fadistas:
> Como não há duas sem três
> - ca falamos portinglês! (337)

The poem effectively plots the marginalizing forces of metropolitan hegemony and voices resistance to it from the margin. Brites places this linguistic production within global Portuguese language, but asserts its validity against the assimilationist forces of standardized metropolitan Portuguese proliferated throughout Portuguese emigrant communities.

The poem begins with a perhaps romanticized view of the importance of language, only then to underscore the inequities that exist within it. Importantly, especially for matters of power and symbolic capital outlined in the poem, the exposition of these begins with "mas dos linguistas as queixas." We can argue that the poem refers to more than just strictly linguists, but to a larger set of social actors and subjects that serve as instruments of surveillance for standard language. Bourdieu locates even more specifically these actors and their relation to official language:

> Produced by authors who have the authority to write, fixed and codified by grammarians and teachers who are also tasked with inculcating mastery, the language is a *code*, in the sense of a cipher enabling equivalences to be established between sounds and meanings, but also in the sense of a system of norms regulating linguistic practices. (45)

Furthermore, "linguistas," and their role within the Portuguese "global nation" (including its systems of production), echoes Antonio Gramsci's theorization of the relationship between intellectuals and hegemony (12). More than serving as the gatekeepers of "correct" Portuguese, the metaphoric linguists also reproduce the social rules and meanings—in this case linguistic norms—that prop up dominant modes of production.

The social actors and forces that rebuke certain lexical loans, such as those deployed by Brites, while permitting others, designate the parameters of adequate and orderly Portugueseness. The lexical loans with which Lídia Jorge's characters grapple in *O Cais das Merendas* have largely become markers of cultural capital within the metropolitan and global markets of Portuguese language, while the loans used within emigrant communities are seen as incompatible with the image of Portugueseness established in the metropolis and disseminated politically and commercially throughout the diaspora. Brites makes this dissonance particularly clear: "Porque diabo o Mayone/que dizem ser português/ anda armado em camone/ com isso do emigrês?!" (337). Orderly Portugueseness, in other words, must be conveyed through conventional normative monolingual practices.

For the evoked "linguistas," the use of *emigrês* thus implies a deficit of Portugueseness, a loss surrendered to the dominance of the host nation's language which, in the global exchange of imperial languages, also exercises prestige value over the Portuguese language. The succumbing to a globally dominant language, however, brings different consequences *vis-à-vis* Portugueseness depending on geographical location and, relatedly, location within global modes of production.[2]

The work of another Luso-American writer, Ramiro Dutra, sheds more light on the relationship between *emigrês* and emigrant experiences of global capital. Like the hotel workers of rural origins in *O Cais das Merendas*, the experiences outlined in Dutra's poem, "Lactifórnia," exist as instruments of wealth accumulation within global capital:

> Meu amor trabalha duro,
> Trabalha na leitaria,
> Chega a casa derreado,
> São três ordenhas por dia.
>
> [...]
>
> Meu amor trabalha duro
> Todos os dias do ano,
> P'ra dar de mamar à América
> Com este leite açoriano. (Dutra 309)

The linguistic production contained in the poem emerges, therefore, from these experiences of labor and production, rather than from bourgeois consumption that informs metropolitan code-switching and the integration of loanwords into conventional Portuguese.

> A Sandra faz "baby-sitting",
> Cozinha que é um encanto,
> E há-de um dia coroar
> No Senhor Espírito Santo.
>
> [...]
>
> A vaca é a nossa vida,
> A nossa sustentação,
> Põe a comida na mesa,
> Paga os "bills" e o camião. (Dutra 310)

Lexical loans, such as that in the stanzas above, typically integrated into Portuguese phonological patterns, circulate within a Luso-American sphere of meanings where socioeconomic challenges coexist with, and in many ways inform, traditional ceremonies (such as Espírito Santo festivals) and how they are performed. Dutra's poem thus gives expression to a form of Portugueseness on the margins of both the global nation and global capital; while also demonstrating how the latter informs the former.

As Brites's poem underscores, the social forces behind official Portuguese, and dominant notions of Portugueseness recognize this form of linguistic production as disorderly. In doing so, the same forces of exclusion that historically forced the emigration of many Portuguese, thus forming émigré communities, continue to play out in the so-called Portuguese global nation depending on one's place in global capital and production. As Robin Tolmach Lakoff explains, speakers enter discursive realms "with differing amounts of real-world power, authority, and status, and these are translated into differences in permissible linguistic behavior" (44). In other words, it is not the lexical borrowing that marginalizes the speaker, but rather the speaker's marginalized place in capital that impacts how their linguistic production is valued and interpreted in the global nation.

Indexicality and Symbolic Exchanges

The luso- subject is signified through the post-Estado Novo metropolis's construction of the global nation and interpellated via intersecting institutions, such as schools, family, and media. Although the use of Portuguese language is not the singular medium of participation in the global collectivity, orderly/bourgeois-derived linguistic production is nonetheless a nationalist measure of adequate Portugueseness and a criterion for accessing the signifying process of the Portuguese global national narrative. The same is true for residents of both the metropolis and of communities abroad. As Emanuel da Silva explains, discourses surrounding global Portuguese nationalism tend to "gloss over internal divisions based on unequal capital (be it linguistic, regional, cultural, economic, gendered, or generational)" (190). Although strategically neglected at the level of official discourse, these divisions, as the literary texts above illustrate, consistently emerge and inform subjectivity within the Portuguese global nation.

The linguistic production of the luso- subject resides within a larger field of global Portuguese language and, relatedly, global late capitalism. A linguistic variety, such as the emigrês, or a style like bourgeois speech, exists within the constellation of meanings of local and global matrices of power. As Dermeval da Hora notes, moreover, "avaliar a variação associada ao estilo implica avaliar a identidade do usuário" (20). Eckert delves further into the relationship between identity, style, and ideology by positing ideology "at the center of stylistic practice:

one way or another, every stylistic move is the result of an interpretation of the social world and of the meanings of elements within it, as well as a positioning of the stylizer with respect to that world" (456). Using Bourdieu's theoretical terminology, different styles or varieties exist within a linguistic market—in this case that of Portuguese. This market is, furthermore, always in contact with other linguistic markets and is part of the circulation of languages within global matrices of power, such as that of, and leading to, late capitalism. We can, therefore, talk about a global linguistic market within late modernity in which different languages circulate carrying different exchange value in a cultural economy framed by centuries of empire. Within the global linguistic market, and the language-specific markets (as well as different local markets) contained therein, one finds "an economy of symbolic exchanges" (Bourdieu 37) where power, privilege, and subalternity are performed, recognized, and policed.

Concisely put, the indexical field is the series of connotations (tied to socioeconomics, race, sexuality, gender, (dis)ability) attributed to different variants—phonetic, lexical, prosodic, orthographic, and syntactic. As Eckert phrases it, the indexical field "is an embodiment of ideology in linguistic form" (464). The terminology of "indexicality" became an integral part of sociolinguistic theoretical parlance through Michael Silverstein (2003) and Eckert's work over the last two decades. The terms *index* and *indexical* were introduced to semiotics far earlier by Charles Sanders Peirce who referred to "indexical signs" (IV 359).[3] The indexical sign shares a connection to the object "as a matter of fact and by also forcibly intruding upon the mind" (IV 359). Peirce uses the weathervane as a metaphor for the indexical sign—one that points toward an entity (physical or otherwise) beyond it.

The study of indexicality examines how a subject's linguistic practice is ensnared into the field of social meaning where power and subalternity are discursively constructed and rendered legible. In this sense, linguistic production becomes a form of identity performance in which what we say, and how we say it, makes us legible to the aforementioned field of meaning and other interlocutors contained therein. These connotations, socially attached to variables, are never permanently fixed, however. As the bourgeois lexical borrowing in Lídia Jorge's novel illustrates, these connotations emerge through and reproduce existing power relations between speakers. This is where Bourdieu's concept of cultural capital is particularly helpful: subject-positions carrying significant cultural capital by way of their place in global and local matrices of power appropriate and integrate variants (foreign-language words, in this case) into their identitarian performance.

Greater power in the economy of capital and production correlates to greater power in the economy of symbolic exchanges in which privileged subjects can accumulate and resignify variables, imbuing them with what is called "prestige"—a term used in sociolinguistics, most famously by William Labov's studies in linguistic variation and social stratification in New York City (1966, 1972) to designate variants that tend to index markers of high social capital, such as education, wealth, and residence in affluent areas. This is, moreover, what Bourdieu would call a symbolic act of power. Jorge's novel thus traces for us the birth of a particular Portuguese prestige variant, emerging through a subject-position carrying sufficient cultural capital to transform a non-standard linguistic variant into one of prestige, and ultimately into conventional standard language, the case of *hotel* being just one example.

The subject-position voicing *emigrês*, on the other hand, exists in a place within capital and its field of meaning that is largely divergent from Jorge's bourgeois subject. This discrepancy ultimately underscores the notion that the speaker shapes and reproduces the indexical field through the linguistic signs that are voiced, written, or signed. This also speaks to the complexity of the relationship between the identity of the speaker and the field of social meaning in which indexicality, power, and prestige circulate. Notably, the same word, or lexical loan, carries different meanings and indexical value depending on the speaker's identitarian value in the global/imperial/capitalist economy of bodies. An example mentioned earlier illustrates precisely this: while the word *shopping* has become part of standard (global) Portuguese, the term *mall* remains stigmatized and labeled as illegitimate linguistic production, the opposite of a prestige variant.

Rather than defiantly using such lexical loans, as proposed by Brites, the luso- subject is taught to read the indexical field in accordance with the hierarchy of values attributed to each style—intersecting with social hierarchies—by the forces of social domination that posit particular styles in conjunction with power. Through institutional and corporate media forces, the luso- subject is guided away from the lexical borrowing of *emigrês* and toward standard Portuguese found in the Portuguese school classroom in the host country (usually funded and staffed by the institutions mentioned earlier) and in metropolitan mainstream media. In following the broadly disseminated style—the normative/standard—the *luso-* subject is more symbolically integrated into the constructed center of the global nation.

Moreover, for the bourgeois characters in *O Cais das Merendas*, inaugurating and utilizing a new variable does not "simply reflect or reassert their particular pre-ordained place on the social map" (Eckert 464). Rather, it implies an "ideological move" (Eckert 464) that adds to the semiotic repertoire of bourgeois identity performance. The linguistic sign, such as that used through bourgeois loans, is added to the world of signs as the subject performs the ideological maneuver of identity. This performance and introduction of a sign carries more value because of the speaker's initial transformation into a sign. As Eckert further elaborates, "the use of a variable is not simply an invocation of a pre-existing indexical value but an indexical claim which may either invoke a pre-existing value or stake a claim to a new value" (464). It is in this regard that the indexical field is always shifting, the dynamic nature of a language's lexicon being merely one example. Similarly, *emigrês* also stakes a claim to a new value by defiantly (in relation to metropolitan standard language) building upon an indexical field corresponding to Portuguese emigrant linguistic markets. Within the larger linguistic markets of the global nation and *Lusofonia*, however, these ideological moves diverge in value according to the speaker's place in the existing matrix of power.

Through socioeconomic stratification (and its intersections with other modes of exclusion) access to indexical value is also stratified with unequal participation in the economy of symbolic exchanges. This is, of course, evidenced in the linguistic production found within spheres of power—political, cultural, business, and financial—in which lexical loans have become part of everyday mainstream vocabulary. The instances of borrowing seen in *O Cais das Merendas*, as well as others in mainstream metropolitan media and popular culture index not only cultural capital by accessing foreign vocabulary, but also full participation in late modernity's modes of production (including cultural) and consumption. As such, they subsequently also index access to shaping dominant culture through such modes.

Bourgeois lexical borrowing, therefore, not only contributes to a collection of signs through which dominant identities can be performed, but also becomes integrated into dominant culture, as evidenced by the loans often found in news media, television programs, and other media. These are, of course, vehicles of staging normativity—be it linguistic, gender, ethnic, racial, or corporal, while simultaneously obscuring discursive processes of othering along these lines.

Furthermore, the perpetual elaboration of dominant culture—in this case, normative Portugueseness—also contributes to the field of meaning in which power is embedded, reproduced, and misrecognized. Regarding dominant culture and misrecognition, Bourdieu lays out the connection between these and language:

> ideologies serve particular interests which they tend to present as universal interests, shared by the group as a whole. The dominant culture contributes to the real integration of the dominant class (by facilitating the communication between all its members and by distinguishing them from other classes); it also contributes to the fictitious integration of society as a whole, and thus to the apathy (false consciousness) of the dominated classes; and finally, it contributes to the legitimation of the established order by establishing distinctions (hierarchies) and legitimating these distinctions. The dominant culture produces this ideological effect by concealing the function of division beneath the function of communication: the culture which unifies (the medium of communication) is also the culture which separates (the instrument of distinction) and which legitimates distinctions by forcing all other cultures (designated as subcultures) to define themselves by their distance from the dominant culture. (167)

Bourdieu's last sentence certainly applies to many subaltern experiences born of western expansion and imperial endeavor. It is also observable in José Brites's deployment of *emigrês*—defining Portuguese emigrant, and Portuguese-speaking linguistic production, by its distance to the linguistic production proposed and enforced by "os linguistas." Through this distance between marginal and dominant culture/speech the discrepancy in indexical and prestige value is reproduced, and so are dominant notions of valid Portuguese expression and identity that impact both Portuguese emigrant communities and under-privileged metropolitan citizens.

Disparate Capital, Disparate Subjectivities

As noted above, the value of a variant such as a lexical loan is contingent upon the speaker's value within the realm of signs composing the semiotic existence of the Portuguese global nation, which is in turn inextricable from the larger semiotic existence of global power relations. The speaker, or subject, is, in other words, also a sign composed of meaning attributed to labor, race, geographic location, gender, ethnicity, age, sexuality, and (dis)ability.

As a participant in the field of meaning, the subject exists and is interpreted through the circulation of signs that compose said field—what Jacques Lacan calls the symbolic realm—or "the universe of symbols" (*Seminar II*, 29). Notably, Voloshinov refers to this realm as "the world of signs" (10); and "without signs there is no ideology" (9). As power relations can only exist ideologically—through meaning given to power, and power given to meaning—there is a vested interest in reproducing the symbolic realm. The symbolic is also the place of language and subjectivity in which the subject exists as sign among other signs, linguistic, corporal, or otherwise. With regard to this particular relationship, Lacan claims that "the system of egos [is] entirely comprehended within [language]" (*Seminar II*, 278). Emile Benveniste comes to a similar conclusion when arguing that "it is in and through language that man constitutes himself as a *subject*, because language alone establishes the concept of 'ego' in reality" (224) [author's emphasis]. Moreover, Peirce, in a vein similar to Lacan's, argued decades earlier that "the word or sign which man uses is man himself [...] Thus my language is the sum total of myself" (V 189).

To exist as a subject in the symbolic realm, the process of identity is crafted and articulated through the semiotic fabric of this realm even before birth through social forces such as family, school, and other institutions. For the luso- subject as a body/sign this occurs, in addition to language, by way of symbols indexing their own Portugueseness including home decorations (such as the *galo de Barcelos*), soccer club affiliation, cuisine, quotidian interpersonal practices (i.e., membership in Portuguese social clubs), and participation in different rituals (as in the case of Portuguese-language Catholic mass or annual Portuguese diaspora festivals). State initiatives thus operate in tandem with different markets of goods and artifacts arising from diaspora, driven in either private or public sectors. These sorts of semiotic phenomena constitute the endless economy of signs into which the luso- subject is placed. These are, in other words, examples of the repeated moments in which the subject is confronted by the sign which it is to occupy in the symbolic/world of signs. As Voloshinov elaborates, "consciousness becomes consciousness only once it has been filled with ideological (semiotic) content, consequently only in the process of social interaction" (11). The body turned into a sign (i.e., the luso- subject), through signs, then circulates within the world of signs—becoming another link in the signifying chain of power. State and private initiatives look to guarantee that the luso- subject is legible as such to the authoritative gazes of orderly Portugueseness.

Value and Connotation in the Translingual Sign

Voloshinov's theorization of ideology as a constellation of signs effectively takes into account the relationship between power and language, and especially the role of the subject within the world of signs. For him, the nature of the sign is not fully understood without considering its ideological functions—the complex components comprising the word as a "social sign" (14). This invites us to consider the politics of lexical loans as "translingual signs" in order to account for the use and/or conventional integration of a linguistic sign from one language into another. This process of integration implies issues of indexical value and connotation that have been discussed in this essay. The conventionality of these loans suggests a borrowing not only at the level of individual speakers, but at the supra-level of an entire official language, the limits of which are elaborated and policed by agents of dominant culture. Subsequently, the integration of the sign makes its use in speech a marker of modern (that is, post-Estado Novo) Portugueseness.

The term "translingual" has been widely used in the realm of translation studies in contexts of shifting meanings, namely signifieds, from one language to another, especially in reference to a subject's experiences across different languages. The translingual sign at work in contemporary standard Portuguese entails far more than the evoked signified, summoning meanings that circulate beyond the sign. At the same time, thinking of lexical loans as linguistic signs sets up a theoretical trajectory through which to interrogate the semiotic, and therefore political, complexities that involve translingual integration. Distinguishing the conventional/orderly loanword *shopping* from the disorderly nonce loan *mall* thus serves to designate the inequity between the two; the former being a marker of privilege and born of the accumulation of capital, whereas the latter is denied legitimacy in the global nation. Understanding the emergence of the translingual sign demands an awareness of the workings of meanings that exist beyond it, but that are also central to its construction.

Regarding meanings that exist beyond the sign, and evoked by it, Roland Barthes notably works with a significational model that accounts for different relationships between signifier, signified, and the larger realm of meaning. Drawing on the work and model proposed by Louis Hjelmslev, Barthes is concerned mainly with the relationship between denotation and connotation of the sign. In challenging the authenticity of denotation, Barthes dismantles the fantasy of the totality and containment of meaning within the sign. This fantasy thus establishes a hierarchy positing denotation over connotation: "there is no reason to make this system the privileged one, to make it the locus and the norm of a primary, original meaning" (6).

The conventionality of *shopping* over *mall* offers an example of connotation impacting the emergence (or rather, selection) of a signifier and denoted referent. The connotation or indexical value of the signifier determines its reference to the signified in the language into which it is integrated. The appropriation of bourgeois foreign terms in *O Cais das Merendas* suggests that connotation, in a way, precedes denotation in its integration into Portuguese. The connotation of *hotel*, for instance, in being perceived as tied to a foreign bourgeois subject carrying significant cultural capital, is understood first through the subject speaking it. *Hotel* is a signifier that is chosen, because of its cultural capital, to denote the same as *estalagem*. In the cultural politics of lexical borrowing in Jorge's novel, connotation (namely bourgeois late capitalist consumption) is the criterion through which a signifier is appropriated and ultimately integrated into standard Portuguese. Voloshinov comes to a similar conclusion when refuting the "strict division between referential denotation and evaluative connotation" (105), arguing that such a division fails:

> to note the more profound functions of evaluation in speech. Referential meaning is molded by evaluation; it is evaluation, after all, which determines that particular referential meaning may enter the purview of speakers — both the immediate purview and the broader social purview of the particular social group. (105)

Value, in other words, is not extrinsic to the sign, whether it is the linguistic sign or the sign pertaining to a socially constructed body. Value, as a form of signification, emerges through historicized relations of power, global and local. It is thus the higher value placed on bourgeois foreign speakers over the existent marginality of working-class Portuguese emigrants that informs the higher indexical value attributed to bourgeois lexical loans in relation to the loans deemed "disordered" used by the emigrant *luso-* subject.

Conclusion

As often overlapping discursive projects, *Lusofonia* and the Portuguese global nation are constructed collectivities, within which emigrant identities with connections to Portugal or its former colonies are subsumed. Through the critical frameworks of indexicality, we can interrogate the imbalances and social disparities in power that the discursive project strategically glosses over. Such disparities are once again obfuscated under mainstream depoliticized and dehistoricized narratives of nation and language. In the realm of speech, the everyday performance of metropolitan linguistic centrality through particular lexical borrowing (among other linguistic phenomena) simultaneously inscribes the border between disorderly and normative speech between that which is permitted to metropolitan Portuguese speakers and that which must be policed by authorities of orderly Portugueseness.

It is in the semiotics of social life that disciplines may converge and offer nuanced understandings of Portugal's project of global nationality and *Lusofonia* as discursive projects that inevitably interact with the larger world of signs in which global and local forms of power are embedded. A complex critique of the imperial-esque expansion of the Portuguese language demands an examination of how those that speak the language are socially and culturally situated within it, and which forces do the situating. How do the criteria for "adequate" Portugueseness or sufficient Lusophony intersect with larger modes of exclusion? In interrogating value within linguistic production and exchanges across the Lusophone World, we arrive at larger questions of power, and the reasons for which *Lusofonia* and the Portuguese global nation continue to be so problematic.

NOTES

1. While several volumes have been published on *Lusofonia*, the volumes themselves, or the essays contained therein, have tended to be disciplinarily segregated between linguistics and cultural studies. For instance, *Lusofonia and Its Futures* (*Portuguese Literary & Cultural Studies* 25) contains only one essay by a scholar who identifies as a linguist, meanwhile all contributors to *Global Portuguese: Linguistic Ideologies in Late Modernity* situate themselves disciplinarily within linguistics.

2. Code-switching and lexical borrowing in other Portuguese-speaking immigrant communities has been well-documented such as in Brazilian (Araújo) (Bensabat-Ott) (Castellarin) and Cape Verdean (Carvalho) communities in the United States.

3. While Peirce uses the term *interpretant* as synonymous with referent, similar to Saussure's *signified*, Peirce's term leaves room for discord between sender and recipient. For Peirce, the sign is "something which stands to somebody for something in some respect or capacity. It addresses somebody, that is creates in the mind of that person an equivalent sign, or perhaps a more developed sign. That sign which it creates I call the *interpretant* of the first sign (II 135) [author's emphasis].

WORKS CITED

Almeida, Miguel Vale de. *An Earth-Colored Sea: "race," Culture, and the Politics of Identity in the Postcolonial Portuguese-Speaking World*. New York: Berghahn Books, 2004. Print.

Althusser, Louis. *Lenin and Philosophy and Other Essays*. Ben Brewster (trans). New York: Monthly Review Press, 1972. Print.

Araújo, Luísa. "Code-Switching among a Portuguese-English Bilingual Family." *Delaware Working Papers in Applied Linguistics*. 3. 1991. pp. 21-31. Print.

Bakhtin, Mikhail. *The Dialogic Imagination: Four Essays*. Austin, Texas: University of Texas Press, 1981. Print.

Barthes, Roland. *S/Z*. New York: Hill and Wang, 1974. Print.

Bensabatt-Ott, Mary. *Portuguese-English Code-Switching: The Brazilian Community in the Greater Washington, D.C. Area*. Ann Arbor: UMI Press, 2001. Print.

Benveniste, Emile. *Problems in General Linguistics*. Coral Gables: University of Miami Press, 1971. Print.

Bianco, Bela Feldman. "Multiple Layers of Time and Space: The Construction of Class, Ethnicity, and Nationalism among Portuguese Immigrants." *Community, Culture and the Makings of Identity: Portuguese-Americans along the Eastern Seaboard*. Dartmouth: University of Massachusetts Dartmouth, 2009. pp. 51-93. Print.

Bourdieu, Pierre. *Language and Symbolic Power*. Cambridge: Harvard University Press, 1994. Print.

Brites, José. "Emigrês e Portinglês." *Ecos de Uma Viagem*. Franciso C. Fagundes (ed). Providence, RI: Gávea-Brown Publications, 1999. pp. 337. Print.

Carvalheiro, João Ricardo Pinto. "Media Representations and Second-Generation Discourses: The Nuanced Identities of Portuguese Descendants in France." *Interdisciplinary Journal of Portuguese Diaspora Studies*. 3 (2): 317-337. 2014. Print.

Carvalho, Julio C. de. *The Uncertain Journey: The Diasporic Effects on the Identity, Education, and Achievement of Cape Verdean Immigrants*. Saarbrücken: VDM Verlag, 2009. Print.

———. "The Exodus of Cape Verdean Immigrants to the Northeastern United States." *Research on the Influences of Educational Policy on Teaching and Learning*. Cynthia Sunal and Kagendo Mutua (eds). Charlotte: Information Age Publishing, Inc. 2013. Print.

Castellarin, Stephanie S. "Code-Switching in Portuguese Print Media of Brazilian Immigrant Communities in Massachusetts." *Bridgewater State University Undergraduate Review* 11. pp. 31-35. 2015.

Cordeiro, Albano. "La communauté portugaise aujourd'hui." *Portugais de France, citoyens d'Europe: État des lieux et avenir*. Albano Cordeiro (ed). Damarie-les-Lys: Assises de la Communauté Portugaise de France, 1997. pp. 28-39. Print.

Dias, Eduardo Mayone. *Falares emigreses: Uma abordagem ao seu estudo*. Lisbon: Instituto de Cultura e Língua Portuguesa, 1989. Print.

Dutra, Ramiro. "Lactifórnia." *Ecos de Uma Viagem*. Franciso C. Fagundes (ed). Providence, RI: Gávea-Brown Publications, 1999. pp. 309-10. Print.

Eckert, Penelope. "Variation and the Indexical Field." *Journal of Sociolinguistics* 12/4, 453-76. 2008. Print.

"Episódio 194." *Espelho d'Água*. Sociedade Independente de Comunicação. Lisbon. 28 November. 2017. Television.

Ferreira, Sónia. "Media e Migrações: A Língua Enquanto Património Identitário na Produção de Conteúdos Mediáticos na Diáspora." *Interdisciplinary Journal of Portuguese Diaspora Studies*. 3 (2): 339-359. 2014. Print.

Gramsci, Antonio. *Prison Notebooks*. New York: Columbia University Press, 1992. Print.

Hill, Jane. "Language, Race, and White Public Space." *American Anthropologist*. 100 (3): 680-89. 1998. Print.

Hora, Dermeval da. "Estilo: uma perspectiva variacionista." *Variação Estilística: Reflexões teórico-metodológicas e propostas de análise*. Edair Maria Görski, Izete Lehmkuhl Coelho, Christiane Maria Nunes de Souza (eds). Florianópolis: Editora Insular, 2014. pp.19-30. Print.

Jorge, Lídia. *O Cais das Merendas*. Sintra: Publicações Europa-América, 1982. Print.

Kaufman, Helen. "Is the Minor Essential?: Contemporary Portuguese Fiction and Questions of Identity." *Symploke*. 5 (1-2): 167-182. 1997. Print.

Klimt, Andrea & Holton, Kimberly DaCosta. "Lusophone Studies in the U.S." *Community, Culture and the Makings of Identity: Portuguese-Americans along the Eastern Seaboard*. Dartmouth: University of Massachusetts Dartmouth, 2009. pp. 9-24. Print.

Klimt, Andrea. "Divergent Trajectories: Identities and Community among Portuguese in Germany and New England." *Community, Culture and the Makings of Identity: Portuguese-Americans along the Eastern Seaboard*. Dartmouth: University of Massachusetts Dartmouth, 2009. pp. 95-124. Print.

Labov, William. *The Social Stratification of English in New York City*. Washington, D.C.: Center for Applied Linguistics, 1966.

———. *Sociolinguistic Patterns*. Philadelphia: University of Pennsylvania Press, 1972.

Lacan, Jacques. *The Seminar, Book II: The Ego in Freud's Theory and in the Technique of Psychoanalysis, 1954-55*. New York: Norton; Cambridge: Cambridge University Press. 1988. Print.

Lakoff, Robin T. *Talking Power: The Politics of Language in Our Lives*. New York: Basic Books, 1990. Print.

Larkosh, Christopher. "'Ex-Centric' Lusofonias: On Remembered Language and Its Possible Futures in Portuguese-American Culture." *Portuguese Literary and Cultural Studies* 25. 42-65. 2013. Print.

Leandro, Maria Engrácia. *Au-delà des apparences: Les Portugais face à l'insertion sociale*. Paris: L'Harmattan, 1995. Print.

Lourenço, Eduardo. *O Labirinto da Saudade*. Lisbon: Gradiva, 2000. Print.Moita,

Lopes L. P. *Global Portuguese: Linguistic Ideologies in Late Modernity*. New York: Routledge, 2015. Print.

Moser, Robert H, and Antonio L. A. Tosta. *Luso-american Literature: Writings by Portuguese-Speaking Authors in North America*. New Brunswick, N.J: Rutgers University Press, 2011. Print.

Peirce, Charles Sanders. *Collected Papers*. Cambridge: Harvard University Press, 1931, Vols. I-VIII. Print.

Poplack, Shana. "Sometimes I'll start a sentence in Spanish y termino en español: toward a typology of code-switching." *Linguistics* 18 (7/8): 581-618. Print.

Rocha, João Cezar de Castro Rocha. ed. *Lusofonia and its Futures. Portuguese Literary and Cultural Studies* 25. Amherst, MA: University of Massachusetts Press, 2013. Print.

Rowland, Robert. "A cultura brasileira e os portugueses." *Trânsitos Coloniais: Diálogos Críticos Luso-Brasileiros*. Bela Feldman Bianco, Cristiana Bastos, Miguel Vale de Almeida (eds). Campinas: Editora da UNICAMP, 2007. pp. 397-409. Print.

Saussure, Ferdinand. *Course in General Linguistics*. New York: McGraw-Hill Book Co, 1966. Print.

Silva, Emanuel da. "Humor (re)positioning ethnolinguistic ideologies: 'You tink is funny?'." *Language in Society* 44: 187-212. 2014. Print.

Silverstein, Michael. "Indexical order and the dialectics of sociolinguistic life." *Language and Communication* 23: 193-229. 2003. Print.

Voloshinov, Valentin N. *Marxism and the Philosophy of Language*. New York: Seminar Press, 1973. Print.

DANIEL F. SILVA is Assistant Professor of Portuguese at Middlebury College where he is also a Faculty Fellow at the Center for the Comparative Study of Race and Ethnicity and a contributing member of the International and Global Studies Program. He is the author of *Anti-Empire: Decolonial Interventions in Lusophone Literatures* (Liverpool University Press, 2018) and *Subjectivity and the Reproduction of Imperial Power: Empire's Individuals* (Routledge, 2015). He is also the co-editor of *Imperial Crossings: Writings on Race, Identity, and Power in the Lusophone World* (Liverpool University Press, Forthcoming); *Decolonial Destinies: The Post-Independence Literatures of Lusophone Africa* (Anthem Press, Forthcoming); *Emerging Dialogues on Machado de Assis* (Palgrave, 2016); and *Lima Barreto: New Critical Perspectives* (Lexington Books, 2013). He is co-editor of the book series, *Anthem Studies in Race, Power, and Society* published by Anthem Press; and has published scholarship in *Hispania*, *Chasqui*, and *Transmodernity*.

FABIO SCETTI

Being Portuguese in Montreal: Cultural and Traditional Practices as Markers of the Community's Identity

ABSTRACT: This article aims to present the cultural practices that mark Portuguese identity in the Portuguese community of Montreal. This community, established primarily in the district of Saint-Louis, is an example of an ethnic district where Portuguese traditions thrive, and the Portuguese language serves as a vehicle of communication. Portuguese migrants arrived there in the 1950s and created their own space, while also integrating within the urban linguistic landscape of French or English. The research presented here is based on an ethnography that illustrates how dynamic the community is and how language practices in Portuguese evolved and are used within the group mainly during cultural activities and traditions. In addition, discursive analysis is used to examine elements relating to community members' cultural and linguistic awareness with the process of identity (re)construction. This research shows how the Portuguese language and its representations may help in understanding the complex process of defining the group's identity through cultural and traditional practices.

KEYWORDS: Cultural Practices, Portuguese Migration, Montreal, Language and Identity, Representations and Imaginaries

RESUMO: Este artigo tem como objetivo de mostrar como a comunidade portuguesa em Montreal mantem-se ativa hoje-em-dia. Esta comunidade, instalada no distrito de Saint-Louis, é um exemplo de distrito étnico onde as tradições vivem e a língua portuguesa é um veículo de comunicação. Os migrantes portugueses chegaram desde a década de 1950 e criaram um espaço próprio, mesmo integrando mais com a sociedade francófona ou anglófona dentro da paisagem linguística urbana de Montreal. A pesquisa etnográfica que nos serve como base, permite observar como a comunidade é dinâmica e como as práticas linguísticas em português evoluem dentro do grupo, juntamente com atividades culturais e tradições. Além disso, a análise discursiva fornece alguns elementos que relacionam a consciência cultural e linguística dos membros da comunidade com o processo de (re)construção da identidade. A pesquisa mostra como a língua portuguesa e as suas representações podem ajudar na compreensão do processo de definição da identidade do grupo através de práticas culturais e tradicionais.

PALAVRAS-CHAVE: Práticas culturais, Migração portuguesa, Montreal, Língua e Identidade, Representações e Imaginários

---

1. Introduction

Montreal, the largest city within the province of Quebec, Canada, has been described as a city where diversity is key to promoting intercultural rapprochement (Gouvernement du Québec La diversité). Interculturalism is a neologism in Quebec (Rocher, et. al.) and it contrasts with the multiculturalism that has been promoted since the 1970s by the 1988 Canadian Government – Multiculturalism Act. There is no official definition of interculturalism as there is for multiculturalism, but it was defined at the time of the "Quiet Revolution" in Quebec (Linteau), that started with the raising of awareness of the diverse population that resulted from the waves of immigration in the 1960s. This meant a consideration of how Quebec can be distinguished from other Canadian provinces by its large territory, its historical path, its Francophone identity and culture, its Catholic tradition and the specificity of its political, legal and economic system (Bouchard).

    The historical dominance of English in the urban area was underlined by the fact that many Allophone[1] immigrants chose to speak English rather than French. That is why the question of the education of allophone immigrants has been considered one of the major points mentioned by the Commission Gendron[2] in a report that examined the situation of the French language and linguistic rights in Quebec (Gouvernement du Québec "Loi 22 et Loi 101"). English occupied the position of an international language and the main language for many companies and the business world, in general. It was also the most frequently adopted language at home by Allophones (Gouvernement du Québec La situation). The Quebec government then adopted preventive measures to affirm the status of the French language. Bill 101 or « Charte de la langue française » (1977)[3] marked a milestone in the history of the province of Quebec and its new model of intercultural integration and created a divide between immigrants who arrived in Quebec before and after 1977 (Mc Andrew).

Portuguese migration to Montreal is interesting to observe because it started in the 1950s and it reached its peak during this period of change in Quebec. Montreal is also interesting because it serves as a meeting point between policies: intercultural policy in Quebec and Canadian multiculturalism. Canada was the first country in the world to adopt multiculturalism as an official policy in 1971, under Prime Minister Pierre Elliott Trudeau. This policy encourages each citizen to preserve their values and their historical and ethnic background, Francophones, Anglophones, First Nations peoples and immigrants. Diversity thus became a strong marker of Canadian identity; it was seen as an asset. Since then, new citizens, immigrants, no longer feel obliged to assimilate and renounce their cultural, linguistic or religious/spiritual heritage; they can choose to naturalize as Canadians while retaining their own values. In this country with two official languages, French and English, cities such as Montreal or Ottawa, which remained bilingual and bicultural (English and French) within the public space, open their doors to ethnic groups which created their own districts, an enclave (McAll).

Saint-Louis is a piece of this multicultural and multilingual puzzle where different unofficial languages found their spaces within the landscape of the city of Montreal. Located near the city center, Saint-Louis represents the heart of the Portuguese community for those Portuguese and Portuguese descendants living in Montreal, around the metropolitan area, and across the province. In 2016, the Canadian Census identified 76,705 people in Montreal of Portuguese ethnic origin (Statistics Canada, 2016).

The Portuguese community first settled in this district in 1953 (Moura and Soares) and founded their own association and a church. The church, Missão Santa Cruz, is the engine of Portuguese cultural and associative life in Montreal. Today, the church remains the soul of the community's history and identity.

An ethnographic study conducted between 2011 and 2016 has made it possible to observe daily life within the group, oral practices in Portuguese and in both English and French, and discourses promoted by members on communitarian identity (Scetti "Évolution de la langue portugaise"), questioning whether identity is a real individual process or whether it is truly chosen. Moreover, observations of cultural activities and traditions, such as *a festa do Santo Cristo*, provide an experience of life within the group. Examples will help readers to understand better the experience and the discourses of imaginaries and representations that circulate. All interviews were conducted in 2011. Examples are authentic, punctuation was added, and some corrections were made to improve readability and understanding of an oral practice of the language. This shows how practices are evolving. The name of the speaker, the generation (1G – first generation with the date of arrival; 2G – second and 3G third generations), profession and level of education (1st level – primary; 2nd level – secondary and University) are placed in parentheses.

2.1. Living the Portuguese Community of Montreal

In Montreal, Saint-Louis is one of the pieces of a multiethnic puzzle. Along Boulevard Saint-Laurent, also called La Main, the city enfolds China Town, the Jewish district of Mile End, Little Italy and Parc-Extension, the Greek neighborhood. Walking along that street, we can feel the history of each community and we can taste and smell aromas from their countries of origins. Languages are living within each group, which makes this trip more interesting and gives it a sense of authenticity.

Saint-Louis is not just a district but a life experience. For the Portuguese, it represents the center of economic life where commercial activities have developed a thriving and complex community business (Robichaud). There, we can find associations, clubs, institutions, professional activities and Portuguese companies based in Montreal.

Portuguese community life in Montreal is important, and according to some members, it is better organized and united than in other Portuguese communities in North America. For instance, Sílvia (2G – 1989, Student, University) underlines: "quando eu vou a Toronto ou nos Estados Unidos é diferente, não é a mesma coisa. Aqui somos todos juntos, uma grande festa."[4] She facilitated an understanding of how the Portuguese community, called *comunidade*, is defending and promoting its own identity through the action of local institutions, associations and clubs, in comparison to other communities in North America.

Community members highlight the concentration of Portuguese facilities, businesses and activities, and comment positively on their ability to use Portuguese on a daily basis within the group. For the future of the community, it is important to have friends and contacts living in the group in order to help find a job within the district, to support ethnic businesses and to participate in activities organized by local clubs and associations. The activism of the church, Missão Santa Cruz (MSC), is crucial as Mário (2G – 1967, Services, Cégep) states: "já tínhamos aqui a igreja; também ajudou a integração, com a catequese pronto e encontrar-se com outros jovens aqui."[5] This network helps integration of newcomers within the group.

2.2. The Main Institutions of Montreal's Portuguese Community
The associative life within the group is animated by four different types of organizations: mutual or benefit, recreational, religious and educational (Da Rosa and Laczko).

Among the mutual or benefit organizations, which are voluntary associations, we find, for example, the Centro de Acção Sócio-Comunitária de Montreal, an organization of Portuguese volunteers who care for the needs of the members of the group, and the Caixa de Economia dos Portugueses, a credit union or cooperative bank founded in 1969, serving many Portuguese and their descendants; after 1983, the bank welcomed non-Portuguese clients. It is now known as Caisse Desjardins Portugaise, part of a prominent financial network of credit unions in Quebec. This illustrates the integration of the Portuguese into mainstream Quebec society.

Recreational organizations, local associations and clubs maintain and continue to promote the spirit of union, festivity, and folklore of the neighborhood. These associations and clubs are located mainly in Saint-Louis, but also in the surrounding areas, for example in Sainte-Thérèse, Laval (off-island suburbs) and Montreal North (a borough of the city of Montreal). The oldest of these is the Associação Portuguesa do Canadá (APC), founded in 1956. It is the first Portuguese association created in Canada and constitutes one of the pillars of the Portuguese community in the city; it is located near another pillar: the church MSC. It is important to recall that APC established the first Portuguese-language newspaper in Canada, *Luso-Canadiano*, in 1958. Following a split within the APC, *Luso-Canadiano* became the voice of another association, Casa dos Portugueses de Montreal, an anti-Salazarist association created in 1961. For that reason, APC launched the newspaper *Voz de Portugal* (http://www.avozdeportugal.com) on April 25, 1961, which became the conservative voice of the community and is now the oldest weekly newspaper of the Portuguese community throughout Canada. Due to the lack of interest of some of its members, the Casa dos Portugueses de Montreal ceased its activities in 1963 (Moura and Soares), but was reborn in 1965 under the name of Club Portugal de Montreal (CPM). This club, together with APC, represents one of the main institutions promoting traditional and cultural activities for the communitarian life within the district. Both APC and CPM feature in their activities the folkloric *rancho* group and focus on transmitting Portuguese cultural heritage to younger generations.

Virgílio (1G 1980 – 1954, Services, 1st level), president of APC, predicts the decline of communitarian and associative life: "não direi a pequeno prazo mas a longo prazo isto, todas as associações vai morrer tudo, já os clubes têm indo a morrer lentamente aqui e agora começam as associações."[6] He accuses the younger generations of inactivity in terms of participating in the community's life. We could observe what he said three years later, in 2014, the date of the second fieldwork visit to the community. APC activities were less productive, and engagement of young descendants is one of the main causes of this decline.

Among recreational associations, we also find Casa dos Açores, an example of a regional cultural association, where people from the Azores meet, especially on Friday evenings, for a typical meal prepared and offered to members of the association.

Of all the types of organizations, religious and educational institutions are regarded as the most powerful ones in terms of cultural promotion within the community. Mainly composed of Catholics, the community initially moved from church to church in order to find mass services in Portuguese. Nevertheless, since 1964, with the foundation of the Missão Santa Cruz (MSC), this institution also found a fixed location where members could participate in religious services (mass, catechism, preparation for sacraments) in Portuguese. Subsequently, various non-Catholic churches with services in Portuguese have been created: Igreja Baptista Portuguesa, Luz para as Nações, Igreja Batista Vida Nova, Assembleia de Deus da Nova Unção and Igreja Pentecostal Portuguesa, which tend to target predominantly Brazilian and Luso-African communities.

Among educational institutions, the most prominent is the Portuguese language school Escola Santa Cruz created in 1971 within MSC, one of the first in Montreal. This school teaches students from six to twelve years of age. Today, it has merged with the secondary school Lusitana, created in 1975 by Professor José de Barros, which offers more advanced Portuguese language instruction for students from twelve to eighteen years of age. Both schools operate on Saturdays and provide instruction in Portuguese language, culture, history, geography and literature, among other subjects.

2.3. The Missão Santa Cruz's Mission

The Missão Santa Cruz (MSC), also called Centro Comunitário Santa Cruz or simply Santa Cruz, is the religious center of Catholic life in the community. Since

1984, it has been located a few steps from the APC, at the corner between rue Rachel and Saint-Urbain. This institution represents the point of convergence of Portuguese community life even for the many families who live in the surrounding areas of the city (Teixeira and Da Rosa). In fact, people within the group seldom interchange names, calling MSC simply Santa Cruz or *comunidade*, which shows how MSC is considered the principal entity of the entire community.

MSC has two missions today: first, to transmit the Catholic faith in Portuguese (in fact, Catholic mass services, catechism and introductory seminars on the sacraments, from baptism to marriage, are offered in Portuguese), and, second, to teach and transmit the Portuguese language and culture to young descendants. At the initiative of the church, other groups were created, a folkloric dance group or *rancho*, a youth group called Os Jovens, and a prayer group and choir called Nossa Fé. Of all the church's initiatives, the MSC's Portuguese communitarian school, considering both the primary school Escola Santa Cruz and the secondary school Lusitana, represents the institution to promote the Portuguese language and figures as the defender of the prestige of the Portuguese language norm, or standard European Portuguese (EP), together with official Portuguese institutions, i.e., the Consulate, or local radio stations and newspapers. The inscription "a minha pátria é a minha língua,"[7] paraphrasing the writer Fernando Pessoa, is written on bluish azulejos and welcomes students every Saturday. Esmeralda (2G – 1966, Services, University) remembers how hard it was to go to normal school within the Quebec education system all week long, and even on Saturdays for Portuguese classes at the communitarian school, when she was a child, but she observes how it is beneficial for her son, today, to have the chance to study Portuguese: "Agora a gente obriga os nossos filhos também porque a gente vê o resultado."[8] For her, this underlines the level of fluency of the Portuguese spoken by her son, at home and within community life.

However, life is not easy for the communitarian school today. In fact, according to the school's own statistics (Eusébio), student enrollment peaked in 1982–83 with nearly 1,000 students, but after the year 2000, enrollment has significantly decreased. On the contrary, Lusitana had its peak attendance in 1993–94, but since then, attendance has been declining as well. In 2018, we counted 300 students total in the two schools. Among pupils of these two schools, we notice a strong presence of children whose parents are from continental Portugal (MSC: 89% of the fathers and 84% of the mothers, Lusitana: 96% of fathers and

91.5% of mothers), mostly from the north and the central regions of Portugal. Few parents are originally from the islands of Madeira and the Azores, despite the major presence of Azoreans in Montreal (Eusébio). In fact, Azoreans are one of the major groups in Montreal, together with *continentais* (Continental Portuguese People). In other Portuguese communities around the country, Azoreans are generally more numerous. Statistics from MSC may demonstrate the dominant position of *continentais* within MSC, and the choice of the formal norm of Portuguese, *norma-padrão* or EP, taught at school and used as the "good" one for many activities. For that reason, other varieties of Portuguese, such as those from Madeira and the Azores suffer from negative stigmatization within the group (Scetti "Variation dialectale du portugais"). In this extract, for example, Elijah (3G – 2000, Student, 1st level), who was eleven years old during the fieldwork visit in 2011, mentioned his paternal grandparents: "as vezes não estou a perceber o que é que ele (grandfather) está a dizer; ele tem um sotaque."[9] He assumed impossible to understand his grandfather and that his Portuguese is different from the one taught at school.

MSC was the first institution to teach and promote Portuguese and its norm, its church and school are the heart of the group and the public space where this language is spoken on a daily basis. Life around these institutions maintains a desire for continuity of the *comunidade* toward the future. The church is a place for shared values and for opportunities to build new families. "O último banco da igreja é um lugar de encontro para os jovens da comunidade,"[10] argued the priest José Maria Cardoso. The school, on the other hand, is a place of conviviality and union, where peers with a common family history and the same cultural background can meet. Meanwhile, since the population of the group is aging, the priest created in 1999 the Universidade dos Tempos Livres, also called UTL, which is responsible for educating the oldest members of the community by offering them different courses: French and English language courses (for those who had no time or need to learn them before), and many other kinds of courses in Portuguese, namely, dance classes and music, computing, history, religion and morality, cooking and handicrafts. The activities of UTL for elderly people are well known not only within Saint-Louis, but also among other Montrealers who are interested in Portuguese language and culture and who may enroll in the courses. The interest of non-Portuguese Montrealers in these courses shows how well the group is integrated in Montreal with people from different origins.

3. An Ethnographic Approach to the *comunidade*

The data presented here is based on an ethnographic study realized between 2011 and 2016 in Montreal. It was necessary to live within the community in order to carry out the author's doctoral research in sociolinguistics about the evolution of oral language practices in Portuguese, analyzing its intergenerational transmission. This research was divided into two fieldwork sessions. The first fieldwork visit was undertaken in 2011 (for 7 months) in order to collect data in oral Portuguese. This allowed observation of how oral practices have evolved and identification of seven elements of weakness in the linguistic structure of spoken Portuguese within the community (Scetti, "Évolution de la langue portugaise"). The second fieldwork visit was realized in 2014 (for 4 months) and focused more on observing discourses that circulate among community's members about the Portuguese language and its practices, in relation to ideologies and representations of a collective identity of the group.

This combined analysis, linguistic and discursive, aimed to examine the question of identity among members of the group in relation to language practices. For that reason, identity has been studied in its process of (re)construction, while defining new markers of a collective identity. Results of the Discourse Analysis showed how important it is to speak Portuguese within the group and in activities related to communitarian life. The Portuguese language is perceived as a dominant language in the world market of languages (Calvet) and finds its position as a tool for the future of the members of the group (Scetti, "O português"). Jaime (3G – 1995, Student, 2nd level) wants to focus on the power of the language underlining the international position of Portuguese today, promoted by many institutional and official discourses, such as within the local communitarian school MSC: "A 7a língua mais falada do mundo."[11]

Moreover, this research showed how the Portuguese language is evolving and how the norm of prestige, the standard European Portuguese (EP), is being questioned. Forms are evolving, and speakers give importance to the use of what they define as the "good" Portuguese, learned at school, instead of the Portuguese used within families, which is considered as "not good" and "dialectal." In this particular context of language contact in a city where two languages are dominant, a process of attrition (see: Scaglione, Scetti "Évolution de la langue portugaise") is observed in oral Portuguese spoken within the community, which shows the importance of contact with the two dominant languages in Montreal: English and French.

Oral Practice Observations, realized daily, permitted an understanding of the use of the three languages in different situations, due to speakers, places and conditions. Different practices, such as Code-Switching, Code-Mixing or different interferences (structural, lexical and phonetic), are considered as phenomena of the context of Language Contact and then analyzed, while questioning language practice as an identity marker. "O meu português é taratata,"[12] explains Florbela (2G – 1970, Education, University), who feels her Portuguese is not "pure". This practice may be seen as negative and may be seen as a weak point when considering oneself a "real" member of the community and in a projection as a "real Portuguese." This may refer to an ideology of purity of the language, based on discourses, perceptions and beliefs about a language and its positions, all constructed by members in the interest of a group (Woolard).

Portugueseness is then observed as a main element for the building of a collective identity. Language practices along with cultural awareness, knowledge of the culture and the history of the group and of Portugal, or participation in communitarian life are strong markers of identity that one should fulfill if one wants to be a member of the group, a real "act of identity" (Le Page and Tabouret-Keller).

While observing daily life within the *comunidade*, we could see how the Portuguese language is a vehicle of communication mainly between older members of the group, and in which spaces this language is used. This element is important when describing the vitality of the group.

In general, during communitarian activities, Portuguese is the main language. Members of the community speak Portuguese during all other practices, cultural and religious. For this reason, it was of major interest to observe in detail some activities organized by the MSC. This research focused on how activities were organized, in which way group members related to each other and which languages were used. We could observe that the main activities organized by MSC were mainly related to religious life. As an observer of these events, I could describe in detail the vitality of the Portuguese language and its presence spoken and written. Members of the organization committee within MSC speak mainly Portuguese and communication is maintained entirely in Portuguese.

4.1. The vitality of the group

The *comunidade* is known in the city of Montreal for its vitality and liveliness (Scetti, "Langues et migrations"). Throughout the year, especially during the summer, Montrealers and tourists can attend a succession of events based on religious holidays related to the Catholic tradition. They can participate in processions, shows, dances and eat Portuguese cuisine in the forecourt of the MSC's church. Notable festivals include those of Nossa Senhora do Monte, organized by Madeirans, the Espírito Santo, Senhor Santo Cristo dos Milagres (Santo Cristo), Santo António, São Pedro and São João.

During ethnographic observations, we attended many festivities and parties related to these religious events. Those activities contributed to the discussion of my position as an ethnographer, of the ways to interpret data, and of the position of the ethnographer as neither an insider nor an outsider (Mullings). The Santo Cristo festival provided a good opportunity to observe integration within the community as well as the integration of the group and its neighborhood within the city of Montreal.

4.2. A Long Day within the comunidade:
A Festa do Santo Cristo **(May 18, 2014)**
The celebration of *Senhor Santo Cristo dos Milagres* takes place on the fifth Sunday of Easter in the Roman Catholic calendar.

It is often warm in Montreal at this time and the streets are generally empty on Sundays. Around 4:00 p.m. on this day, a crowd gathers in front of Missão Santa Cruz church and prepares to follow the first procession of the season for the community.

The priest leads the procession. He leaves the church, and everything seems organized and prepared. There is a presenter who announces in Portuguese the departure of each group following along Clark Street to the intersection with Boulevard Saint-Joseph. Each group represents an institution: Escola Santa Cruz, Lusitana and Universidade dos Tempos Livres. Associations and clubs are also present. The different folkloric groups (*ranchos*) perform their main activities during the parade. The Grupo Coral Santa Cruz marches between the different institutions accompanied by the music of three orchestras founded in the community.

There is an eye-catching festival of flags in front of each orchestra. The flags show the identity and belonging of each group. The first to appear is the Filarmónica do Divino Espírito Santo from Laval under the flags of Canada, Portugal and Quebec. Then, in the middle of the procession, the Banda da Nossa Senhora dos Milagres from Montreal enters under the flags of Portugal,

Quebec and the Azores, but surprisingly without the Canadian flag. Finally, to conclude the parade, the Filarmónica Portuguesa de Montreal marches and plays behind its five flag-bearers. The flags appear as follows: Portugal and the Azores Islands on one side, the city of Montreal in the center, and the flags of Quebec and Canada on the other side.

The march is long, many Portuguese and descendants of Portuguese migration come from all over Quebec to attend this popular and religious festival. From Quebec City, some travel more than 250 km to relive the traditions of Portugal. For instance, Joana (2G – from Quebec City) comments: "a gente aqui é muito involvida na vida da comunidade" and continues, "sinto-me quase em casa, em Portugal."[13]

The statue of Christ is carried in procession by men wearing a red cloak and followed by barefoot women who sometimes carry large white candles or ropes on their shoulders, recalling the penances suffered by Jesus Christ. The crowd follows behind them in silence. While returning to the church, people rush to the statue, grab the rope in their hands and pray. Men in the crowd are mainly dressed in black suits with dress shoes. Women are well dressed in honor of this first festive Sunday. I feel like I am in Portugal, having the impression of moving in time and space, in another reality. It seems a perfect representation of a procession in a local village in Portugal. The only thing changing is the landscape of the Canadian city, organized in its large and perpendicular streets and boulevards.

According to the priest, it is only the beginning of the summer holidays and religious festivities. One of the functions of the church, as the center of the union of the community, is to put on these events. Santo Cristo has been maintained for decades as a moment of communion. People meet, mostly elderly people, but also young descendants participate, share and realize how significant this event is for the group's life and for the existence of the group in time.

4.3. Discourses on Language and Cultural Awareness

The Santo Cristo event shows how the Portuguese district has become part of Montreal's urban landscape bringing its culture, symbols, cuisine, traditions and language into the public sphere. The *comunidade* plays the role of reference in the discourses of its members. Identity negotiation is interesting to observe in the public sphere. There is a common ideology on a collective ethnic identity, even though this process remains complex to define and dynamic (Norton and Toohey). We can observe a construction of different identities (Moore and Brohy 289), considering this plural definition as more open and malleable for members to join, that is also why during our interviews we can observe varied nominations such as Portuguese-Canadian, Luso-Canadian or even Luso-Quebecker.

Our research shows how important the Portuguese culture is for members of the group. "Living in a Portuguese way" is important to feel like a "real" Portuguese. It is also important to underline how staying halfway between Portugal and Canada assigned a dual identity that can be the result of a complex and never-ending individual journey through identity representations. Sílvia (2G – 1989, Student, University), for example, repeats that: "é metade, não me identifico mesmo como ser portuguesa realmente, sou canadiana de origem portuguesa."[14] She wants to underline how she adapts to different spaces, situations and territories. The construction, or daily reconstruction, of identity is the result of the negotiation between one self's choice and the result of an imposition; an attributed identity. In this extract, Dora (2G – 1979, Services, University) underlined how she is considered as Canadian when she is on vacation in Portugal, and how she is identified as Portuguese when she meets her husband's friends and family, in Montreal: "O meu esposo que é canadiano e quando estou com a malta dele, eu sou portuguesa, mas eu sou canadiana porque nasci aqui também e quando vou a Portugal, não sou portuguesa porque sou canadiana."[15] From this extract, we can assume how the identity negotiation depends on context and situation, as well as on participants to the interaction.

According to our Discourse Analysis, speaking Portuguese is a mark of belonging to the group, like sharing a common family history of migration or finding the same cultural traditions. All of these elements are important in a group to define who is a member and who is not. This involves many questions regarding membership in the group. The choice to speak a language can become an "act of identity" (Le Page and Tabouret-Keller, 1985) by which speakers express their personal affiliation to the group.

Being Portuguese is not synonymous with living in Portugal or often traveling there. Being Portuguese does not exclude being part of the new context in Montreal, in Quebec and in Canada, as well: "mesmo que a gente se considera português a gente faz parte do Canadá"[16] (Mário, 2G – 1967, Services, 2nd level). So, maybe we should redefine new core statements of the common identity within Saint-Louis, in terms of language practice. A linguistic ideology refers here to the situated, partial, and interested character of conceptions and uses of language (Errington).

When analyzing discourses, we see how important it is for a group created from a migration process to maintain the link with the past and origins. Identity as a product of successive socializations (Dubar) must be observed as a process based on a common past, an origin, the contribution of an inheritance, and a contact with different people. The link with Portugal is not severed and different sentiments emerge from these discourses, especially among speakers of the 1st generation (1G), including patriotic *orgulho* ("pride"), feeling fully Portuguese (Lurdes, 1G 1974 – 1951, Services, 1st level) or feeling a deep love for the home country, *até morrer* ("until death") (Vítor, 1G 1989 – 1952, Services, 2nd level). All of these images are the result of an individual process fueled by collective ideologies: being oneself *eu* ("I") as a member of a *nós* ("we"). *Eu* and *nós*, in the process of identity negotiation, shape from time to time in each discourse, showing the importance of the plural, collective identity, even if this notion of diasporic identity may be imaginary and ideologic (Rosa and Trivedi).

4.4. Living between Flags

When questioning whether identity is a real individual process or whether it is truly chosen, research seems to indicate that the individual process must continuously deal with adaptation to a mixture of compensations and constraints dictated by the group. Andrée Tabouret-Keller explains, in fact, that the identity of a group is delimited by boundaries that are established between those who belong or do not belong to the group (1997: 316). The individual must then adapt to these collective impositions, being nobody without the others (Kaufmann).

Within the *comunidade*, even if members of the 1st generation (1G) are more closely attached to the image given to the Portuguese flag, as observed during the Santo Cristo event—representing the language, the culture and traditions—new flags (of the city or of the new country) are not strange anymore and represents their integration into the new context. Members of the 2nd generation (2G), also called *geração-ponte* (bridge generation)—descendants of the first Portuguese immigrants in Montreal who did not necessarily live in Portugal—remain closely linked to a common heritage from this country by a set of representations and imaginaries of identity, and it is starting from this generation where all flags may be seen as necessary for identity negotiation. In fact, a common identity is seldom represented and based on ideologies. For example, Dora (2G – 1979, Services, University) explains how Portuguese people are in general: "muito abertos, muito sociáveis, bons viventes, as pessoas que gostam de gozar da vida, de socializar. Mas somos também pessoas patriarcas, mas do bom sentido, acordamos muita importância à família, tentamos ser uma família unida, temos bons valores. Guardamos a nossa religião que é uma coisa que é muito difícil aqui em Montreal."[17] This kind of image seldom refers to some aspects related to a common *nós* ("we") and emphasizes the link between culture, roots and language. However, this ideal "we" also relates to the strong role of MSC in creating and propagating discourses on images regarding the link between identity and religion. The desire to transmit this knowledge and these feelings to future generations is repeated by some members, in discourses and representations promoted through the MSC's actions. Descendants of the next generation (3rd and 4th generations), in fact, are influenced more by discourses generated inside the common space, mainly within clubs, associations and institutions. Language practices remain a fundamental value of the group throughout the identity process. For example, Elijah (3G – 2000, Student, 1st level) defines Portuguese as his first language, "his" language, the one he first spoke with his grandparents, highlighting its importance in daily practices at home (grandparents and parents) and at school (friends from a Portuguese background). Language practices, together with music, food and religion, helps in defining the group itself and the group's identity. According to Esmeralda (2G – 1966, Services, University), it is important to live within the *comunidade* and to keep these traditions and symbols in order to feel Portuguese, sometimes even more Portuguese than people living in Portugal: "eu sinto-me muito portuguesa, toda a gente diz que sou portuguesa de mais até. Acho que até sou mais portuguesa que os portugueses em Portugal porque a gente mora aqui nesta comunidade e a gente guarda aquelas coisas antigas, não sei os costumes. Eu acho que sem a comunidade era muito difícil."[18] Without the *comunidade* it is difficult, she repeated, underlining the important role of the group and mainly the role of MSC in maintaining this sense of Portugueseness.

5. Conclusion

In a context of migration and integration it is difficult to raise cultural awareness. Considering both the heritage as well as the new culture (receiving for 1G members and home culture for members born in Montreal), the ultimate goal is to integrate into the new context as well as into the communitarian context. The process of integration into intercultural Quebec or multicultural Canada requires constantly negotiating identities during a review of life experiences. When Virgílio (1G 1980 – 1954, Services, 1st level), for instance, says: "eu sou canadiano e português,"[19] he asserts his definite choice to be both and to show his two flags, if we want to maintain this symbolism. However, he needed to justify his choice and noted how the new context was favorable to him since his arrival and defended how he feels connected to Canada, as a Canadian. Meanwhile, he also needed to justify his attachment to Portugal, saying he wanted to return to Portugal one day, for any choice showing a sustained reason.

Choices of identity and attributions are mixed according to the situation and different spaces. They all can be described as "acts of identity" (Le Page and Tabouret-Keller). These choices and their explanations show that it is possible to be Portuguese, Luso-Canadian or Luso-Quebecker or simply to be Canadian or Quebecker. Different elements are established in the list of identity markers, adapted and set up according to the experience of each speaker. Language remains an important element, both in practices but especially in the representations and imaginaries mobilized through discourses that are built around it. With it, other practices, cultural and traditional, are also considered as markers of the community's identity.

In conclusion, ethnographic research shows how important it is for the researcher to participate in the "common" life within the *comunidade*. In fact, for members, it can be important to go to school on Saturdays or go to mass on Sundays, and to participate in a religious festival, such as Santo Cristo, but it is also important to participate in folkloric *rancho* dances, to join an association or a club, to buy bread at a Portuguese bakery or eat in a Portuguese restaurant. The responsibility is everyone's in order to ensure the maintenance of the district in the future, to recall the history of the group's migration and to prevent the loss of the Portuguese language in the future.

The description of Santo Cristo celebration demonstrates how important the union of the community can be. Through this religious celebration, many other groups within the *comunidade* are visible, and try to be visible as well, within the community and urban life. Many flags were present during the Santo Cristo celebration, but sometimes those flags were not all included in representation of some of the groups. Each flag was a symbol for all the *comunidade*, regarding a region (Quebec and the Azores), a country (Portugal and Canada) or even the city of Montreal, where the community is included. However, flags do not stand alone. During our observations, flags were waving together, showing an image of plurality, where identity is performed and where exclusivity is replaced by multi-alternativity.

NOTES

1. Allophone – A person who, in a given territory, has for his or her first language another language than the official language or languages

2. Commission Gendron – Commission of Inquiry on the Situation of the French Language and Linguistic Rights in Quebec, founded in 1968.

3. Bill 101 – It is a Fundamental Law which is part of the statute of the French-speaking province of Quebec together with other statutes: Charter of Human Rights and Freedoms (1975) to guarantee the cultural rights of citizens and the Declaration on the interethnic and interracial relations (1985).

4. "When I go to Toronto or to the United States it is different, it is not the same thing. Here we are all together, a big party."

5. "The church existed here already; it also helped for integration, with catechism it gives the possibility to meet other young members."

6. "I will not say soon but in few years, all these associations will die, clubs have already dying slowly here and now it is the turn of associations."

7. "My home is my language."

8. "Now we force our kids (to study Portuguese), because we see the result."

9. "Sometimes, I do not understand what he says; he has an accent."

10. "The last pews of the church are considered a good place for glances' exchange between young members of the community."

11. "It is the 7th most spoken language in the world."

12. "My Portuguese is *taratata* (not good)."

13. "People here are very involved in the life of the community. I feel almost at home, in Portugal."

14. "It's half-way. I do not really identify myself as a Portuguese. I am Canadian of Portuguese origins."

15. "My husband is Canadian and when I am with his friends I am Portuguese, but I am Canadian because I was born here. And when I am in Portugal, I am not Portuguese because I am Canadian."

16. "Even if we are Portuguese, we are part of Canada."

17. "Very open, very sociable, people who love to live, people who like to enjoy life, to socialize. But we are also patriarchal people but in a good sense, we give a lot of importance to the family, we try to be a united family, we have good values. We keep our religion which is something that is very difficult here in Montreal."

18. "I really feel Portuguese, everyone says I'm Portuguese even more. I think I'm even more Portuguese than Portuguese people in Portugal because we live here in this community and we keep those old things, I do not know, usages, traditions. I think without the community it would have been very difficult."

19. I am Canadian and Portuguese.

WORKS CITED

Bouchard, Gérard. L'interculturalisme. Un point de vue québécois. Boréal, 2012.

Calvet, Louis-Jean. Le marché aux langues: les effets linguistiques de la mondialisation. Plon, 2002.

Da Rosa, Victor M.P. and L.S. Laczko. "Ethnic organizational completeness: a discussion of trends in Montreal's Portuguese Community." A Bilingual Journal of Portuguese-American Letters and Studies, 1984, pp. 5–8.

Dubar, Claude. La socialisation: construction des identités sociales et professionnelles. Armand Colin, 1991.

Errington, Joseph. "Ideology". In Key terms in language and culture, edited by Alessandro Duranti, Blackwell, 2001, pp. 110–112.

Eusébio, Joaquim. Falando Português em Montréal. Quebec World, 2001.

Gouvernement du Québec. La situation de la langue française au Québec. Rapport de la Commission Gendron. Vols. 1–3. Office de la langue française, 1972.

———. "Loi 22 et Loi 101." Office Québécois de la Langue Française, 2002. https://www.oqlf.gouv.qc.ca/charte/reperes/reperes.html.

———. La diversité : Une valeur ajoutée. Politique gouvernementale pour favoriser la participation de tous à l'essor du Québec. Ministère de l'Immigration et des Communautés Culturelles – MICC Québec, 2008.

Kaufmann, Jean-Claude. L'invention de soi: Une théorie de l'identité. Armand Colin, 2004.

Le Page, Robert B. and Andrée. Tabouret-Keller. Acts of identity: Creole-based approaches to language and ethnicity. Cambridge UP, 1985.

Linteau, Paul-André. Brève Histoire de Montréal. Boréal, 2007.

McAll, Christopher. Class, ethnicity, and social inequality. McGill-Queen's UP, 1992.

Mc Andrew, Marie. "La loi 101 en milieu scolaire." Revue d'aménagement linguistique, no hors-série, 2002. http://www.oqlf.gouv.qc.ca/ressources/bibliotheque/ouvrages/amenagement_hs/ralo1_charte_mc_andrew_vf_%2009-22_1.pdf.

Moore, Danièle, and Claudine Brohy. "Identités plurilingues et pluriculturelles." In Sociolinguistique du contact. Dictionnaire des termes et concepts, edited by Jacky Simonin et Sylvie Wharton, ENS Éditions, 2013, pp. 289–315.

Moura de Almeida, Manuel, and Imitério Soares. Pionniers. L'avant-garde de l'Immigration Portugaise, Canada 1953. Direcção Geral dos Assuntos Consulares e Comunidades Portuguesas, 2003.

Mullings, Beverley. "Insider or outsider, both or neither: Some dilemmas of interviewing in a cross-cultural setting." Geoforum, 30, 1999, pp. 337–350.

Norton, Bonny, and Kelleen Toohey. "Identity, language learning, and social change." Language Teaching 44, 4, 2011, pp. 412–446.

Robichaud, Denis. "La création du quartier portugais de Montréal. Une histoire d'entrepreneurs." Géographie Économie Société 6, 4, 2004, pp. 415–438.

Rocher, François, Micheline Labelle, Ann-Marie Field, and Jean-Claude Icart. "Le concept d'interculturalisme en contexte québécois : généalogie d'un néologisme." *Commission de consultation sur les pratiques d'accommodement reliées aux différences culturelles*, décembre, 2007.

Rosa, Jonathan, and Sunny Trivedi. "Diaspora and language." In *The Routledge Handbook on Migration and Language*, edited by Suresh A. Canagarajah, Routledge, 2017, pp. 330–346.

Scaglione, Stefania. *Attrition: Mutamenti sociolinguistici nel lucchese di San Francisco*. Franco Angeli, 2000.

Scetti, Fabio. "Variation dialectale du portugais parlé au sein de la communauté de Montréal." *Géolinguistique*, no. 17, 2017, pp. 151–175.

———. *Évolution de la langue portugaise dans sa dynamique de transmission au sein de la « communauté portugaise » de Montréal*. PhD Dissertation. Université Paris Descartes, 2016.

———. « O português não é só a língua do passado e dos avós, mas é também uma nova língua do futuro! » *Atas XII CONLAB, 1° congresso da Associação Internacional de Ciências Sociais e Humanas em Língua Portuguesa*, FCSH – Universidade Nova de Lisboa, 2015, pp. 6443–6451.

———. « Langues et migrations – groupes minoritaires et visibilité: La communauté portugaise à Montréal et à Paris ». *Actes du Colloque « Les minorités invisibles : diversité et complexité (ethno)sociolinguistiques »* – Université Paul Valéry Montpellier 3 / Laboratoire DIPRALANG, 25-27 Octobre 2013, 2014, pp. 269–77.

Smolicz, Jerzy J. "Core values and cultural identity." *Ethnic and Racial Studies*, vol. 4, no. 1, 1981, pp. 75–90.

Statistics Canada. "Census of Canada 2011: Immigration and ethnocultural diversity." Industry Canada, 2016. http://www.12.statcan.ca

Tabouret-Keller, Andrée. *Le nom des langues, I. Les enjeux de la nomination des langues*. BCILL 95. Peeters, 1997.

Teixeira, Carlos, and Victor M.P. Da Rosa. *The Portuguese in Canada: Diasporic Challenges and Adjustment*. Toronto UP, 2000-2009.

Woolard, Kathryn A. "Introduction: Language ideology as a field of inquiry". In *Language ideologies*, edited by Bambi B. Schieffelin, Kathryn A. Woolard and Paul V. Kroskrity (Eds.), Oxford University, 1998, pp. 3–47.

FABIO SCETTI holds a PhD from the Université Paris Descartes (Sorbonne – Paris – Cité). He is currently an Associate Researcher at the Université Sorbonne Nouvelle – Paris III – Laboratoire Clesthia (France). His doctoral research focuses on the evolution of the Portuguese language spoken by Portuguese immigrants who settled in Montreal. Since 2015, he has also been an Associate Researcher in Lexicography, working on the conception of two dictionaries of Endangered Languages (project VOLF at the Istitut Cultural Ladin, Vigo di Fassa (TN), Italy, and project VVV in Val Masino (SO), Italy). He is also a member of the organisation committee for the interdisciplinary group: *Diversidade Linguística do Português* (DLP) and organizes annual round-tables focusing on topics related to the Portuguese language and variation.

BENJAMIN LEGG

Angolamania: Affective Bonds with Angola in the Music of the Cabo Verdean Diaspora

ABSTRACT: The relationship between the Cabo Verdean diaspora and Angola has undergone transformations in the past half-century. Angola was long a destination for Cabo Verdean emigrants, particularly when both countries were Portuguese colonial possessions. Despite historic tensions between these migrants and the indigenous population in Angola itself, the Cabo Verdean community in New England today manifests a strong affection toward Angola and Angolan music. This paper will investigate the way that this affective relationship presents itself in the world of popular music, with a particular focus on the music of the Mendes Brothers, based in Brockton, MA, and the Angolan singer Bonga's connections to the Cabo Verdean diaspora in Rhode Island. This analysis will be contextualized by research on the Cabo Verdean diaspora in the social sciences as well as by personal interviews conducted by the author with Cabo Verdean community activists and music industry representatives. This article will highlight the role of personal affective connections in discussions of Cabo Verdean diasporic identity and pan-Lusophone African solidarity.

KEYWORDS: migration, diaspora, New England, Cabo Verde, Angola, popular music, pan-Africanism, ethnic identity, Mendes Brothers, Bonga.

RESUMO: A relação entre a diáspora cabo-verdiana e Angola tem transformado bastante nas últimas cinco décadas. Angola sempre foi destino para emigrantes cabo-verdianos, sobretudo quando os dois países ainda eram sob domínio português. Apesar das tensões históricas entre estes migrantes e a população indígena de Angola, hoje em dia, a comunidade cabo-verdiana de Nova Inglaterra manifesta uma forte relação afetiva com Angola e a música angolana. Este artigo investigará a maneira em que esta relação afetiva se revela pelo meio da música popular, com enfoque especial na música dos Mendes Brothers de Brockton, MA, e nas ligações do cantor angolano Bonga com a comunidade cabo-verdiana de Rhode Island. Para estabelecer os contextos desta análise, se emprega pesquisas sobre a diáspora cabo-verdiana oriundas das ciências sociais, além de entrevistas conduzidas pelo próprio autor com organizadores da comunidade cabo-verdiana em Nova Inglaterra e representantes da indústria musical de tal região. Essa pesquisa enfatizará a importância das ligações afetivas pessoais nas discussões da identidade diáspórica cabo-verdiana, e da solidariedade luso-africana.

PALAVRAS-CHAVE: migração, diáspora, Nova Inglaterra, Cabo Verde, Angola, música popular, movimento pan-africano, identidade étnica, Mendes Brothers, Bonga.

1. Introduction

Among my earlier memories of the visible presence of the Lusophone diaspora in southeastern New England is an Angolan flag displayed proudly across the DJ's table at a hip hop show in Providence, RI, when I was a teenager. The group that was performing, Busted Fro, included notable players on the New Bedford hip hop scene in the early 2000s, several of whom were of Cabo Verdean descent. I mentioned the display of the Angolan flag to an acquaintance of mine who grew up in the Cabo Verdean community of southeastern Massachusetts, and I was surprised by her response. She complained that one of the group's members with whom she was acquainted had appropriated an Angolan identity, despite his Cabo Verdean roots. "I was born in Angola too, but you don't see me waving an Angolan flag," she remarked. This interested me for a number of reasons. First, I had never known that this friend, whom I had always associated with Cabo Verde, was born in Angola, a country that was figuring more and more in my own studies of the Lusophone world. Second, I didn't understand why she would want to separate herself from her connections with the land where she was born. It was among my first encounters with the intricacies of identity politics in the Cabo Verdean diaspora.

I have since grown fully aware of the deep bonds between Cabo Verde and Angola. A Cabo Verdean student that I tutored talked about trips to Angola to visit relatives when he was younger. I continued to meet more and more Cabo Verdeans who had been born in Angola and emigrated to the United States or Portugal as children. Above all, I noticed the presence of Angola in Cabo Verdean music. Listening to Cabo Verdean music produced both within Cabo Verde and in the diaspora one heard constant references to Angola. Similarly, I began to realize that much of what I thought was Cabo Verdean zouk that was played on the radio or in clubs was actually performed by Angolan musicians. It was becoming clear that a strong connection between Cabo Verde and Angola existed that went beyond the bureaucratic and diplomatic sphere of the *Comunidade dos Países de Língua Portuguesa* (Community of Portuguese-Language Countries or CPLP)

A full analysis of the multifaceted links between Angola and Cabo Verde would be an undertaking beyond the limits of this article. Nevertheless, an examination of even some minimal elements of these linkages helps forefront lessons we can learn from the Cabo Verdean experience, both in the archipelago and around the world. Cabo Verdean culture and identity, predicated on a mixture of African and Portuguese influences, and strongly molded by a history of migration, is a rich illustration of Paul Gilroy's interpretation of double consciousness in his seminal work *The Black Atlantic* (1993), which begins with a sentence referring to DuBoisian thoughts on consciousness: "Striving to be both European and black requires some specific forms of double consciousness" (1). The Cabo Verdean experience—born in the violence of the encounter between Portuguese slaver and enslaved African, shaped by Cabo Verdeans' continual journeys from their islands to places like the United States, northern Europe, and Portugal's other African colonies, and informed by a multitude of relationships with other African and African diasporic cultures, as well as the cultures of not just one, but several imperial metropolises—has created a prismatic array of consciousness throughout Gilroy's theoretical Black Atlantic.

Beyond its explicit illustration and potential for expansion of definitions of a Black Atlantic, the Cabo Verdean experience of multiple consciousnesses and migration can also inform our own ways of interpreting migration's role in the forging of identity. Luís Batalha and Jørgen Carling support this view: "The ubiquity of migration in Cape Verdean society, cultural heritage, and family life facilitates the study of processes that are also present in other parts of the world, but often in a more subtle way. Moreover, Cape Verde represents an astounding diversity of migration experiences..." (Batalha and Carling 29). The sheer magnitude as well as the disperse nature of the Cabo Verdean emigrant community, which can be found not only in Portugal, the former metropolis, but also in the Netherlands, in the United States, and in African countries like Senegal, Angola and Guinea-Bissau, builds a diversity of dialogues with pan-African political thought, with continental and insular Portuguese cultures, with Afro-American and Afro-European identities, and with more specifically Lusophone African trends in literature, music and popular culture.

In this article, I will at times refer to the Cabo Verdean community as a diaspora, a usage that partially contradicts Deirdre Meintel's claim, "Labour migration from the Cape Verde over the last century-and-a half corresponds more closely to the transnationalism model; however, as our historical review in the following section will show, the concept of diaspora is also pertinent in some ways" (26) Nevertheless, in a recent article on the power of narrative in the Cabo Verdean community, Gina Sánchez-Gibau writes, "To understand the African diaspora as a site of historical memory to which Cape Verdeans are connected is to acknowledge original conceptualizations of diaspora (i.e., dispersal from and connection to the homeland), while recognizing the continual re-creation of diasporic communities in the present" ("Telling our Story" 112). She further argues, "Indeed, in some ways, the notion of "telling our story" is one rooted in the very nature of the term *diaspora*—a term that signals the ties of responsibility engendered between a nation and its emigrants abroad" (112). James Clifford's influential definition of diaspora itself, as Meintel maintains, does support the term's utility in describing the Cabo Verdean communities scattered across the world: "Decentered, lateral connections may be as important as those formed around a teleology of origin/return. And a shared, ongoing history of displacement, suffering, adaptation, or resistance may be as important as the projection of a specific origin" (306). Gilroy himself comments on the way that the wide distribution of the African Diaspora through a Black Atlantic world produces broad repercussions:

> The fractal patterns of cultural and political exchange and transformation that we try and specify through manifestly inadequate theoretical terms like creolization and syncretism indicate how both ethnicities and political cultures have been made anew in ways that are significant not simply for the peoples of the Caribbean but for Europe, for Africa, especially Liberia and Sierra Leone, and of course, for black America. (15)

In this article, I intend to illustrate, through the examination of popular musicians, that affective relationships and cultural activity amongst Cabo Verdean and Angolan musicians in Atlantic locations as diverse as southeastern New England, the Netherlands, Angola and Portugal have had impacts beyond the world of clubs, concert halls and recording studios.

My background is in literary and cultural studies, and in this article I owe a debt to the work of anthropologists like those cited above and ethnomusicologists, who have strongly informed my thinking. What follows is a brief overview of the Cabo Verdean presence in Angola, which is necessary to better understand these ties. After this overview, I examine the presence of Angola in Cabo

Verdean popular music produced in New England, and to a lesser extent Cabo Verde's reciprocal impact on Angolan popular music. This examination will be undertaken through close readings of song lyrics, as well as the reporting of interviews with Cabo Verdean community members in New England. Although the incorporation of such interviews is less conventional in literary and cultural studies work, Sánchez-Gibau reminds us of the importance of storytelling in the Cabo Verdean community: "An examination of Cape Verdean diasporic identity formation is irrevocably tied to stories, both individual and collective" ("Telling our Story" 112). Despite my departure from familiar methodological territory, it is my intention to bring a cultural studies perspective to the study of a community that is pivotal to broader understandings of Black Atlantic consciousness, the role of migration in the shaping of identity, and the power of diaspora.

2. Cabo Verdeans in Angola/Cabo Verdeans in the United States: The Intricacies of Identity

As mentioned above, Angola has long been among the most prominent destinations for the Cabo Verdean diaspora, and its attraction grew as more Cabo Verdeans moved there in the period after the Second World War (Batalha and Carling 21). In Batalha and Carling's work they present the Cabo Verdean song "Terezinha" as evidence of Angola's prominence as a destination for Cabo Verdeans in the 1940s, 1950s, and 1960s, for the colony already appeared in musical portrayals of migration (21). Cabo Verdeans occupied a unique position in colonial Angola, one that was at times fraught with connections to the colonial regime. In his study of Angola under the Portuguese, Gerald J. Bender discusses those who migrated to Angola during the last decades of Portuguese rule: "It was hoped that these individuals, whom the Portuguese considered perfect racial and cultural intermediaries between Africans and Europeans, would help stabilize the multiracial *colonatos*" (110). Despite this enhanced colonial status, Cabo Verdeans did not always occupy an elite position, and could be found inhabiting Luanda's shantytowns, or *musseques,* like Sambizanga (Moorman 90). Cabo Verdeans in Angola, rather than identifying with the autochthonous African populations, maintained their own identity, an identity that many perceived to be aligned with that of the Portuguese colonial masters. Marissa Moorman mentions this in her 2008 work on Angolan popular music, when she cites Ilídio do Amaral's descriptions of the Cabo Verdean presence in Luanda's late colonial *musseque* quarters, particularly in informal commerce (67).

In Bender's book, he mentions riots that occurred in the slums of Luanda in 1974, after which both white Portuguese and Cabo Verdean slum dwellers eventually decided to flee (201). Moorman also references this violence when she describes the participation of some Angolan musicians in these riots: "Musicians like Chico Coio got involved in the spontaneously formed self-defense militias in the musseques. Such militias defended against attacks from Portuguese merchants, Cape Verdean volunteer forces working for the Portuguese police, and FNLA militants" (195). In footnotes to his book, Bender further claims, "Almost all of the approximately 40,000 Cape Verdeans who were in Angola before the April 1974 coup resembled Cape Verdeans in the U.S. in that they identified with the Portuguese in the colony, not with the Africans" (203). Bender's commentary here on Cabo Verdean identification with the Portuguese as reflecting patterns in the United States stands out, and this topic will be addressed later in this article. Rather than painting a picture of a Cabo Verdean community harmoniously integrated into indigenous Angolan society, both Bender and Moorman portray a community in an ambiguous position. How, then, have Cabo Verdeans developed the affective connections with Angola that are discernible in the New England diaspora, when such connections may have been more tenuous in Angola itself? Bender's statement also points to a response to this question. He connects the Cabo Verdeans of Angola with Cabo Verdeans in the United States, and makes the debatable claim that both groups identified at the time more with the Portuguese than with Africans or Afro-descendants. As a native of southeastern New England who was raised in proximity to a large Cabo Verdean community that clearly identified as a community of color, separate from the white Portuguese, statements like Bender's come as a surprise. Nevertheless, scholars like Deirdre Meintel have also documented this identification: "Cape Verdeans were described as fluent speakers of Portuguese, mostly literate, free of racism, and as bearers of a culture whose Portuguese roots were the only ones recognized, one that set them apart from African-Americans (Meintel 1981:1984a)" (35). A 2009 article by Marilyn Halter documents this phenomenon in greater detail.

Halter's article explores the changing dynamics of racial and ethnic identification in Cabo Verdean communities of New England. She writes, "In the first decades of the 20th century, although Cape Verdean settlers sought recognition as Portuguese-Americans, white society, including the other Portuguese immigrants in the region, excluded them from their social and religious associations. At the same time, the Cape Verdeans chose not to identify with the native-born black population" (Halter 531). Halter continues, claiming, "And despite over thirty years as an independent nation of Africa, the great majority of both Cape Verdean immigrants and the American-born still resist the label of African" (535). This attempt to avoid connection with the black community in a country where racial binaries are a determinative aspect within culture and society perhaps has contributed to a liminal status for Cabo Verdeans in the United States. In an article on race and ethnicity in the Cabo Verdean community of Boston, Gina Sánchez Gibau quotes a woman named Wanda: "There are Black people and there are White people and you were trying to be Grey, somewhere in the middle, and there was no Grey. So, I identified with who, you know, I wanted to be like" ("Contested..." 484). Although some Cabo Verdeans in the U.S. may have wished to maintain a separate identity from Afro-Americans, they were also rejected by white society, thus prompting the creation a distinctly outside and somewhat hidden status, one memorialized in the title of Claire Andrade-Watkins's 2006 documentary on the Cabo Verdeans of Providence, *Some Kind of Funny Porto Rican*. Marilyn Halter claims that a focus on multiculturalism beginning in the 1970s presented an option for a separate and hybrid identity that was not available in the United States that Bender had in mind when he compared Cabo Verdeans in Angola to Cabo Verdeans in the United States (Halter 542). Furthermore, since 1975, Cabo Verde has been an independent nation that has affirmed a distinct identity from that of Portugal. The Cabo Verdeans that were in Angola during the colonial period were part of a political and cultural system that did not allow for the creation of explicit affective relationships with the host colony. It is only in the post-independence world of diaspora that these relationships can be fully articulated and celebrated.

In Halter's article she discusses the relationships between Angolans and Cabo Verdeans in contemporary Massachusetts. She describes the trajectory Cabo Verdean descendants who were born in Angola and have now found themselves in the United States. These diasporic denizens have lived a particularly transnational experience, with some having migrated from Angola back to Cabo Verde and then to the United States and others joining the wave of *retornados* to Portugal and then migrating to Massachusetts. Some non-Cabo Verdean Angolans have also obtained political asylum from the United States and emigrated as well. All of these communities have tended to emerge in places like Brockton, Massachusetts, where an existent Cabo Verdean community meant that, "they have been able to take advantage of a Portuguese-language infrastructure, social services, medical professionals, and co-ethnic employment and housing networks originally set up for the Cape Verdean newcomers" (546–547). Halter also discovered that good relations exist between Cabo Verdeans and recently arrived Angolan immigrants in Brockton. While there may be some tension between the two communities in Portugal, in Brockton they coexist well, and many of the Angolans in fact learn Cabo Verdean *kriolu* to better assimilate into the existing Cabo Verdean community (547). The fact that Angolans and Cabo Verdeans need to coexist in a broader Lusophone African diasporic community may have prompted the affective relationship evidenced in music. In the United States, the two communities find common ground with their dependence on the Portuguese-language community infrastructure, while in Portugal they find common ground as postcolonial migrants of color. By being grouped together, Angolans and Cabo Verdeans have created more positive connections than they may have had during the colonial years, when the Cabo Verdean community was connected to the apparatus of colonial power. These connections can even be seen in Angola itself. On a recent visit to Angola, a functionary for the *Partido Africano para a Independência de Cabo Verde* (African Party for the Independence of Cabo Verde or PAICV) noted that, "the Cape Verdean community looks very well integrated into Angolan society" ("Comunidade cabo-verdiana"). For a variety of reasons, Angolans and Cabo Verdeans appear to have created a stronger affective cultural bond, at least in southeastern New England, than that which existed when the Luanda riots of 1974 took place. An exploration of the musical manifestations of this bond will provide a deeper insight into the topic.

3. "Angolamania"

Cabo Verdean music is often studied as a creative expression of the migratory experience. Many Cabo Verdean songs narrate displacement, and scholars have studied Cabo Verdean songs as an insight into a national identity predicated on diasporic dispersion. In an article about the role of images of emigration in Cabo Verdean music Juliana Braz Dias writes:

> Cape Verdean music has had a strong role in the process of construction and reconstruction of social identities. It is an essential tool in the formation of the idea (and feeling) of what it means to be Cape Verdean, and aids the adaptation of Cape Verdeans to foreign lands, as well as in their re-adaptation when they return to the homeland. (174)

Given music's prominent role in the creation of a Cabo Verdean identity, it becomes essential to listen to that music to find answers to our questions about that identity, such as affective links to Angola. This section will examine both scholarly works about Cabo Verdean and Angolan music and songs produced by diasporic musicians to illustrate Angola's position in Cabo Verdean discourses of identity. It is important not only to focus on the representation of Angola that is created in songs, but also to understand the impact that Angolan popular music itself has had on Cabo Verdeans in the diaspora. Furthermore, a discussion of the transnational nature of Cabo Verdean popular music and its varied influences will help reinforce the significance of inter-diasporic relations, such as those referenced by Halter, in the creation of Cabo Verdean identity.

Cabo Verde has become known globally for its rich musical culture. Artists like Cesária Évora and Maria de Barros have gained followings around the world since the 1990s. What many foreign fans of Cabo Verdean music may not realize is that much of the music that they consume originates in a diasporic musical network. Rui Cidra writes, "Migrants who settled in different migrant communities built musical production networks that enabled migrant and non-migrant musicians to record their music. Until recently, all recordings of Cape Verdean music were made entirely outside of the country" (190). Given the material poverty of Cabo Verde and the fact that there was already a well-established diasporic network in more economically developed countries, it not surprising that the production and recording of Cabo Verdean music would become a global enterprise. Musicians needed the more advanced production technology available in countries like Portugal, the United States and the Netherlands, and were able to take advantage of these through pre-existent migrant communities.

A side effect of this process of transnational musical creation was the opportunity to work with musicians from other countries who would have an influence on Cabo Verdean music. Cidra discusses the importance of Rotterdam as a recording center for Cabo Verdean musicians in the 1960s. This Dutch city had a large Cabo Verdean migrant population and was home to the influential record label Edições Casa Silva (later known as Morabeza Records). Though the majority of artists on this label in those early years were Cabo Verdean, this record label presented another point of dialogue between Cabo Verdeans and Angolans outside of the confines of the moribund Portuguese Empire. In his article, Cidra writes of the pro-*Partido Africano da Independência da Guiné e Cabo Verde* (African Party for the Independence of Guinea and Cabo Verde, or PAIGC) political leanings of the founders of Casa Silva, and uses this to explain these nascent links between the Cabo Verdean and Angolan popular music scenes in that decade of anti-colonial struggle in both countries. Cidra explains:

> Casa Silva was also connected to the 'anti-colonial struggle' and PAIGC propaganda activities. With these political leanings, it published recorded poems of Cape Verdean writers and intellectuals and political speeches by party leaders, as well as the *Angola '72* LP by the Angolan singer Bonga, who was then exiled in the Netherlands, and who was backed by Humbertona and the Angolan Mário Rui Silva. Records with political content were put into sleeves belonging to other records and transported covertly to African countries by Cape Verdean and Angolan sailors. (194)

While in Angola itself there may have been tensions in the early 1970s between Cabo Verdean migrants and Angolans who were ready for independence, within a broader Lusophone African diaspora, musicians with similar political leanings were working together to better spread their message.

Though his message was unmistakably linked to the Angolan independence movement (and particularly with the UNITA party (Moorman 241)), the above-mentioned singer Bonga has gained considerable popularity among Cabo Verdeans. A Bonga concert that I attended in East Providence, RI, in 2010 was attended mostly by first and second generation Cabo Verdean-Americans. Among Bonga's most popular and enduring songs is "Mona Ki Ngi Xiça," a song from *Angola '72* sung in Kimbundu, that discusses the sorrow of leaving a child behind when one needs to migrate. This song lives on as an iconic symbol of Angola's struggle for independence. While most Cabo Verdeans do not speak Kimbundu, Bonga's performance of this song at the concert was accompanied by silence and even tears from some members of the audience. There was no way of knowing how many of the people in the audience were born in Angola or had connections there, but it was striking to see the way that an iconically Angolan cultural product affected a crowd of Cabo Verdean listeners. Despite the creation of separate national identities, it was clear that Bonga's supremely Angolan creation also spoke to Cabo Verdeans' experience of migration and identity formation.

One explanation for the Cabo Verdean interest in the music of Bonga and other Angolan musicians of his generation can be found in Moorman's work. She describes the way that an appreciation of the popular music produced in Luanda's *musseques* transcended racial and class divisions in the colony's final years:

Music in late colonial Angola took private grief and by performing it publicly made it collective. The sound, and perhaps even the process, was attractive to whites as well, and in an ironic twist on the lusotropical narrative, by the early 1970s, whites made their way to the musseques in sizeable numbers to hear Ngola Ritmos and other popular bands play. In the end, it was Angolan music and Africans who succeeded in producing a culture, both cosmopolitan and African, that attracted European audiences. (137)

Whereas the Cabo Verdeans may not have identified with local African populations, they were part of this colonial cosmopolitanism described by Moorman, and would have been involved in the music scene as actively as Luanda's whites were. Furthermore, as a colonial people also facing an independence struggle against the Portuguese, the collective airing of grief that Moorman posits would have perhaps had particular resonance.

A 2010 interview I conducted with Yvonne Smart, a worker at the Cape Verdean Museum Exhibit in East Providence, RI, focused on the connections between Bonga and the Cabo Verdean community of southeastern New England. Smart hosted Bonga when he first came to perform in the United States in 1974. In her interview, she stated that she believes his tour of the United States at the time was the first exposure that many Cabo Verdean-Americans had to Angolan culture. Bonga had come to perform at the United Nations for a memorial service in commemoration of the recently assassinated PAIGC leader Amílcar Cabral. According to Smart, this tour was sponsored by the PAIGC support committee in the United States. Bonga and his band played in a variety of the venues in the United States during this tour, including Brown University in Providence, Southeastern Massachusetts University (now University of Massachusetts Dartmouth), and the Cape Verdean Progressive Club in East Providence. Since little money was available to sponsor this group of musicians, members of the Cabo Verdean community like Smart hosted them and provided them with food. Smart remembers that the group of musicians was diverse, and included musicians from Angola, Mozambique, Cabo Verde, Brazil, and even Martinique. Songs were sung in Kriolu, Portuguese, and a variety of African languages: "It was world music before they called it world music," as she put it. She remembers the emotional impact of Bonga's concerts at the Cape Verdean Progressive Club on the audience: "My mother, when he came, was in her 80s, at the time, and she went to that concert and I remember it really moving her." Smart has since befriended Bonga, attending all of the shows that he has performed in the region.

She says that Bonga feels an affinity for Cabo Verdeans, claiming that the Cabo Verdean community of Lisbon embraced him when he first moved to Portugal from Angola. He had gone to Portugal as an athlete and, according to Smart, eventually defected, living illegally with help from Cabo Verdeans in Lisbon. Smart recalls that at the same time when Bonga was staying with her and performing in the United States, there were tensions between Cabo Verdeans and Angolans in Angola. "There was trouble because the Cape Verdeans came over to Angola to be middle men. The Angolans thought that Cape Verdeans were on the side of the Portuguese government, even if they weren't" (Smart). Despite this, according to Smart, Cabo Verdeans in both Lisbon and New England embraced the singer. Bonga's performance in the United States to commemorate Cabo Verdean and Bissau-Guinean independence hero Amílcar Cabral sent a strong message of solidarity between the various independence struggles of Portuguese-colonized Africa, and laid the groundwork for future expressions of solidarity between Cabo Verdeans and Angolans.

The Mendes Brothers are a musical group rooted in the Cabo Verdean community of Southeastern New England that continues this performance of solidarity in a more contemporary context. The Mendes Brothers are João and Ramiro Mendes, two brothers from the Cabo Verdean island of Fogo who settled in Brockton, MA, the community mentioned by Marilyn Halter as a point of encounter between Cabo Verdeans and Angolans in the United States. Starting in the early 1990s, the brothers began a prolific musical career. Their music was popular both with the local Cabo Verdean community and with non-Cabo Verdean listeners who were interested in the burgeoning world music scene of the era. They are mentioned in the 1994 *Rough Guide to World Music* as, "the hot new names in the U.S.-based Cape Verdean scene" (Peterson 280). During the 1990s and much of the 2000s, the brothers also ran a record label out of Brockton called MB Records that was influential in the North American Cabo Verdean music scene, releasing albums by local Cabo Verdean artists and even breaking some Angolan artists, like the Kafala Brothers and Waldemar Bastos, into the U.S. market. The Mendes Brothers themselves have released several songs that deal with Angola as a primary topic. In a 2010 interview with Callie Crossley on the Boston radio station WGBH, the Mendes Brothers discussed their connections with Angola, stating that they have recorded over twelve songs that deal with the theme of peace and unity in Angola (*Callie Crossley Show*).

This interview invites the listener into these musicians' transnational experience. They discuss their experiences touring in Angola in the 1990s and singing songs with themes of peace and reconciliation. In the interview, one of the musicians describes Angola as, "a sister country that speaks the same language and was a former colony of Portugal as well" (*Callie Crossley Show*). This statement will be analyzed more closely after a discussion of the songs of the Mendes Brothers. Their experience with the use of music as a peace-building tool led the musicians to create a foundation in the 2000s called The Music and Life Foundation that supports efforts to build peace through music. Among the most salient features of the Mendes Brothers' music is that it functions as a commentary on global crisis, something exemplified in several of their earliest songs. Their first album from 1993, *Palonkon*, contains two songs that discuss Angola, "Angola na Paz" and "Angola Beleza Natural." The first of these songs deserves analysis, as it is an unequivocal statement of solidarity between Cabo Verdeans and Angola.

The song has a sound that shows influences from both Cabo Verdean and Angolan popular music genres. The rhythm of the song is much like mid-tempo Cabo Verdean *coladeira* music, while the instrumentation reflects an Angolan sound, as it features the high-tuned electric guitars that were popular in much of the late colonial Angolan music that has been researched by Moorman. Musically the song can appeal to both audiences. The lyrics are sung in Kriolu, and begin,

> Angola, Angola/ Dja bu sufri tcheu nes mundo/ Sufrimento ta kaba/ Tudo na paz e harmonia/Angola, Angola/ Tudo bo dor tambem é nha dor/ Bu sufrimento é nha lamento/ Bu alegria é nha contentamento.
> Angola, Angola/ You've suffered much in this world/ The suffering is ending/ All in peace and harmony/ Angola, Angola, all your pain is also my pain/ Your suffering is my lament/ Your joy is my contentment. (Mendes Brothers "Angola Na Paz")

Angola, which was experiencing a tenuous peace in 1993, had, at the time of the song's release, suffered through seventeen years of civil war. The Mendes Brothers express their sorrow at the suffering that Angolans had undergone during the years of war, and, by reaffirming the end of hostilities, make an appeal for peace in the strife-torn country. The chorus of the song is a plea for national unity, "Um só povo um só nação/ Um só povo um coração/ Um só povo um direção/ Angola na paz é midjor//Just one people just one nation/ Just one people one heart/ Just one people one direction/ Angola at peace is better"

(Mendes Brothers "Angola Na Paz"). Although they themselves are not Angolan, the Mendes Brothers plead directly with their fellow Lusophone Africans to unite. Later in the song, they appeal to various factions of the conflict including, President "Zedu" dos Santos, Jonas Savimbi, and "forças estrangeiras" (Mendes Brothers "Angola Na Paz"). While the song displays solidarity with Angolans, it is important to note that the lyrics contain *bo* (your) in reference to Angola and *nha* (my) in reference to the Cabo Verdean singers. The singers show their concern with Angola, but they do not claim the conflict and suffering as their own. It is an interesting song in that it clearly separates the Cabo Verdean singers from their Angolan subject matter, while at the same time encouraging Angolans and reinforcing empathy and support from Cabo Verdeans around the world.

The other song from this album with Angola as a theme is "Angola Beleza Natural," a song that discusses the natural beauty of the country. This paean to Angola describes it as a land with "beleza natural/ natural beauty," and "riqueza natural/ natural riches" (Mendes Brothers "Angola Beleza Natural"). The chorus of this song reveals the affective relationship that the Mendes Brothers have established with Angola as both nation and concept. The singer claims, "Angola intrega meu coração/Angola makes my heart whole," and also that, "Angola fica na recordação/ Angola stays in one's memory" (Mendes Brothers "Angola Beleza Natural"). These declarations confirm that Angola holds an essential role in the Mendes Brothers' configuration of their self-identity. Though the brothers are not Angolan, the nation makes their hearts whole and stays in their memories. In a study of Portuguese *retornados* from Angola living in northern New Jersey, Kimberley DaCosta Holton notes similar emotional responses to Angola from these white former colonists and claims:

> They have never 'gotten over' Angola, and contrary to commonly held perceptions, this longing for past lives has little to do with material wealth. Some came to the United States in search of a surrogate Africa. Others came to escape what they characterize as the social toxicity…All still dream of returning to Angola, either permanently or for a visit" (503).

The Mendes Brothers display a similar affective reaction to the country that perhaps stems from the influence of Cabo Verdean *retornados* who fled Angola and present similar feelings as the Portuguese *retornados* detailed by DaCosta Holton. Marilyn Halter already has documented the presence of Cabo Verdean *retornados* in Brockton, MA, the city where the Mendes Brothers are based. Just as time spent in the diaspora helped to shape Bonga's reaction to Cabo Verdeans in Lisbon in the 1960s, so proximity to people who had spent time in Angola in the Brockton Cape Verdean community may have led to a deeper interest in that nation on the part of the Mendes Brothers. This is an interesting connection to ponder, and it would be important to interview the musicians about it.

The Mendes Brothers continued publicly to manifest their affection for Angola, discussing the nation in the above-mentioned interview on the *Callie Crossley* show and playing a sample from a song recorded in the late 1990s called "Angola Kuia". In 2006, they released a compilation CD of their songs specifically dedicated to the topic of Angola called *Para Angola com um Xi Coração*. The album contains both of the songs discussed earlier in this paper, in addition to several other songs exploring the theme of peace in Angola. The next year they recorded an album called *Cabo Verde* which, nevertheless, still includes two songs about Angola, one entitled "Luanda" and the other, "Angolamania." The latter song is particularly interesting as it displays a consciousness of the group's fixation on Angola, utilizing the titles of several other songs including "Angola na Paz" and "Angola Beleza Natural" in the lyrics. The song's final verse features the artists singing the names of various cities and towns in Angola and repeating the chorus, "Ai amor, Angolamania/Oh love, Angolamania" (Mendes Brothers "Angolamania"). Angola has now achieved the peace that the brothers had so actively hoped for in their earlier songs, but it has not lost its hold on them as a source of musical inspiration. Though they may have established a relationship of *bo* and *nha* with Angola, they still feel that it is important to refer to Angola, and to embrace their own "Angolamania."

While it would be an exaggeration to refer to Cabo Verdeans in New England as having "Angolamania," the popularity of Angolan music in the community cannot be denied. In a 2010 interview, Djuca Baptista, a concert organizer and club promoter in the Cabo Verdean community of Providence, RI, describes the magnitude of this popularity. Djuca works with Jambaby, a production company that had, at the time, organized at least three Angolan music events in Providence. These events included a *kuduro* dance night, a concert by Bonga, and another concert by the Angolan *kizomba* star Don Kikas. According to Baptista, these events drew large audiences. When asked if he thought that the audiences were mostly comprised of Angolans and/or Cabo Verdeans who had lived in Angola, he responded, "No, they had everybody from the community." Much like Yvonne Smart's mother's emotional reaction to Bonga in the 1970s, these

Cabo Verdeans from Rhode Island in the 2010s were attracted to Angolan music without any direct personal connection to Angola.

Don Kikas himself presents an interesting case of the multi-faceted identities that manifest themselves in the Lusophone African diaspora. A particularly illustrative point is his 1999 hit *kizomba* song "Angolanamente Sensual" (Angolanly Sensual). *Kizomba* is an Angolan genre of dance music that shares many auditory features with *zouk*, a genre of music that originated in the French Antilles but that has become a powerhouse musical genre among Cabo Verdeans from around the diaspora. JoAnne Hoffman has written about the popularity of *zouk* with Cabo Verdeans and discusses its initial boom in the Cabo Verdean community of Rotterdam, while also tracking its growing popularity in the diaspora as well as in Cabo Verde itself. Speaking about the genre, she claims that, "The roots of *cabo-zouk* lie in a combination of local and global factors that crossed paths at a particular time, in a particular place and answered a particular need—the popularity of Antillean *zouk* intersected with a community of musicians that related to its rhythm and the related dancing" (Hoffman 218). Don Kikas represents a further extension of the genre, now from the Cabo Verdean diaspora to Angola itself, where songs influenced by Antillean and Cabo Verdean *zouk* have become the basis for the success of the now internationally-renowned *kizomba* genre of music and dance.

Don Kikas was born in the city of Sumbe, Angola, but moved to Brazil with his family at a young age (Vaz). According to Djuca Baptista, he was based in Portugal in the 2000s. He is another product of migration, and while his song "Angolanamente Sensual" may feature an explicit reference to Angola, it also has references to a transnational Lusophone identity that overflows the confines of the former empire. The video for the song begins with the musician flying his private plane, the DON K 2000, on a course that goes from Boston to Lisbon to Luanda. The song ends with the singer praising the sensuality of a variety of primarily Lusophone countries: "Moçambicanamente/ Caboverdeanamente/ Guineensemente uí/ Sãotomensemente/ Portuguesamente/ Brasileiramente uí/ Mexi-mexi-mexi-canamente/ PALOP-PALOP-PALOPamente/ Universalmente// Mozambicanly/Cabo Verdeanly/ Guineanly/ São Tomeanly/ Portuguesely/ Brazilianly/ Mexicanly/ PALOP-ly/ Universally" (Don Kikas). The reference to the term PALOP, a Portuguese-language acronym for Officially Portuguese-Speaking African Countries (Países Africanos de Língua Oficial Portuguesa), is noteworthy, as it posits a cultural unity among the former Portuguese colonies of Africa.

This echoes comments by the Mendes Brothers about Angola being a sister country that shares a language with Cabo Verde. While Cabo Verdeans take pride in their own language, Kriolu, the comments by the Mendes Brothers and Don Kikas's mention of the PALOPs also affirm Cabo Verdean identity within a larger community of Portuguese-speaking African countries. Based on Djuca Baptista's description of the large crowd at the Don Kikas show in Providence, the Cabo Verdean community there certainly does not see a problem with identifying with other Portuguese-speaking African countries. Although "Angolamania" may be an exaggeration, the examples detailed in this section certainly illustrate an "Angolaphilia" in the Cabo Verdean community of southeastern New England.

4. Conclusions

In their interview with Callie Crossley, the Mendes Brothers discuss a song from their album entitled "Porton di Regresso" (Gate of Return). They claim that this song addresses people from all over the "Atlantic diaspora," and invites them to cultivate closer contact with Africa. They say that, "Africa is very lonely. They're looking for the connection. They're looking for their sons and daughters in particular to reconnect to the continent" (*The Callie Crossley Show*). Based on the examples that have been studied in this paper, there is indeed an attempt on the part of many Cabo Verdeans and Angolans to try to reinforce connections between Cabo Verde and the African continent, a reinforcement in which the southeastern New England Cabo Verdean community plays a role. As posited in the introduction to this paper, the Cabo Verdean migrant experience is one that illustrates and expands on Gilroy's influential discourse on the Black Atlantic. We can see the ways in which the college campuses, theaters, recording studios and dance clubs of southeastern New England have been spaces that have fostered the cultivation of a multiple consciousness among Cabo Verdean migrants and their descendants, which strengthen connections with Africa and the African Diaspora. In his book, Gilroy discusses the dual consciousness that many Afro-descendants develop, a consciousness that entails recognition of belonging within both a national community and a broader African diaspora. When I asked Djuca Baptista about the connection that Cabo Verdeans feel with Angola in relation to those with other African countries he answered, "The connection with Angola isn't different from the one with other countries in Africa" (Baptista). This response was interesting, because the examples of the presence of Angola in some elements of Cabo Verdean popular culture, not to mention the special connection that Bonga felt with Cabo Verdeans, seem to indicate that there is indeed a special bond between the two nations. Nevertheless, Baptista implied that the connection that Cape Verdeans felt with Angola was part of a broader cultural approximation to Africa. As scholars like Marilyn Halter and Gina Sánchez-Gibau have shown, there has been a growing trend among Cabo Verdeans in the United States as well as the diaspora in the past half-century to identify more with Africa.

Social scientists of all political stripes, ranging from Brazil's reactionary Gilberto Freyre in his articulations of Lusotropicalism to Portugal's more radical Miguel Vale de Almeida and his *"mar da cor da terra"* (earth-colored sea), have posited the existence of a Lusophone "Brown Atlantic" that contrasts with Gilroy's Anglo-centric Black Atlantic. These discourses often focus on ideas of "exceptionalism" in the context of Portuguese imperialism. In this article I hope to have made the case that the particularly multi-faceted discourses of identity encountered in the Lusophone world do not merely stem from a Portuguese imperial exceptionalism, but rather from the genuinely multi-faceted migratory experiences of groups like the Cabo Verdeans. By following the directive so eloquently investigated by Gina Sánchez-Gibau and referenced in the introduction to this article, scholars must investigate people's specific stories of migration, diasporic affiliation, and transnational affect. I hope that my brief analysis of the work of specific musicians and community organizers is a small step in this direction.

In a migratory and mobile world, people develop diverse ties with a variety of other nations and cultures. Bonga left Angola to live in Portugal where he was embraced by the Cabo Verdean community of Lisbon, an event that led to an affection toward Cabo Verdeans. Yvonne Smart, a member of the New England Cabo Verdean community with connections to the political struggle in the archipelago itself, brought a voice from one Lusophone African struggle for independence into a community that had long been ambivalent about its connection to Africa. The Mendes Brothers lived in a city in the United States where a large community of Cabo Verdean *retornados* from Angola had also settled, possibly sparking an interest in Angola. Their dedication to the use of music as a peace-building tool heightened Angola's role as an inspiration to their music. Don Kikas has lived in Brazil and Portugal, making him more connected to the larger Lusophone world than other Angolans may be. Each of these artist's and activist's unique diasporic paths have contributed to their unique musical and cultural products. The transnational lives that are becoming increasingly common will lead to a wide variety of affective feelings toward different countries and cultures for different individuals. The stories, whether told, or sung, of Cabo Verdeans in New England, with their noteworthy history of migration and displacement, have much to teach us about the ways in which these ties develop.

WORKS CITED

Almeida, Miguel Vale de. *Um mar da cor da terra: "Raça", cultura a política da identidade.* Oeiras: CELTA, 2000.

Batalha, Luís and Jørgen Carling. "Cape Verdean Migration and Diaspora." *Transnational Archipelago: Perspectives on Cape Verdean Migration and Diaspora*, edited by Luís Batalha and Jørgen Carling, Amsterdam UP, 2008, pp. 13–31.

Baptista, Djuca. Personal Interview. 10 Dec 2010.

Bender, Gerald J. *Angola under the Portuguese: The Myth and the Reality.* University of California Press, 1978.

The Callie Crossley Show. Narr. Callie Crossley. Subj. João and Ramiro Mendes. WGBH, Boston. 17 Aug 2010. Radio.

Cidra, Rui. "Cape Verdean Migration, Music Recordings and Performance." *Transnational Archipelago: Perspectives on Cape Verdean Migration and Diaspora*, edited by Luís Batalha and Jørgen Carling, Amsterdam UP, 2008, pp. 189–203.

Clifford, James. "Diasporas." *Cultural Anthropology.* Vol 9, No. 3 (Aug, 1994), pp. 302–338. JSTOR.

"Comunidade de imigrantes cabo-verdianos "muito bem integrada" na sociedade angolana" *Jornal de Angola Online.* Jornal de Angola. 18 Oct 2010. Web. 11 Dec 2010.

DaCosta-Holton, Kimberly. "Angola Dreaming: Memories of Africa among Portuguese Retornados in Newark, NJ." *Community, Culture and the Makings of Identity: Portuguese-Americans along the Eastern Seaboard*, edited by Kimberly DaCosta-Holton and Andrea Klimt, Tagus Press, 2009, pp. 497–524.

Dias, Juliana Braz. "Images of Emigration in Cape Verdean Music." *Transnational Archipelago: Perspectives on Cape Verdean Migration and Diaspora*, edited by Luís Batalha and Jørgen Carling, Amsterdam UP, 2008, pp. 173–187.

Don Kikas. "Angolanamente Sensual" *Xeque Mate.* Zona Música, 1999. CD.

Freyre, Gilberto. *O mundo que o português criou.* 1940. É Realizações, 2010.

Gilroy, Paul. *The Black Atlantic.* 1993. 4th Pr. Harvard UP, 1996.

Halter, Marilyn. "Diasporic Generations: Distinctions of Race, Nationality, and Identity in the Cape Verdean Community, Past and Present." *Community, Culture and the Makings of Identity: Portuguese-Americans along the Eastern Seaboard*, edited by Kimberly DaCosta-Holton and Andrea Klimt, Tagus Press, 2009, pp. 525–553.

Hoffman, JoAnne. "Diasporic Networks, Political Change, and the Growth Cabo-Zouk Music." *Transnational Archipelago: Perspectives on Cape Verdean Migration and Diaspora*, edited by Luís Batalha and Jørgen Carling, Amsterdam UP, 2008, pp. 205–220.

Meintel, Deidre. "Cape Verdean Transnationalism, Old and New." *Anthropologica*, vol. 44, no. 1, 2002, pp. 25–42. JSTOR.

Mendes Brothers. "Angola Beleza Natural" *Palonkon*. MB Records, 1993. CD.

———. "Angola Na Paz" *Palonkon*. MB Records, 1993. CD.

———. "Angolamania" *Cabo Verde*. High Times Records, 2007. MP3.

Moorman, Marissa. *Intonations: A Social History of Music and Nation in Luanda, Angola from 1945 to Recent Times*. Ohio UP, 2008.

Peterson, David. "Sweet Sorrow: The Music of Cape Verde." *The Rough Guide to World Music*, edited by Simon Broughton, Mark Ellingham, David Muddyman and Richard Trillo, Rough Guides Ltd, 1994, pp. 274–281.

Sánchez Gibau, Gina. "Contested Identities: Narratives of Race and Ethnicity in the Cape Verdean Diaspora." *Community, Culture and the Makings of Identity: Portuguese-Americans along the Eastern Seaboard*, edited by Kimberly DaCosta-Holton and Andrea Klimt, Tagus Press, 2009, pp. 461–495.

———. "Telling our Story, Because No One Else Will: Cape Verdean Transnational Identity Formation as Knowledge Production." *Mande Studies*, vol. 16/17, 2015, pp. 107–117. JSTOR.

Smart, Yvonne. Telephone Interview. 10 Dec 2010.

Vaz, Pedro. "Don Kikas." *Mwangole.net*. 22 June 2009. Web. 11 Dec 2010.

BENJAMIN LEGG is a Senior Lecturer and Language Coordinator of Portuguese at Vanderbilt University in Nashville, TN. As a native of southeastern New England, he was exposed to the diverse Portuguese-speaking populations of that region, an experience that led to his interest in the Lusophone World. He currently researches questions of Brazilian national identity and U.S.-Brazil relations, Brazilian culinary traditions and food culture, and queer activisms and visibility throughout the Lusophone World.

BONNIE S. WASSERMAN

Judeotropicalism[1]: Jewish Transculturations in the Lusophone New World

ABSTRACT: This paper conceptualizes Sephardic Jewish survival in the Iberian Peninsula and the so-called New World through the lens of Lusotropicalism, syncretism, transculturation and *mestizaje*. Beginning with the Edict of Expulsion in Spain and forced conversion to Catholicism in Portugal, New Christians face the violent side of transculturation. After the Inquisition is set up in Portugal, New Christians develop syncretic methods to worship as both Jews and Christians. Under a united peninsula between 1580-1640, Conversos flee to Holland where they unite with other Jews and become the *Nação*, a community whose identity is both religious and financial. This group goes with the Dutch West India Company to Recife where some Portuguese New Christians become Jews once again. After the Portuguese retake Recife, the Jews of the *Nação* flee to Suriname, developing *mestizo* communities there and in some of the Caribbean islands. Other Jews from Recife arrive in New Amsterdam (New York) where they establish a thriving community. After 500 years, the influence of these groups can still be felt in the synagogues built in New York, the creole language Papiamentu/o spoken in Curaçao, Aruba and Bonaire, and the tombstones in Suriname, Curação and Barbados, among other things.

KEYWORDS: transculturation, Lusotropicalism, Gilberto Freyre, Judeotropicalism, New Christians, Holland, Sephardim, synagogues

RESUMO: Este artigo investiga várias teorias usadas para explicar a mistura de raças e culturas como o Lusotropicalismo, transculturalismo, sincretismo religioso e miscigenação para examinar a sobrevivência dos Judeus sefarditas depois da Expulsão de 1492 da Espanha e das conversões forçadas em Portugal em 1497 até hoje em dia. Durante a Inquisição em Portugal, comunidades Judaicas desenvolveram métodos sincréticos de praticar religião como Judeus e Cristãos. Sob a península unida entre 1580 e 1640, muitos destes Cristãos Novos saíram de Portugal e foram para Holanda, onde voltaram a praticar Judaísmo com outros Judeus e tornaram-se num grupo financeiro e religioso muito unido e influente chamado "a Nação." Este grupo viajou com a Companhia Holandesa do Oeste para Recife e outras colônias no Caribe. Depois de Portugal recapturar Recife, os Judeus da Nação fugiram a Suriname e formaram comunidades mestiças lá e no Caribe. Outros Judeus de Recife chegaram em Novo Amsterdão (Nova Iorque), onde estabeleceram uma comunidade vibrante. Depois de 500 anos, a influência deste grupo ainda existe nas sinagogas e comunidades que eles construíram nos Estados Unidos, a língua crioula de Papiamentu/o falada em Curaçao, Aruba e Bonaire, e nas pedras tumulares em Suriname, Curaçao, Barbados entre outras coisas.

PALAVRAS-CHAVE: transculturação, Lusotropicalismo, Gilberto Freyre, Judeotropicalismo, Cristãos Novos, Holanda, sefarditas, sinagogas

---

On the corner of 70th Street and Central Park West in New York City stands a majestic building with a prominent cornerstone that reads 1654. The date seems incongruous amongst the brownstones built primarily in the late nineteenth century. However, the structure and the year inscribed on it correspond to a significant moment in both Portuguese and American history, and its presence reminds us how Lusophone culture is still very much alive here in the twenty-first century. It was in 1654 that twenty-three Jews arrived in the Dutch colony of New Amsterdam from Recife, Brazil after the Portuguese had recaptured it.[2] Though the Jewish refugees were not welcomed by the governor, Pieter Stuyvesant, who wrote to the Dutch West India Company for permission to bar them from settling, the Jews remained in Manhattan and later established Congregation Shearith Israel.[3] Today, the congregation includes Sephardic Jews whose ancestors originated in Iberia, as well as families that come from the larger Ashkenazi or Eastern European Jewish population in New York City. While the majority in the synagogue do not speak Portuguese, though there are a few native Brazilians and Portuguese, their rituals, including the way prayers are chanted, derive from the Western Sephardic Traditions that began in Portugal and Spain amongst the descendants of the New Christians who had been forcibly converted to Catholicism in the fifteenth century, and later evolved in Amsterdam amongst Ashkenazi Jews and Italian Jews. While many historians and Judaic scholars have written extensively about this topic, this paper examines how a Lusophone concept used to explain the mixture of races and cultures in Brazil, Lusotropicalism, can ironically be adapted as "Judeotropicalism" to study both the thriving and declining Sephardic communities in the Western Hemisphere.

Lusotropicalism and racial democracy are two terms associated with Brazilian sociologist Gilberto Freyre's 1933 book, *The Masters and the Slaves* (*Casa-grande e Senzala*).[4] These expressions refer to miscegenation or the mixing of races—the former to the predisposition of the Portuguese in colonizing tropical areas and having children with women of color because the Portuguese themselves are descendants of Moors, and the latter to the supposed equality amongst races in Brazil due to this resulting mixture (Freyre 12). When Freyre wrote his treatise, social scientists believed that there was a racial hierarchy in which whites were superior to blacks as well as those of mixed backgrounds. Racial determinism was a standard in academia and was used to fuel the Fascist policies of Nazi Germany. Freyre, however, had studied with Franz Boaz, a renowned Jewish anthropologist at Columbia University, who saw the growing anti-Semitism in Europe at the time and believed that culture rather than race should be emphasized in the study of societies (Maybury-Lewis lxxxiii). Today, scholars consider Freyre's work to be extremely chauvinistic; however, historian Thomas Skidmore points out that he was innovative for his era because his work focused attention on the inherent value of Africans as the representatives of a high civilization in their own right. Freyre was thus furnishing, for those Brazilians who might want to take it that way, a rationale for a multiracial society in which the component 'races'—European, African and Indigenous—could be seen as *equally* valuable (22).

The Brazilian sociologist also wished to differentiate Brazil from the United States where he had traveled extensively. He believed that in his country there was "a marked absence of post-manumission institutionalized racism (e.g., segregation & Jim Crow law(s), (and) a general absence of race-based group violence (e.g., lynching, race-based hate crimes)" compared to North America (Peña, et al 749).

Since its publication, Freyre's theories have been refuted, for racism does indeed exist in Brazil, and it seems a little far-fetched to claim that North African ancestry made the Portuguese any more likely to have sexual relations with women in the countries they colonized than other European men. Moreover, Lusotropicalism was used by the Portuguese government to excuse their colonization in Africa well into the twentieth century. According to the historian David Birmingham, "When fascism fell out of favor in 1945, Salazar's spin doctors pretended that interracial breeding proved that the Portuguese had never been racists in the Nazi or Afrikaner mold" (24). Nevertheless, Freyre's work preceded other theories of racial and cultural mixture that can be used in the study of Sephardic Jews in the Western Hemisphere.

One theory that can be utilized to address cultural "merging" is transculturation, which was developed by Cuban anthropologist Fernando Ortiz in 1947 (Paul 241). Anthropologist Fernando Coronil explains that, "transculturation is used to apprehend at once the destructive and constructive moments in histories affected by colonialism and imperialism" (xv). Ultimately, aspects of both cultures are gained and lost in the violent process of creating something new. Transculturation is often associated with *mestizaje* or the mixture of Europeans and indigenous peoples specifically in Latin America and can also be used to explain the development of Creole languages as well as religious syncretism.

The term "syncretism" originally derived from the Greek prefix "syn-" meaning "with" or "reunion" with "Cretan" a group that was an adversary of the ancient Greeks (Sathler and Nascimento 96). Syncretism by definition has an aggressive or militaristic undertone and when applied to religion, it denotes how one religion is imposed on another by forced conversion. In the so-called New World, different syncretic religions developed amongst the enslaved Africans who were forced to become Christians. As a result of coerced conversion, syncretic religions ultimately blend, though usually with one being "masked" or hidden. Syncretism or cultural mixing is perceived differently depending on which group is imposing itself on the other.

This paper argues that, in order to subvert Portuguese religious policies, overcome prejudice and ultimately survive until the present day, Sephardic Jews used tactics such as syncretism, transculturation, and *mestizaje*. It is important to note that in some instances, however, the Sephardic Jews themselves were the ones who dominated and subjugated others. One of the first examples of transculturation and syncretism occurred after the Jews were expelled from Spain. Three months after their resounding victory against the Moors in Granada that culminated in the Reconquista, King Ferdinand II of Aragon and Queen Isabella I of Castile ordered the expulsion of all Jews and Muslims from their borders on March 31, 1492, to be carried out by July 31, 1492. Both groups could stay if they converted to Catholicism but would face death if they continued to observe their faiths.

The historian Lu Ann Homza notes that although "the number of Jews who left Spain cannot be calculated with any reliability, the figure of 150,000 to 165,000 has been suggested. There are no reliable statistics either, for the Jews who chose to remain and convert" (xxi). Many went east to the Ottoman Empire where they were welcomed by the Sultans who valued their skills in trade and languages.

It was in the Ottoman Empire that the Jews practiced the same traditions that they had in Spain and spoke Judeo-Spanish or Ladino, a Romance language influenced by Hebrew. Others ventured south to North Africa to reside alongside the Muslims with whom they had lived in Iberia for centuries. Many other Spanish Jews, an estimated 70,000, fled west across the border to Portugal where they joined the 30,000 or so Portuguese Jews who already lived there (Melammed 2).

The Jews who crossed the Portuguese frontier from Spain were at first welcomed by King John II, who saw them as beneficial to the nation's economy at a time when the country was expanding its empire and competing with Spain. Indeed, the Spanish Expulsion order came during the so-called period of discoveries and both countries were seeking new trade routes to Asia. The King viewed the wealth and education of the Spanish Jews as a way to build up his nation and though he had them taxed upon their arrival to fill his coffers, he allowed them to practice their religion in order to encourage them to stay in Portugal. This policy changed drastically in 1497 when his successor, King Manuel I, was pressured to evict the Jews as part of an agreement to marry the daughter of King Ferdinand and Queen Isabella.

Damião de Góis, a humanist and historian, wrote chronicles describing how there were opponents to the expulsion who "brought forth a battery of spiritual and material arguments" including the fact that even the Pope permitted Jews to live in his lands (Soyer 184). Other arguments against the expulsion included the fact that the Jews would help the Muslims by providing them with technological information regarding the manufacturing of armaments (Soyer 184). Ultimately, the Portuguese king only expelled the Muslims and forcibly converted the Jews by taking away Hebrew books, confiscating properties, and kidnapping Jewish children and placing them with Catholic families (Soyer 8). According to the historian François Soyer, King Manuel "had two very different aims and ambitions in the first years of his reign: his eagerness to finance a voyage of exploration to India and his obsession with the launch of a new crusade against the Muslims in Morocco" (8). Keeping the Jews and their wealth within the kingdom and not alienating Spain by converting them seemed to solve the king's problems. Moreover, after their conversion King Manuel directed the Old Christians not to inquire into the faith of the New Christians for thirty-five years.

The conversion of the Jews was not accepted by the general populace and in 1506 the resentment that the Old Christians felt toward the New Christians turned to violence as over 2,000 New Christians were massacred in Lisbon.

Melammed explains that, "the king was certain that despite the forced nature of the conversions, the converts or their descendants would eventually assimilate into the Portuguese Catholic society. There had been no plan for establishing an inquisition or for discriminating between Old and New Christians" (6). The theory of transculturation can explain the hostile reaction toward the converts. Transculturation is often a forceful process when two cultures come into contact with one another. King Manuel attempted to force the merger not only of two communities—that of the Portuguese Jews with the Portuguese Catholics—but also a third, the Spanish New Christians, who in addition to having a Jewish background were not welcomed because many were wealthy and came from Spain, Portugal's arch rival. Ultimately, in 1536, the Inquisition was instituted in Portugal to find and punish heretics as well as Judaizers, or those who spread Judaism. The Inquisition institutionalized the transcultural process by creating an atmosphere of fear to force the merger of a minority community within a larger one. Whereas it was successful in some respects as countless New Christians abandoned their traditions, it also led to a different strategy of survival, that of syncretism.

Many New Christians who did not wish to lose their Jewish heritage and assimilate completely became Crypto-Jews who secretly practiced Judaism while outwardly following Christianity. They fled to places that were far from the Inquisitional headquarters in Lisbon and Évora, such as the northeastern part of Portugal and lived in tiny villages in the Beiras and Trás-os-Montes. In these small communities, Crypto-Jews observed Jewish rituals clandestinely while still going to church to dupe their Christian neighbors. They also blended some aspects of both religions, as long as they didn't threaten their Jewish identity. One noted group that maintained its Jewish heritage for over five hundred years lives in the village of Belmonte in the Beira Baixa region of Portugal. Though they were obliged to publicly practice Catholicism, the Jews of Belmonte observed many Jewish religious rites and rituals within their homes and intermarried amongst themselves. Because of their isolation, the Belmonte Jews believed that they were the only Jews left in the world until a Polish-Jewish mining engineer named Samuel Schwarz "discovered" them in 1917 (Gerber, et al 276). In his 1926 book about their closed community he wrote that the Crypto-Jewish traditions were "jealously guarded and revealed only after gaining the complete trust of the outsider" and that only after he "recited the *Shema* prayer ("Hear, O Israel") for them, they recognized the name *Adonai* ("the Lord"), apparently the only Hebrew word they knew; this word magically opened their doors for him" (Melammed 143). Schwarz learned that the traditions were passed on orally by the women as there were no synagogues where the men could officiate (Melammed 145). The Belmonte Jews also incorporated Catholic elements in their life. They prayed to different saints, such as Saint Raphael, and celebrated a number of Christian holidays, such as the Feast of Corpus Christi (Melammed 145).

The Jews of Belmonte are an excellent example of syncretism as they maintained their religion in a hostile environment by retaining aspects of it and passing these on for generations. According to Melammed, "essentially the Belmonte community had mastered the art of living in two worlds simultaneously, adopting two mentalities, both of which were normative for them" (146). After Schwarz published his book, other Jews visited Belmonte with the intention of converting them to normative twentieth century Judaism. In the 1990s Israeli rabbis of Moroccan descent went to the village to "Judaize" the Crypto-Jews. They built a synagogue, brought someone who could perform circumcisions (*mohel*) and built a ritual bath (*mikveh*) (Melammed 153). Melammed notes further that "While the men now have an institution of their own, namely, the synagogue, the women have not relinquished all their "traditional" roles. The women still marry within the fold, and the Passover picnic is still the annual community affair" (154). The "reconversion" of the Crypto-Jews in Belmonte reflects the transculturation of a syncretized group. The Moroccan rabbis did not regard the Crypto-Jews as true or "real" Jews and felt the need to convert them. "Despite the fact by the standards of the outside world, two-thirds of them converted and are full-fledged Jews, the "Last Marranos" seem determined to retain the Marrano part of their identity as well" (154). It is ironic that some of the Crypto-Jews who for centuries hid amongst their Catholic neighbors for fear that they would be converted to Catholicism will now need to hide from Jews who wish to "re-convert" them to a different form of Judaism.

Amsterdam and the "Hebrews of the Portuguese Nation"
The Conversos who were not hiding out in far off villages had to wait until the unification of Spain and Portugal between 1580 and 1640 to leave the country en masse. Though the Inquisition was still in place, thousands fled from Portugal across Spain to France and eventually to Holland. The Dutch allowed freedom of religion after having been subjugated by the Spanish for decades. According to historian Miriam Bodian, "The appreciation the early Portuguese-Jewish émigrés

in Amsterdam felt for the religious freedom granted them was one of the factors that contributed to the rapid growth of the community" ("The Geography" 254). So many Conversos were crossing the border through Spain that the Spanish thought that all the Portuguese in their midst, whether they were Catholic or not, had some Jewish origin (Bodian Hebrews 13).

Once they reached the Netherlands, the New Christians became part of a community called the "Hebrews of the Portuguese Nation" or the *Nação*. In Amsterdam, all foreign ethnic and religious populations were called "nations" and the Portuguese Nation or *Nação* were the Conversos and Crypto-Jews who had come from Portugal (Bodian Hebrews 7). The *Nação* spoke Portuguese and were involved almost exclusively in trade. They also defined themselves as "*homens de negócios*, or 'men of affairs'" (Melammed 14). In this sense, their identity integrated faith with finance. The members of the *Nação* helped each other out because,

> In the long run, the economic structure created by the Portuguese Conversos was based on the notion of group solidarity. The amazing degree to which they supported and cooperated with one another precisely because they all belonged to "the Nation" was one of the outstanding characteristics of the Portuguese *converso* (15).

According to Melammed, rather than creating a *Catholic* identity, the mass conversions and the establishment of the Inquisition were instrumental in making a viable *Jewish* identity that could survive in other countries and adapt to difficult circumstances. Thus, transculturation can be used to explain how the virulent persecution faced by the Conversos at the hands of the Portuguese Catholics actually helped create a *new* Lusophone identity, one that identified itself as Iberian, spoke Portuguese and practiced Judaism. Moreover, it was extremely unified and would eventually challenge their country of origin by becoming part of a trade network for their competitors, the Dutch.

Recife, the First Jewish Community in the Western Hemisphere

During the seventeenth century, the Dutch were expanding their empire and many Jews of the *Nação* joined the ranks of the Dutch West India Company to increase trade with newly established colonies. After the Dutch had colonized parts of northeastern Brazil in 1630, the *Nação* petitioned to go to Pernambuco in 1635 (Feitler 123). The Jews that arrived there built the first synagogue in the Western Hemisphere in Recife in 1636 called Kahal Zur Israel. During the time that Jews were in Recife, a fascinating development occurred. According to the historian Bruno Feitler, the

> Dutch conquest did not necessarily create a more diversified community. Instead, it changed the percentage of first generation Portuguese and Brazilian natives within the community. In effect, the creation of Dutch Brazil led to an unprecedented set of circumstances: A Catholic territory inhabited by New Christians where Judaism was permitted, and which was subject to Calvinist rule (125).

Many Portuguese New Christians living in Recife viewed the arrival of the "Dutch" Jews as an opportunity to return to the religion of their forefathers and began attending services at the synagogue as well as partaking in other rituals, such as circumcision. Soon, the community grew as New Christians with a Jewish background "merged" into the Nação. Others did not become Jewish and continued to practice Catholicism even though their background would cause them to be suspect by the Portuguese Inquisition that would soon monitor the colony after the Dutch left.

When the Dutch capitulated to the Portuguese after years of war, they, along with the Jews, were given three months to leave Recife and the other parts of "Dutch" Brazil. Whereas many Jews went back to Amsterdam, others went to Dutch colonies in the Caribbean, such as Suriname and Curaçao, and others petitioned Oliver Cromwell of Great Britain to go to British colonies in the Caribbean (Portner). At the time, Jews were not openly permitted to live in England, but Cromwell allowed them to go to Barbados under the stipulation that they pay a heavy tax and observe restrictions, such as not owning plantations, slaves, or offering testimony in court. As mentioned earlier, twenty-three Jews ended up settling in New Amsterdam or New York, a city that eventually became home to one of the most influential Jewish communities in the world.

Jews of the Dutch Caribbean

After Pernambuco, Suriname became the largest Jewish community in the New World and received Jews not just from Recife but from Amsterdam and Eastern Europe as well (Ben-Ur, "Still Life," 35). Suriname is located at the northernmost point of South America between Guyana, Brazil and French Guiana and is considered to be part of the Caribbean. It was colonized by both the British, from 1650 to 1667, and the Dutch, between 1667 and 1975. The Ashkenazim and the

Nação lived separately in Suriname and did different types of work. The Ashkenazi community of European Jews lived primarily in the capital of Paramaribo and were merchants, worshipping in the Neve Shalom synagogue that was constructed in 1719. The Sephardic Jews lived primarily in the Jodensavanne or the Jewish Savannah, where they worked in sugarcane cultivation along the river. It was there that they built the Kahal Kadosh Beracha Ve Shalom synagogue in 1685. Later, some Jews from the Jodensavanne moved to Paramaribo and built the Zedek ve Shalom synagogue in 1736. In 1817, 82% of the Jews moved to Paramaribo to escape the unrest amongst the maroons or runaway former slave communities in the rural areas (Ben-Ur "A Matriarchal Matter" 153). Whereas the Portuguese and the Eastern European Jews did not mix, many of the former had children with their enslaved Africans.

It was in Suriname that we find an example of Jewish *mestizaje* as well as religious syncretism amongst the enslaved. Though it is well-known that many slave owners throughout the New World coerced their female slaves to have sexual relations with them, there are many documented cases of enslaved Surinamese seeming to have had consensual relations with their Jewish masters (though it is questionable that the power dynamic of master and slave would ever allow for consent). Though the children of non-Jewish women (in this case enslaved) and Jewish men are not considered Jewish by Jewish Law, in the case of the Surinamese Sephardic Jews, many of the enslaved females and their children were converted and considered by the Nação to be Jewish. According to the historian Ben-Ur, the Jews "seem to have taken the lead among whites in converting slaves to the household religion" ("A Matriarchal Matter" 158). This resulted in the birth of a large mixed race Jewish community that, although treated as second-class citizens, still practiced Judaism (Cohen 161). In *Jews in Another Environment*, the historian Robert Cohen describes conflicts that the mixed race Jews had with the white Jews of the Jodensavanne, beginning with the right to be buried in the Jewish graveyard (Cohen 167). With the decline of agriculture at the end of the eighteenth century, both white and mixed race Jews moved to the city. Language and artistic expression were also affected by the two cultures living in close proximity.

The mixing of the Jews with non-Jews in Suriname as well as in Curaçao led to the creation of Papiamentu/o, a Creole language. According to Ben-Ur,

> The mingling of Jews with the local [sic] African descendant population exerted a profound linguistic impact. Partly because they were among the

earliest white settlers in the Caribbean, Sephardim had a significant impact on creole languages, including Papiamentu, the lingua franca of Curaçao by the 1740s, and Suriname's Sranan Tongo, formerly known as Negro English (*neger engels*) ("A Matriarchal Matter" 167).

Papiamentu has influences from Portuguese, Spanish, Dutch, Hebrew and Niger-Congo languages. The closest linguistic cousin is Cabo Verde Creole where there was also a population of Portuguese Jews who arrived via Morocco (Jacobs 64). Another result of the mixture of cultures in Suriname and Curaçao can be found in the iconography of the gravestones.

Iconography can demonstrate the cultural mixture that took place in the Caribbean amongst the Jews, non-Jews and Africans. Throughout the Caribbean, there are headstones in cemeteries with skulls and crossbones, hourglasses, and hands spread in a priestly blessing with two fingers pointing in different directions. Though there are no explanations for these images, Ben-Ur has found some correlations between the names of the deceased and some carvings. For example, there is a grave of a woman named "Meza" who has a loaf of bread on her headstone as "a charming pun on the family name" (Ben-Ur, "Still Life," 53). Some carvings reflect the syncretic religions living in the Caribbean. There are Christian symbols, such as trumpets and cupids or grapevines that, "provided an opportunity for former Crypto-Jews to transform a familiar Christian symbol into one eminently Jewish" (Ben-Ur, "Still Life," 56). One of the most striking images on many stones is that of an arm coming down from the skies and chopping a tree in half. These images tended to appear on tombstones of people who died young or in the prime of life (Ben-Ur, "Still Life," 65). Ben-Ur also believes that there are allusions to Jews of West African animist religions on some of the stones with the images of cottonwood trees (Ben-Ur, "Still Life," 57).

In addition to living together in Suriname, Africans and Jews were at times discriminated against as well. For instance, in 1775 a theater once banned both groups, yet later, in 1945, the country decreed, "Every Jew who can escape Europe is welcome in Suriname" (Macdonald). Just as the Portuguese Jews of the Nação fled Europe for Dutch territories centuries ago, the Dutch Caribbean provided a haven for those needing safety in the twentieth century.

Curaçao differs from Suriname in that it is an arid island and the Jews who lived there were mostly involved in trade rather than sugarcane plantations. Portuguese Jews arrived from Recife and Amsterdam and built the magnificent synagogue, Mikvé Israel-Emanuel, in 1730. Of all the synagogues of the Caribbean, this one most resembles the central Esnoga synagogue of Amsterdam. It has beautiful blue stained glass windows and an ark made of mahogany. The floors are made of sand—some say to remind the congregants of how Crypto-Jews needed to muffle their voices from the Inquisition. Next to the synagogue is the Jewish Historical Cultural Museum with artifacts from the community, including a memorial to George Maduro, a young man who fought against the Nazis and was killed in a concentration camp. The Museum also contains copies of the most striking headstones from the cemetery, Beit Chaim Blenheim, where over 2,500 Jews are buried. Acid rain from an oil refinery next to the cemetery has eroded most of the headstones.

Jews of Barbados

Though Oliver Cromwell allowed Jews to settle in Barbados, they were taxed and had to live under restrictions, such as prohibitions on owning slaves and land. In Barbados, many became merchants and lived in the capital of Bridgetown on a street called "Jew Street," later known as Swan Street. According to the historian Holly Snyder, "the market was a singular avenue to affluence for the Jewish merchant, and cultivating customers was the appropriate modus vivendi for the achievement of success" (74). However, this changed when the Jews became involved in the cultivation of sugarcane by introducing technology that the Dutch had used in Pernambuco. Ze'ev Portner notes: "The modern windmill, crucial for sugar cane production, was introduced to Barbados by a Sephardic Jew, David de Mercado, and within a short space of twenty years, the economic phenomenon known as the sugar revolution had transformed Barbados forever." By the mid-nineteenth century, dozens of windmills dotted the island and helped make Barbados the richest British colony in the Western Hemisphere. For almost three centuries, the Portuguese Jews of Barbados continued the religious practices of their ancestors, building three synagogues and maintaining traditions from Amsterdam via Recife as well as London.

Two of the synagogues were constructed in Bridgetown, the capital. Another was built in Speightstown, but it was destroyed during a riot. The Bridgetown synagogue is called Nidhe Israel or the "Scattered of Israel". The first one, built in 1654, was demolished by a massive hurricane in 1831 that destroyed much of the island and killed 1,500 people. The second synagogue was rebuilt soon after. By then, some of the community had moved to England and in the next few decades the Sephardic Jewish community of Barbados slowly assimilated into the general population.

One of the ways the transculturation of the Jewish community into Barbadian culture can be seen linguistically is on the headstones of the cemetery that surrounds the synagogue. The earliest stones are written in Hebrew and Portuguese. Over time, they are in Hebrew and Old English, giving way to Modern English. When the last practicing descendant of the Portuguese Jews died in 1929, the synagogue closed and the religious artifacts were sent for safekeeping at the Bevis Marks Synagogue in London. Over the next few decades the old synagogue fell into disrepair and the government wanted to use it as a courthouse. Instead, under the leadership of Sir Paul Altman, a descendant of Jews that arrived from Poland in the 1930s, the synagogue was renovated and a museum was created in what was believed to be the rabbi's house. In 2008, a *mikveh* or ceremonial bath fed by an underground spring was uncovered next to synagogue and archaeologists believe that it may have been buried by debris from the hurricane of 1831. During the cooler months, services take place in the old synagogue. However, during the hot months an air-conditioned house serves as a place of worship.

Few people can remember the days when the first Ashkenazi Jews arrived in Barbados. In a series of personal interviews with me in the spring of 2011, Rose Altman, a Polish immigrant who came to the island in the 1930s, described life on the island for Jews from Eastern Europe as well as Canada and Belgium. At first, some were merchants, but slowly others became involved in real estate development as well as industry. Before the restoration of Nidhe Israel (The Scattered of Israel), the community celebrated Sabbaths and holidays at another location, a house in a residential neighborhood. Aunty Rose, as she was called, reminisced about having large Passover seders at her nearby home where she prepared gefilte fish using Barbadian flying fish, a "transcultured dish." She also described how parents were fearful that their children would marry non-Jews and would therefore send them to boarding schools in Canada, England or the United States. Though there are a few white Jewish Barbadians descended from the original families, a number of black Barbadians have more recently converted to the faith with the assistance of the American conservative movement. Some whites, including Stephen Altman, Rose Altman's son, believe that in the long run, "the converts may turn out to be the saviors of the community" (Portner). In this way the process of transculturation will come full circle as black Barbadian Jews will ultimately outnumber white Barbadian Jews.

Jews in the United States

By the eighteenth century, Portuguese Jews were settling not only in Barbados, but also in many other English colonies, including Jamaica, Nevis, and the thirteen colonies that would later become the United States. One group left Barbados and settled in Newport, Rhode Island, which was becoming an important Atlantic seaport at the time. The congregation, called Jeshuat Israel, hired a self-taught architect named Peter Harrison to build the Touro Synagogue. The Touro Synagogue is the oldest synagogue in the United States and became a National Historic Site in 1946. Like Shearith Israel in New York, the congregation also maintains the traditions that originally came from Portugal via Amsterdam. In an interview about the religious practices of the congregation, Rabbi Dr. Marc Mandel wrote,

> At Touro Synagogue we try to maintain the connection with the early founders of the synagogue. We have maintained the synagogue building just as the early Spanish and Portuguese Jews had it. We also try to maintain their customs. We have the men and women sit separately just as they did. As far as the prayers go, we try to maintain their customs as best as we can. Most of our members are not from the Spanish Portuguese Culture (Sephardic) (Mandel).

Though the actual congregants are not of the same background as the founders, they still choose to follow the traditions that the original members practiced centuries ago. In this way, the Portuguese Nation has an enduring legacy in modern day Rhode Island.

The congregation also celebrates what they feel is a contribution to the establishment of the Bill of Rights in America. Just as the Conversos who arrived in Amsterdam were grateful to the Dutch authorities for allowing them the freedom to practice their religion openly after years of persecution in Iberia, so were the first Portuguese Jews who came to the United States of America. In 1790 George Washington visited Rhode Island along with other members of the cabinet, including Thomas Jefferson, to discuss the ratification of an amendment to the Constitution allowing the freedom of religion. After meeting with leaders of many faiths, Moses Seixas of the Newport Synagogue Yeshuat Israel wrote a letter to the President (qtd. by Twohig 286, on the Touro Synagogue website) expressing how much the Jewish community of Newport respected him and was thankful for his considering the separation of church and state. He wrote:

Deprived as we heretofore have been of the invaluable rights of free Citizens, we now (with a deep sense of gratitude to the Almighty disposer of all events) behold a Government, erected by the Majesty of the People—a Government, which to bigotry gives no sanction, to persecution no assistance—but generously affording to All liberty of conscience, and immunities of Citizenship: deeming every one, of whatever Nation, tongue, or language, equal parts of the great governmental Machine.

Soon after Seixas sent the letter, the community received a reply on August 21, 1790 from the president himself in which he wrote, "May the children of the stock of Abraham who dwell in this land continue to merit and enjoy the good will of the other inhabitants—while everyone shall sit in safety under his own vine and fig tree and there shall be none to make him afraid" (Washington). Though it is not known just how much the letter from a descendant of Portuguese Jews had on shaping U.S. policy, the congregation celebrates their encounter with the first president of the United States by reading his letter every year.

In conclusion, Lusotropicalism provides an entry to discussing cultural mixing in the New World and the ability of Sephardic Jews to survive and thrive under difficult circumstances. Though many comment on Gilberto Freyre's allusion to Moorish blood in the Lusophone body, he also lauds the Jewish contribution to the Portuguese temperament. He describes the contributions of the "Israelites" or Jews who had fled to Portugal after being expelled from Spain and had a remarkable capacity to adapt to new places (9). According to Freyre, "It was the Semitic element, mobile and adaptable as no other, that was to confer upon the Portuguese colonizer of Brazil some of the chief physical and psychic conditions for success and resistance" (10). The Jewish role in shaping the Portuguese character and thus assisting them with colonizing tropical regions throughout the New World is not widely acknowledged in Lusophone history or scholarship. Today, many assume Portuguese Jews do not exist, but are rather the descendants of the New Christians who had been forcibly converted to Catholicism at the end of the fifteenth century, and over time, and under the threat of the Inquisition, became Catholic, or in other words, Portuguese. However, through transculturation, and in the specific case of Jews, Judeotropicalism, the Sephardic Jews maintained their identity and traditions, and they arrived, ironically, in the United States before the Roman Catholic Portuguese.

NOTES

1. The term, "Judeotropicalism" was developed jointly by the author and Christopher Larkosh at UMass Dartmouth.

2. There have been several explanations as to how the Jews from Recife arrived in New Amsterdam, including being lost in a storm or by shipwreck. Historian Ann Helen Wainer quotes Oppenheim when she writes that their ship, the *St. Charles*, may have been "diverted by pirates from their intended voyage from Brazil to Holland" after the Portuguese recaptured Recife (6).

3. The Jews from Brazil also petitioned the director general of the company to stay in New Amsterdam, reminding him that the Jews had lost a significant amount of money when Recife fell, and to help the new arrivals in New Amsterdam (Binder 10).

4. The term "racial democracy" does not actually appear in Freyre's book, yet is implied by his theory on the mixture of races.

5. It has been generally believed that the forced conversion in Portugal began with people going to public squares and having Holy Water sprinkled on their heads, yet it was, in fact, violent as children were taken away from parents, properties were appropriated and books were confiscated (Soyer 8).

WORKS CITED

Altman, Rose. Personal Interview. 20 April 2011.

Axelrod, Paul and Michelle A. Fuerch. "Flight of the Deities: Hindu Resistance in Portuguese Goa." *Modern Asian Studies*, vol. 30, issue 2, May 1996, pp. 387–421.

Bejarano, Margalit and Edna Aizenberg, eds. *Contemporary Sephardic Identity in the Americas: An Interdisciplinary Approach.* Syracuse UP, 2012.

Ben-Ur, Aviva. "A Matriarchal Matter: Slavery, Conversion, and Upward Mobility in Suriname's Jewish Community." *Atlantic Diasporas: Jews, Conversos, and Crypto-Jews in the Age of Mercantilism, 1500–1800*, edited by Richard L. Kagan and Philip D. Morgan, Johns Hopkins UP, 2009, pp. 152–169.

———. "Still Life: Sephardi, Ashkenazi, and West African Art and Form in Suriname's Jewish Cemeteries." *American Jewish History*, vol. 92, no. 1, March 2004, pp. 31–79.

Binder, Frederick M., and David M. Reimers. *All The Nations Under Heaven: An Ethnic and Racial History of New York City*. Columbia UP 1995.

Birmingham, David. *Empire in Africa: Angola and its Neighbors*. Ohio UP, 2006.

Bodian, Miriam. "The Geography of Conscience: A Seventeenth-Century Atlantic Jew and the Inquisition." *The Journal of Modern History*, vol. 89, no. 2, June 2017, pp. 247–281.

———. *Hebrews of the Portuguese Nation: Conversos and Community in Early Modern Amsterdam.* Indiana UP, 1997.

Cohen, Robert. *Jews in Another Environment: Surinam in the Second Half of the Eighteenth Century*. E.J. Brill, 1991.

Congregation Shearith Israel, the Spanish and Portuguese Synagogue website. Accessed 1 March 2018.

Coronil, Fernando. Introduction. *Cuban Counterpoint: Tobacco and Sugar* by Fernando Ortiz. Duke UP, 1995.

Feitler, Bruno. "Jews and New Christians in Dutch Brazil 1630-1654." *Atlantic Diasporas: Jews, Conversos, and Crypto-Jews in the Age of Mercantilism, 1500–1800*, edited by Richard L. Kagan and Philip D. Morgan, Johns Hopkins UP, 2009, pp. 123–151.

Freyre, Gilberto. *The Masters and the Slaves: A Study in the Development of Brazilian Civilization*. Translated by Samuel Putnam, University of California Press, 1986.

Garfield, Robert. "Public Christians, Secret Jews: Religion and Political Conflict on São Tomé Island in the Sixteenth and Seventeenth Centuries." *The Sixteenth Century Journal*, vol. 21, no. 4, Winter 1990, pp. 645–654.

Gerber, Sylvie, et al. "The photoreceptor cell-specific nuclear receptor gene (PNR) accounts for retinitis pigmentosa in the Crypto-Jews from Portugal (Marranos), survivors from the Spanish Inquisition." *Human Genetics*, vol. 107, issue 3, September 2000, pp. 276–284.

Graizbord, David. Personal interview. 20 February 2018.

Homza, Lu Ann, editor. *The Spanish Inquisition, 1478–1614: An Anthology of Sources*. Hackett, 2006.

Jacobs, Bart. "Papiamentu: a diachronic analysis of its core morphology." *Phrasis*, vol. 2, 2008, pp. 59–82.

Kagan, Richard L., and Philip D. Morgan, eds. *Atlantic Diasporas: Jews, Conversos, and Crypto-Jews in the Age of Mercantilism, 1500–1800*. Johns Hopkins UP, 2009.

Lindo, Elias Hiam. *The History of the Jews of Spain and Portugal, from the Earliest Times to Their Final Expulsion from Those Kingdoms, and Their Subsequent Dispersion: with Complete Translations of All the Laws Made Respecting Them During Their Long Establishment in the Iberian Peninsula*. London: Longman, Brown, Green and Longmans, 1848.

Macdonald, Norman. "Six Degrees of Suriname." *AramcoWorld*. Vol. 66, No. 4. July/August, 2015.

Maybury-Lewis, David H.P. Foreword. *The Masters and the Slaves*. Gilberto Freyre. University of California Press, 1986.

Mandel, Marc. Personal Interview. 4 February 2018.

Melammed, Renée Levine. *A Question of Identity: Iberian Conversos in Historical Perspective*. Oxford UP, 2004.

Nogueiro, Inês, et al. "Phylogeographic analysis of paternal lineages in NE Portuguese Jewish communities: Paternal Lineages in the Portuguese Jews."

American Journal of Physical Anthropology, vol. 141, no. 3, March 2010, pp. 373–381.

Ortiz, Fernando. *Cuban Counterpoint: Tobacco and Sugar*. Duke UP, 1995.

Paiva, José Pedro. "The Inquisition Tribunal in Goa: Why and for what Purpose?" *Journal of Early Modern History*, vol. 21, issue 6, 2017, pp. 565–593.

Paul, Sarmila. "Translation as an Agent of Transculturation and Identity Transformation in an Increasingly Borderless World." *Border, Globalization and Identity*, edited by Sukanta Das, Sanatan Bhowal, Sisodhara Syangbo, and Abhinanda Roy. Cambridge Scholars Publishing, 2018, pp. 211–216.

Peña, Yesilernis, Jim Sidanius, and Mark Sawyer. "Racial Democracy in the Americas: A Latin and U.S. Comparison." *Journal of Cross-Cultural Psychology*, vol. 35, no. 6, November 2004, pp. 749–62.

Portner, Ze'ev. "The Barbados Jewish Community: A Tale of Jewish Survival." *Jewish News: Britain's Biggest Jewish Newspaper Online*. November 30, 2015.

Ray, Jonathan S. *After Expulsion: 1492 and the Making of Sephardic Jewry*. New York UP, 2013.

Rosas-Moreno, Tania Cantrell. *News and Novela in Brazilian Media: Fact, Fiction, and National Identity*. Lexington Books, 2014.

Sathler, Josué A. and Amós Nascimento. "Black Masks on White Faces: Liberation Theology and the Quest for Syncretism in the Brazilian Context." *Liberation Theologies, Postmodernity and the Americas*, edited by David Batstone, Eduardo Mendieta, Lois Ann Lorentzen, and Dwight N. Hopkins, Routledge, 1997, pp. 95–124.

Schmidt, Bettina and Steven Engler, eds. *Handbook of Contemporary Religions in Brazil*. Brill 2016.

Skidmore, Thomas E., Peter H. Smith, and James Naylor Green. *Modern Latin America*. 8th ed. Oxford UP, 2014.

Snyder, Holly. "English Markets, Jewish Merchants, and Atlantic Endeavors: Jews and the Making of British Transatlantic Commercial Culture, 1650-1800." *Atlantic Diasporas: Jews, Conversos, and Crypto-Jews in the Age of Mercantilism, 1500–1800*, edited by Richard L. Kagan and Philip D. Morgan, Johns Hopkins UP, 2009, pp. 50–74.

Soyer, François. *The Persecution of the Jews and Muslims of Portugal: King Manuel I and the End of Religious Tolerance (1496–7)*. Brill, 2007.

Touro Synagogue National Historic Site. Accessed 1 March 2018.

Twohig, Dorothy, et al, eds. *The Papers of George Washington: Presidential Series* Vol 6. University Press of Virginia, 1986.

Wainer, Ann Helen. *Jewish and Brazilian Connections to New York, India and Ecology: A Collection of Essays*. Bloomington: iUniverse, 2012.

Winant, Howard. "Racial Democracy and Racial Identity: Comparing the United States and Brazil." *Racial Politics in Contemporary Brazil*, edited by Michael Hanchard, Duke UP, 1999, pp. 98–115.

BONNIE S. WASSERMAN is an Assistant Professor of Africana Studies at the University of Arizona. She has her doctorate in Portuguese from the University of Wisconsin-Madison and has taught Portuguese at a number of universities, including Fordham University and Rutgers University-Newark. She was the recipient of two Fulbright Scholarships (Portugal, 1994-95 and Barbados, 2011). Dr. Wasserman is the author of three books: *Contemporary Afro-Brazil: A Multidisciplinary Anthology* (Cognella 2018), *Cinema for Portuguese Conversation* (Focus 2009) and *Metaphors of Oppression in Lusophone Historical Drama* (Focus 2009). Currently, she is writing a monograph on the Afro-Latin American coming of age novel.

Box Art, Food Science, and Portuguese Protestants: An Interview with Katherine Vaz

Katherine Vaz is the author of two novels and three collections of stories who has drawn on her experiences as an Azorean-American in her writing and become perhaps the most recognizable name in Portuguese-American fiction. Her work has won several awards, including the Drue Heinz Literary Prize and Prairie Schooner Book Award, and has been translated into six languages. She has been leading the Writing the Luso Experience workshop at Disquiet International Literary Program in Lisbon, Portugal, since 2013. Vaz lives in New York with her husband, Christopher Cerf, and agreed to speak with me from her home over the phone. This telephone interview was recorded on October 18, 2017 in New Bedford, Massachusetts, and has been shortened slightly for length.

Hi, Katherine, how are you?
Hi, Maggie. Good to talk to you.

How's your life?
Good. I've just finished a novel I've been working on for twelve years, and I just turned it into my agent, so I'm in that period of trying to distract myself by writing and doing other things. It's a book that started out with research in Madeira, and it's about a group of people who were converted to Presbyterianism on the island of Madeira and were violently driven off the island for religious reasons and were given refuge in Illinois, of all places. The Protestant societies there heard about their hardships as they fled the island and took up residence in Trinidad. So, that was a lot of research, and it's—I would hope it's turning into a sort of *Love in the Time of Cholera*. It's based on the true story of someone who was put in prison and raised in prison in Madeira with his mother, who was condemned to die for heresy. The sentence was commuted, but she did spend two and a half years in prison. He met and courted someone he met in the Lincoln household, which…it's a love story. He went off to the Union army and was injured and basically wandered a long time before he found her again.

This is based on a magazine article I came across, or was actually given to me many, many years ago at the Library of Congress. The woman in charge—and this was in the Hispanic division—the woman in charge was Brazilian, and said "Oh, here's something I think you should see." And it was a map display simply called The Portuguese Protestants of Illinois. So, that was long ago enough that I remember doing my research with a yellow legal pad and going to libraries and writing things down. It was really before googling things was one way to operate, but I am a believer in doing the research with your physical being and going to the places and seeing what it feels like. You put yourself in the position of finding things out you wouldn't otherwise. When I went to Illinois and I was in residence there—in Jacksonville, Illinois, which was one of the sites of the Portuguese settlement—there were all sorts of things I found that I might otherwise not have come across.

There are orchids on the prairie, which I didn't know about. I went on a hike in the prairie and discovered that there are these bowl-shaped indentations all over the prairie that get full of grasses and can act as kindling. I don't think I would have known that if I hadn't gone. One day, I was there and suddenly all these cicadas were hatching all over the place. I was told, oh, it's the thirteen-year cycle of them, and they happen to be here when you're here, raining out of the trees and covering the sidewalks. And I thought, gosh, I don't think I would know to research if I hadn't put myself in the place. So that's kind of a long answer to saying it's been a long project with a lot of research and writing and rewriting. I put it away two years ago, thinking 'I just don't know what to do with it anymore; I've written it as well as I can.' My father was dying at the time, and it just felt like I didn't want to return to it. And then I got it out about a year ago, and I rewrote it from first page to last completely, and that took a year. It's a long book with very short chapters, so that's finished.

Well, congratulations on it being done!
Thank you. It was sort of a long project, and it feels like I just want to write short things now. I did a labor of love creative project, collaborating with a Portuguese painter named Isabel Pavão, who has exhibited her work all over the place. She lives in New York; she's originally, I think, from Coimbra, but she's lived in New York for maybe two decades now, and we got together through this wonderful organization in New York City called the Arte Institute. What the Arte Institute does, with Ana Ventura Miranda, is put artists together who are in the Portuguese community or Portuguese-American/Luso-American communities. I'd admired Isabel Pavão's work, and she wanted to get together. We had no preconceived idea of what we wanted to do when we had lunch and started

talking, and we found out that we both had older husbands who had serious health issues. We just...kind of collaborated in this magical way after that. She pulled all these paintings together, and I wrote these prose poems, and that's something we've just put together.

I guess I always need something to be doing. I wouldn't say that this is a Portuguese or Luso-American project, except that I did collaborate with a Portuguese painter, but my heart—and I guess my artistic identity and source seems to always go back to the well of my Azorean background. The Arte Institute gets a lot of the credit for trying to put all sorts of artists together, and so we did this project recently. You know, it's hard for me. I'm not good at taking days off, I guess. I like to have something going, to have projects to do. I think getting them into the world is a new thing to learn how to do. I'm trying to explore the different ways there are in storytelling now, not just ebooks, but hybrid books, and I like graphic novels, and telling stories on iPhones, and I think there are just really interesting ways of storytelling now. Maybe because my dad was a painter, I like to think visually as well. I'm trying to learn those sorts of things, too.

I do notice that in your newest book, most of the short stories in *The Love Life of an Assistant Animator* seem to begin with an image, mostly collages.
The collages are mine. I did those. I love doing box art, and one thing I love about it, because it's a gear that's just abstract. In other words, in writing you have to think of the character, what's the story here, what's the measure of things, how much weight do I give to description, tangents and so forth. With box art, it's a very confined space, and I just do it instinctively. I tend to do it really quickly, but I don't do it often, for some reason. I sometimes sit down and nope, it's not there. After I lost my dad, I sat down maybe a year later and I did about six or seven box art pieces about him and losing him. I did it in about two weeks, and it was exhilarating and helped me then write about him. It was a tapping the source sort of feeling. I really recommend for writers—there's something good about getting up from the computer and doing something else that feels creative. I'm a good cook, for instance, and I do cooking in between things as a way to be creative. That part of the creative process where you have to stop pushing and let it come to you is a good thing to do. So, box art is something I love to do. I'm a big fan of Joseph Cornell.

And meanwhile, I'm also trying to learn...I just had lunch with this wonderful writer named Claire Cooney who does fantasy and science fiction, and is someone who does reading Audible books and audio books. And I thought, I want to learn more about that, and she wanted to get together with me. I feel like there's a way we keep pushing as writers at trying to do something, and it's good sometimes to step back and to refill, or to let the work come to us in a way that requires a certain amount of patience.

What was the first story or poem that you remember writing?

You know, it's funny. When I was about twelve years old—this is going to sound very funny, but I went to a school called Our Lady of Grace in Castro Valley, California, which is near Oakland. I went to high school in Oakland. And we had an exercise every day where we were supposed to write a paragraph using the vocabulary words of the day, and I remember writing something that seemed to come from another place and made me well up with tears. I still remember that feeling, and I don't remember what I wrote. But I remember that feeling, and I remember deciding that's the feeling I want all the time. And I've told this story a lot, so forgive me if you've already heard it, but also when I was twelve, almost at the same time my godmother's housekeeper—and you know, that whole branch of the family is from the Azores—she got locked out of her house, and my father sent me to let her in. I wondered why she didn't just call us. It was the neighbor who saw her and called my dad. She was not literate in terms of English or Portuguese, but she also couldn't dial a telephone because she didn't recognize what numerals were. My father painted her phone dial; he said, "I think she thinks in color." So, he color-coded her phone and then made blots of color to correspond to, say, the fire department or our house or so on. To me, I instantly thought at the age of twelve that that was like another language, and that I wanted to be able to write or work in a way that I found a language of color. That color as a language, or a metaphor for love, was something that made sense to me. I think that's when I really started out as a writer, but it took a real commitment.

I remember in college, I decided I would write every morning from nine to twelve, because that's what Flannery O'Connor said she did, and I would go to the library and sit in one of those carrels. I don't even know if they even have those in libraries anymore. I think I wrote one essay that was okay, and the rest was stuff I just threw out. I was just teaching myself how to write. I also made a study of how stories were put together. I remember spending two years—I was sending stories out to magazines when I was in my early twenties, and I was getting encouraging letters back, but they were stopping just short of taking them.

And I thought, 'I just want to study how stories are made. I can do images, I can do the description; I want to learn how stories are built.' I taught myself. I watched movies and broke them down to study the bones of a story. I think I was in my mid to late twenties when I sold my first story to a magazine called Black Ice, which no longer exists. It was based on a teacher telling me, "You know, Katherine, you're just trying to write like everybody else. Why don't you tell me a story that's yours? Every time you come in and talk to me about your Portuguese background and your family and what's happened, I just think, why don't you just write that?" So, I went home and I thought, why don't I just write that?

So, I wrote a story called "Original Sin," and I wrote it in one day. Instead of laboring over it, it felt like, alright, let me just say some things I know and that are from my family, from me and what I know. It's very Californian, because that's where I grew up, too. And it ended up in a magazine called Black Ice, which as I've said, they don't exist anymore, but it made me so happy that it was there. And then my second story got picked up by a magazine called The Sun, which is still going strong. And then a friend read "Original Sin" and said, "Why don't you write another one like that?" I wrote something called "Fado," and I put "Original Sin" and "Fado" together, and I submitted it for an NEA and I got it. So I thought, alright, I think I found who I am as a writer, so I'm just going to write some more stories in this vein. I put them together, and that was the Drue Heinz collection—Fado and Other Stories. It's almost like who I *was* was waiting for me to find myself and write about it.

When I was growing up, my father was an historian for the Portuguese community. He wrote a book called The Portuguese in California. My mother was a voracious reader; my mother was born in New York, actually, and met my father in California. She's mostly of Irish background, a voracious reader. I came from an environment where books and painting were encouraged and respected. I think my dad said to me one day, "We have a lot of poets in our community and a lot of historians, but nobody's writing short stories the way you can do." In a way, my parents gave me a lot of encouragement by example, because my father painted a lot and my mother read a lot, novels and short stories. So that's really my beginning, and since this is for a Portuguese journal, it really was when somebody said to me, "You come in and tell me these amazing stories about your family; why don't you write those?" it was somebody saying that to me.

And now, when I teach at Disquiet, I think it's people who I see are in the same kind of position. The stories might be different; I think a lot of us had parents and grandparents who were immigrants, and so there was a bicultural adjusting to it. I'm curious about people who are third generation Portuguese, what do you write about, what do you do? And I've met through Disquiet a lot of wonderful writers of all ages and locations who are exploring that. I feel really gratified by Disquiet, because they've set up something that's unique. People who are of a Portuguese background, or Azorean and Brazilian and Mozambican, and the whole panoply of backgrounds get to say our stories need to be heard, too. I see that I had a similar pathway, it was just forty years ago now.

I don't think I felt like I was allowed to write about Portuguese themes, or things that would directly relate to my family until Disquiet existed.
Well, then that's wonderful news, and I'm happy to have had a role in that because I feel like Disquiet gives me a chance to give back to people who might be in the position that I was in.

Disquiet has changed your relationship with Portuguese-American writers and literature. How has it changed your relationship with Portugal?
Portugal has always been really, really good to me and has treated me like I'm their visiting cousin. Maria Teresa Horta, it's worth mentioning, did a review of the first book I had published there, which was *Mariana*, the novel about the nun who wrote the love letters—although whether she wrote them or whether they were a French invention is under dispute, so it's important to note that I do know that, but I thought, why don't I write a book, a novel, that she is alive—but Maria Teresa Horta was a champion about writing about it and welcoming me to such a degree that I was so touched by that, and she's still my friend. She always asks about what I'm doing and what I'm up to. You know, we writers work supposedly in isolation, but I have always found that the writers who you might say are 'the real thing' are extremely generous and are welcoming and build a community. When she wrote this long piece about an American writing about this nun, she made it okay for me and she welcomed me.

I think it's important to take note of the generosity of writers who open their hearts to other writers, and I think Disquiet, as I say, deserves a lot of credit for giving me the chance to do that with usually younger writers; not all of them are, but usually. Who, as you say, "Gee, I didn't even know I could write about this," that the cultural attitude can change to be, "Yeah, you can." I remember a young woman coming up to me; I was doing a reading, maybe in California, and she said, "You know, I'm from Hayward," which is adjacent to the town where I'm from. I'd set some of my short stories in Hayward, because I'd thought, why not? It's a place on the East Bay. And she said, "It's funny; I never thought I could set a story there," and I said, "May I ask why?" She said, "It just didn't seem possible, because nobody would care or be interested in Hayward." I said, "Well, you need to write an interesting story about Hayward," and she laughed and said, "Yeah, but in fact, I didn't even know that that could be true." Things about that are very nice, because you feel like it not just says what's okay to do in literature or writing or the publishing world, but what's okay as a person for you to step up and do and claim and look at and investigate.

Writing is a long path; it's impossible not to have missteps and disappointments and rejections. It's just part of it, and I think rather than be discouraged by that…when I would send things out when I was younger, it used to be you would put a story in a manila envelope and send it out. I would actually wait to hear back from them, and if I got a rejection, I would just send it right back out again. After a while, you just get to know certain editors, and sometimes they contact you and say, "Do you have anything for me?" And I think it just requires a lot of patience and doing the work. Not being angry or impatient, like why isn't the world noticing me? I think that gets into a very dangerous area where you're mad at the world. You can write when you're angry, and that's good fuel to have, and you can write when you're distressed, that's good fuel. Whatever works. But being mad that your voice isn't being heard can lead to trouble. You just have to think, let me look at this, and what can I write that is going to speak to people? And that's a good thing to do. I'm sure I'm long-winded here and off topic, but I think that it's good to be patient and always willing to learn more about what you do. I don't think you ever get to a point where you know how to write, because each new piece is going to teach you something that you need to learn.

On the line of advice, when you were younger, was there any particular advice, life advice or writing advice, that has stuck with you over time?
In my case, it was somebody saying, "Why don't you tell me some of the things that are yours?" I think that looking for what you have inside you is the place to begin. But then, just studying stories for what they can teach you about what you can do with your own material, because you have to be an original. You cannot write like anyone else. By definition, original means that it has to come from you. So, you learn with the part of your brain that's always trying to learn

more, the way a musician has to be an original, but I've never met a musician who didn't study music, what's being done in the field. Mostly, it's trying to say, "What's my voice, and how do I create it?" If you just want flat-out the best advice I ever got, was one of the nuns in my grammar school saying, "Do not wait for the time that you think you're ready to begin; just begin." And that was the most valuable advice I got.

I do that exercise, just a mini-version at Disquiet, and I used to give it to my workshops when I taught at the various colleges and universities, what I call my *tabula rasa* exercise. To take a day and not do things; not crowd your agenda, don't look at email, don't flip through magazines, don't clutter your brain. Just let the screen down. And very often, you can tap into something that's there for you that you need to say, that you need to express. That's the starting point, going to the internal as a beginning point rather than looking to the external is probably the best advice to give to writers about who they're supposed to be and what they can do with what they have.

And I think, to be generous. I think this is going to be an odd thing to say, but never be jealous of another writer. Never be envious of someone's success, because it implies that there's only a limited amount to go around, and that's not true. And you're looking at someone else, not at yourself. The best writers I know have that generous heart, where they care about—Maggie, you know Denis Johnson, because you got to meet him. He had a generosity that came from who he was, and he extended it to other writers. It illuminated them in a way that was like a gift. I'm an advocate of being like that, and of stepping back to refuel and find out who you are as a writer.

I have a couple of oddly specific questions. One of them is fun and one is serious. Which would you like first?
Let's do the fun one.

Okay, if you could pick any novel to live in, what would you choose?
Now, that's interesting. I fell in love with *All the Light We Cannot See*, but it's set in World War II, so I don't know if I want to be in the novel. *Exit West* is one of my recent favorite novels, that the magical world that he created, I just wanted to be within that world, too, but it's about displacement. That's a funny question, because it implies, am I going to want to be in this world, or do I just want to be in this amazing thing this artist created. If it's that, I would say Tony Doerr's

All the Light We Cannot See really feels like I would want to be in, and *Exit West* by Mohsin Hamid, I would also want to be in. And Elizabeth Strout did *My Name is Lucy Barton*; I just love that as a novel, and I felt like I was in that consciousness in that world, too. But if you're talking about childhood favorite novel, I'd love to be in one of the *Oz* books.

I got that question from my little sister.
Oh, that's really cool. Tell her that's very cool. I guess the easy answer is one of the *Oz* books, because it's when I fell in love and got enchanted by the idea that books created other worlds.

You've mentioned *One Hundred Years of Solitude* before.
That's probably my all-time favorite novel. The world that he created—of course, there again, that's a very dangerous world that he's writing about. In terms of what he created, the work of art, it's like saying, do I want to live in the painting *Guernica*? Yes, in terms of the work of art; I don't want to be in the landscape of a war, except I do like to feel what other people feel. We're stuck in our own consciousness for our whole lives. One of the things that art does is let us feel like we're somebody else, or in another world, which we don't get to do in real life. So that's one of the chief virtues, I think, not just of books themselves but of writing.

Going off of that, my slightly more serious, oddly specific question: In your short story, "The Mandarin Question," which is in the book *Our Lady of the Artichokes*, you describe a girl whose after-school job is playing violin at a slaughterhouse in order to calm the cattle before they're killed, in order to prevent the dark-cutting of the meat. For me, that image, probably more than any other image in the book, is something that has stuck with me over time, and it's something that I think back on a lot. And I've always been curious—where did the idea for that story and that image come from?
Oh, okay. Now, I'll tell you something that's very funny. I put that in my new novel, the Madeiran novel. It's in there, too, because there are slaughterhouses. Slaughterhouses actually started when Chicago was becoming a big hub in this country, and they were trying to figure out, how do you herd cattle from the West and deliver it to the East Coast. Slaughter used to be something that occurred in every town. We get the expression "this room is a shambles," well, that was

the original expression for a slaughterhouse. It's about to me, the metaphor and the reality both, that things occur out of our view that did not used to occur, so we're out of touch with it. The idea itself, I find very compelling. "The Mandarin Question" is an old philosophical problem that, in fact, Eça de Queirós wrote a short novel about called *The Mandarin*. I read that in Portuguese, I think when I was in college, and I thought that would be a wonderful thing, to have the Mandarin question in a contemporary setting. So, there again, oddly enough my Portuguese roots took hold with that. But the slaughterhouse idea, honestly, because I'm interested in cooking.

My parents wrote a Portuguese cookbook when I was young, and I love to cook. I have all those books…I don't remember the title now, but it's a compendium textbook where I discovered what dark-cutting was. It's a real thing, that if an animal is frightened, whatever hormones or I don't even know what it would be, shoot through the blood stream, and the meat toughens or gets darker, and that's a real thing. And so a lot of people come to say, and I think Temple Grandin is one of them, to make slaughterhouses more humane. I'm enough of a vegetarian that I think that's a misnomer, but okay. There is a real thing called dark-cutting. It was just a book about food science, and I discovered it while I was reading through there. So, I just put the Mandarin question together with the slaughter, I guess.

I think sometimes we have ideas. An idea is not a story; an anecdote is not a story. Sometimes these pieces exist in our heads that wait for the right places. They wait to find where they belong in the narrative. It's like, Borges has the idea of the library of the universe, that everything ever known or thought or felt is somewhere in the library there; you just have to pull the right books out and put them together. I think that maybe that's what I did with that one. I'll text you the name of the book where I found this, because it's something that I came across that I thought made a lot of sense. It helped me be a vegetarian, because I thought, well they experience fright and dread.

CHRISTOPHER LARKOSH

Ten Questions for Jarita Davis

1. A lot has changed in this country since the moment Tagus Press published *Return Flights.* **Where do you see yourself now in relation to where you were then?**

Honestly, I've been quite off balance since *Return Flights* has been published. I turned in my final edits for the book right before undergoing brain surgery, and I don't think I ever gave myself the proper chance to fully recover from that. I began 2016 with lots of readings and book signings, and ended it with community outreach, political engagement, and activism. My life has completely changed.

Since then, I haven't done much Writing with a capital "W" because I am not feeling centered enough. I journal almost daily, but that is a different kind of writing. It's a way for me to actively process thoughts and make sense of my day. The "real Writing" is more of a receiving; it's a deeper realization that leaves its mark on the page. My life has been too hectic, and I've allowed myself to be spread too thin to hear the words that make for Writing.

Right now I am trying my best to re-center. I think a lot of us in the United States have felt our lives disrupted by political chaos. The news headlines feel like a sadistic carnival ride, spinning us disoriented and nauseated. It's hard to feel grounded or stable. I'm currently seeking out serenity and patience, not that I think I can make sense of our nation necessarily, but I want to be able to stay anchored through the storm. So far the best ways I know to do this are through meditation and journaling.

2. I can imagine that the current political climate of intolerance and exclusion, especially the increasing normalization of public expressions of racism and anti-migrant sentiment, must be troubling for someone like yourself who has put a lot of thought into questions of race and migration in your writing. How do you see the present configuration of power as it targets the most vulnerable in our society?

What can I say? It's terrifying.

I was walking into the grocery store in January, and a girl about 12 years old asked if I would walk with her because she was afraid she might get snatched. When I was a kid, I was always afraid of being kidnapped, and because I could sympathize I agreed to walk with her. It wasn't until we were in the store and she said something like, "Maybe people will think that you're my mom" that I realized she'd picked me because we were both brown skinned, and it turned out that yes, neither of her parents were documented. So, I don't think it was kidnappers that she was afraid of snatching her, but ICE. This is on Cape Cod, not the Mexican border. Our entire nation has been infected with this horrible culture of anti-immigration anger and terror. The sheriffs of Barnstable County and Bristol County have both entered into agreements with ICE called 287g in which their officers are deputized and have agreed to serve as immigration officers in communities which have large Cape Verdean populations. I do everything I can to protect the safety of these vulnerable members of my community, like fighting for the Safe Communities Act in Massachusetts, but that bill didn't pass. My own State Senator, Vinny deMacedo, voted against it even though he is a Cape Verdean immigrant himself, born on Brava, the very same island as my grandfather.

This is not an abstract idea or some distant threat. This is playing out right beneath my nose. And I'm not just talking about insensitive name calling or bullying; I'm talking about people living in fear for their livelihoods and their lives. People afraid of their families being separated, even afraid to learn what rights they may have because they don't want to call attention to themselves by asking questions. I cannot imagine ignoring or overlooking this problem—it would be unconscionable. I wish I had more answers to help all the people at risk, because whatever I do never seems to be enough.

3. I understand you've started your own political organization out on Cape Cod where you live. Can you tell me a little more about that?

After the presidential election in 2016, some of my friends joked about defecting to Canada or fantasized about becoming expats in Europe. But I said, "I feel like we have a responsibility to stay. A lot of people are going to need help. And these are people who won't have the luxury or financial means to pick up and move overseas." What I didn't realize at the time, was that there would be so many people who need help figuring out how to help. So many people in our town wanted "to do something" but didn't know where to start or how to get involved. I got together with six other women and we started a group called "Engage Falmouth." Our mission is to motivate, mobilize, and empower the community to become a force for progressive change. In a time where a rapid fire series of crises can feel paralyzing, people are happy to make some active effort to be a part of some kind of solution. So, our group shares opportunities for people to connect with groups addressing a myriad of issues and causes under attack: women's rights, LGBTQ+ rights, environmental concerns, social justice, religious freedoms, civil rights, economic justice, and many more. None of us are experts in these areas, but we offer people the tools and skills necessary to work on the concerns that interest them most. We've already outgrown our name-- our membership is strong all over the Upper Cape (Falmouth, Bourne, Mashpee, and Sandwich), and we also have members who live off Cape and on the Vineyard.

4. As you know, I was born and grew up in the Cape and Islands region, an area of the Commonwealth with a number of traditional population groups: not only the Portuguese Americans, but also the Wampanoag Indians, Cape Verdeans, a group that you personally identify with, and more recently the Brazilians. What is it like for you to live, write and engage politically in this kind of diverse cultural environment?

As a native son of this region, you know that this community is very white, which can make nonwhite people feel isolated and sometimes invisible. On the other hand, these other cultures you've mentioned are also present and perhaps being in the minority is what keeps us from taking the value of that culture for granted. It's wonderful to see these groups celebrating their heritage and working to pass it along to the next generations. The Falmouth Cape Verdean Club has been active for almost 75 years now, and people came from all over to go to their dances and events. It was known as "The Big Club." Similarly, the Wampanoags have an impressive language reclamation project where they were able to recreate their lost language by using the religious texts that British colonists created to convert tribal members when they first arrived. The Bible, Book of Common Prayer, and other materials written in the Wampanoag language have survived, and from them enough vocabulary and grammatical structure was recovered to be able to reconstruct the tribe's original language. I've played soccer with Brazilians and Azoreans and Portuguese from the mainland. We're all here. It just takes some looking to find us.

5. In our online conversations, I've noticed that you've also been referencing a number of African-American women writers and thinkers: black feminist

thinker Audre Lorde is just one who comes to mind. Could you talk a bit about the impact of the women of color that were important to you in your intellectual and cultural development?

You have to understand that I cut my aspiring writer's teeth reading Audre Lorde, June Jordan, and Sonia Sanchez. In my writing studio, I have framed black and white photos of Alice Walker, Toni Morrison, and Rita Dove in the 70s. They are young and have full afros and are just starting out. These women have always been my heroes. They are strong and brilliant and defiant. I admire these women because they insist on having their voices heard by making their own way in a world that doesn't have a path cleared for them.

These writers make me feel less lonely. I've also learned so much from them. They are probably the reason I'm a writer.

6. *Return Flights* is a collection of poems that also tells a story: about a young person, whose mother's family is from the Cape Verdean community of New Bedford, and who undertakes a journey from this region to discover more fully the culture of her grandfather. Cape Verdean young people, regardless of whether they migrated here as children or were born in this region. In your readings, there are young Cape Verdeans who are inspired to return as do work to give back to their country of origin? While we probably never imagine that we will become a role model for younger people, so it happens, perhaps precisely because we do not seek it. What has been your reaction to this, and what do you have to share or impart to young Cape Verdean Americans as they begin to take this culture forward?

I had never really thought about how powerful and important representation is. I gave a poetry reading at an afternoon tea for some grade school girls at the Cape Verdean Club in Falmouth. I could see them taking it all in—that someone like them could write about their experiences and have it matter enough that it could be made into a book that others would buy and read. It also turned out that I happened to be seated at a table with three family members from my New Bedford ties. We had no idea that we were related until we sat together that day. The older woman was the one who made the connection. She said, "You're my cousin" and started to cry. Her granddaughter asked, "What does that make me?" and I said, "I guess we're second cousins." She was so excited she couldn't stay seated. She threw her hands up in the air and shouted, "I'm second cousins with a poem-writer!!!" That was the first moment I've ever felt like I had finally found home.

I'm sure a seed was planted for some of those girls who were already curious about what Cape Verde was or means to them, and I hope they let that curiosity grow and explore some more on their own.

7. You were also a participant in the Disquiet International Program in Lisbon and, equally important, its Luso writing workshop. Could you tell me a bit more about your experience in that setting, your relationship with the city of Lisbon as a place for thinking about literature and culture outside of the US context, and of the Portuguese culture as you experienced it from your own set of cultural perspectives?

The Disquiet program was a wonderful experience for me. I was inspired by the ways in which many of the writers in the Luso workshop found overlapping similarities, even though our families were from places as far away as Brazil, Goa, Portugal, Cape Verde, and the Azores. There is an underlying thread that ties us all, and it was exciting to see how a diaspora could have such deep roots.

I had only been to Portugal once before, and it is a beautiful country. I don't think of it as "mine," meaning, it doesn't feel like my birthright, but it is still possible to fall in love with a place that hasn't been passed down to you. My grandfather had never been to mainland Portugal and when he talked about returning to "The Old Country" he was not thinking of Lisbon. Still, literature is such an important part of Portuguese culture, and it is so valued in a way that it is not here in the United States, that as a writer, it won my heart.

8. Luso-American literatures and cultures, especially Portuguese-American works, have drawn both upon canonical Portuguese literary figures and well-known US American writers, though to be frank, mostly from white authors. How might this set of overlapping cultural identity also draw more from African and African-American texts to understand its longstanding relationship with questions of race and radicalization, whether in the context of Portuguese colonialism or US systems of racial categorization?

I would really like to see more Cape Verdeans celebrate revolutionaries like Amilcar Cabral and the PAIGC. We talk about music and food and beauty, but there's a lot we could learn about empowerment from our recent past. The work of African-Americans struggling for civil rights certainly has relevance to that of the political effort it took for Cape Verde to become its own nation.

9. We've had more than a few conversations over the last few years about Cape Verdean Americans and the often ambivalent relationship that many of them apparently have with the fact that Cape Verde is in Africa and yes, that Cape Verdeans themselves have different understandings of their own racial identity, with some identifying as African-American or Black and others not as much if at all? What is your take on this? What if anything is at stake in identifying as Black today?

It's interesting how race, ethnicity, and nationality intersect, and how people choose between them. A Black friend of mine, who is not Cape Verdean, once made a flip comment saying, "I think it's sad when people of color need so desperately to identify with their colonizer." Cape Verde has always been a cultural crossroads, a place where people from far and wide passed through during the navigational explorations, then slave trade, and whaling. When Cape Verdeans distance themselves from Blackness, from being from Africa, they are giving up a part of themselves. I also feel like trying to make a complete break from Portuguese influence is also destructive; it's peeling away another culture layer rather than trying to make peace with it or at least understand how it has come to shape Cape Verdean identity and the nation itself. Rather than defining ourselves by what we aren't, should we be looking at all that we are? I know many Cape Verdeans who would rather identify themselves as "other" or "none of the above" when asked about racial heritage. But wouldn't "all of the above" be much more accurate? And wouldn't it be a better way to think about our culture? To think about all the ways in which we are connected to others across the globe rather than all the ways in which we are separate? If we continue to isolate ourselves further and further, we will only choke off the flow of interaction of that keeps our culture vibrant and alive.

10. If you were to plan another "return flight" to Cape Verde again in the near future, how might your trip be different this next time, knowing what you do now and with more experience behind you? Would you want to travel alone as you did before, or with others? Are there other islands you'd want to see beyond those you visited last time? What sites of cultural, historical or political significance would you want to visit?

I would most like to visit the islands that I have not yet seen. I would especially like to go to Santo Antão, São Vicente, São Nicolau, and Boa Vista. I know that the landscape, people, and culture vary from island to island, and I would like to see more of it for myself. I would spend less time seeking out personal, familial connections, and more time learning about how the people and their lives in a larger context.

JARITA DAVIS is a poet and fiction writer with a BA from Brown University and an MA and a PhD from the University of Louisiana, Lafayette. Her grandfather immigrated to the US from the Cabo Verdean island of Brava. Her work has appeared in the *Southwestern Review*, *Cave Canem Anthologies*, *Crab Orchard Review*, *Plainsongs*, *Verdad Magazine*, and the *Cape Cod Poetry Review*. She lives and writes in West Falmouth, Massachusetts.

Poetry & Fiction

BOBBY MARTINEZ

Three Poems

In the Case of Transparency

"In the case of transparency, if the wall were made of glass, one would see, for example, drawn on the verso, a sign or a figure that fills a gap on the recto."
R. A. Schwaller de Lubicz, The Temple in Man, p.44

When you have three different ideas at the same time
and they walk the dog,
when you turn them upside down and they drift like the crab nebula exploding
when you realize that people are talking backwards, in waves
and it tastes minty green

When you realize that O Milagre do Sol was real, and crucial
but you can't explain why
when the column in the middle becomes a woman with flanking demons
and the cave is lined above with stained glass

And the fuzz around your head is two women, centuries apart, whispering in Pali
saying the most important thing in the world
like in a dream where you have the answer and can't remember it
and it smells like laurel here, after rain

Earth and air - sides of a transparent coin eternally flipped by a laughing Pan,
Dionysus and Athena dispute the shifting hexagrams
when text only becomes more authentic with each mistake, each misunderstanding
when who i am, and who you are becomes confused

When everything is just a little bit transparent
the glass between the yes and no
and you still can't figure out, after a lifetime of long walks

where the light is coming from
and this cool air, and not for the first time in a thousand years of glancing sideways
is more than you have ever expected from life

S. Francesco/Bellini

"St. Francis in the Desert" by Giovanni Bellini, oil on poplar, ca. 1480, Frick Museum, NYC, November 6, 2015

I - Giovanni Bernardone

What did you smell like that morning?
    Your feet smell of sand, your pits smell of oak smoke and ripe earth.
What did your skin taste like that morning?
    Your wounds taste of salt, your skin the bitterness of old roots.
You got up abrupt- as if someone's there, you walked out barefoot.
    I stay under covers, I move to the warm spot that you left.
That great book is closed now on last nights confusion, the birds
    have been about their business long before a thought formed in the half light
and i see you there, a shadow against the sun,
taunt as a steel string, ecstasy and agony so strangely mixed
in your arched back and outstretched arms.
I am lost, i am found, i am with you, i am alone.
    Brother, think of me sometimes, when you speak to god of love.

II- Giovanni Bellini

Did you want it both ways? - both God and the world?
You've sensed this light that's more than sunlight,
you've been surprised in the morning- walked barefoot and alone into dawn
and you've closed the great book after words and more words
of dead worlds made you sad and confused: your heart broken.

So you painted this ass and these flowers, this bird and these rocks.
These are the things you understand, the living beings all around us,
growing things crammed into every inch, between offstage sun
and these three massive rocks.
The fields, the herdsman, this ordinary morning,
the distant, sleepy city of women and men.
And this this dear plain man, Francesco, face lined with agony and alone.

You want to know what he knew, see what he saw, feel what he felt
without giving up this world that you love.

So you painted this picture and have put God-
who even Francesco found a mystery, outside the frame.
And i stand in strange brotherhood with you and God
outside this jewel toned world you've created,
with other hushed museum goers,
in some dead rich man's parlor,
and the woman in the gift shop says
that Franciscans come to see you often
and we all stand in the presence
of this glowing map of your broken heart
wrecked on God's reef of a world you held sacred.

'You Speak About Me'

You speak about me as if i cannot hear.
You write about me as if i cannot read.
I am here, but for you i am a million miles away
behind an invisible film of a past
full of horrors. A past that haunts our
thinking minds like the deadly slivers and shrapnel
of a tornado's logic pulling the world it's shredded for
fifteen thousand years into its I.
Everyone hears everything now.
Everyone reads all that is written.
We are all out here on one field
and it is quiet enough to hear.

BOBBY MARTINEZ is an architect and poet of Portuguese, Ute and Mexican heritage. He has lived in the San Francisco Bay Area for over 45 years, where he is active in queer historical preservation and activism.

Four Poems

With Eyes that Bear the Widowhood of Days
from a line by Beatriz Hierro Lopes

The ceiling of the ocean floor is fat,
with its tidal drop, a mere sandy slope, the
barrenness, now, a symbol, a lost meaning,
to catch, a rule that the Portuguese fisherwomen
on the shore above can attest to, easily
nodding in agreement that they are bound
together, like time they have wagered and lost,
a lifetime of fresh bets and new hands,
grown old with uncertainty, a rule,
a catch, a slip of the tongue and the
courtship will be over, lost to sea journeys far
away from solid-footed Terceira, where black glue
is the medicine of forgetting and a pause
is the known secret inside absence,
and where love is a shy attachment to hope, the
thaw that every woman, waiting here, tempts
with her own fate On shore, they long to don sadness,
like a dark shawl around their forearms.
It is a uniform, encompassing wool, knitted
halfway between loss and joy.
The friendliest girls they used to be,
these women, now waiting on the land,
reveal happiness but with but a slight
mention or a holding note of the wind,
softly reminding them
of the men they used to love.

I've Driven all Night through a Grainy Landscape
—title from a line by Tiago Araújo

All the answers, I used to know,
repeated again and again, as if they were
lines in a political game, trying to talk
someone into believing, as they say
in apples and a banana and then go forth
into a world where there are walls
built across artificial boundaries,
and families torn apart inside the parallel
lines of truth. It is what it is and that
means even if it kills me, I will be true
to my own patience. It's agonizing, I know,
every single time, the visits are painful,
the release is impossible to recreate.
It's a total body experience, granted
and guaranteed to take me somewhere I can
smile and normalize things as they should
be, as I recalled them--just not yesterday.
But, last year, it didn't it take weeks
for the clock to click one minute to
three like when you were a kid, agonizing
to go home. And then there are the waiters,
not food service but those who are patient,
for diagnosis, for tests, for death.
The mid-line boundary between
someone saying everything is gonna be
OK and everything is over. It is the middle
passage, that long journey, that I have
to work myself up to face, to make it
through hard borders and boundaries, week after
week for the past year, a life lived,
sawed in half like a magic trick. I am
perched on the edge of the bed, ready to
nod or to run. Waiting makes you swear

someone was loved and kind once, and
that to make it all OK again, there is
wishing, a hope for it to be as it was,
when it was perceived to be all right
but perhaps it never was. And, so,
to normalize interactions, the daily hellos
we take for granted, the guarantees we
make with each other must be labeled,
seared into agreements that we promise
each other, to be civil or polite, the nods
at the bus stop, basic remnants of life
in front of a modicum of human happiness.
But, my heart also breaks. In truth, it hurts a lot
because the heart knows what my
job is. The hurt is the pain above
it all, the others keep moving away, to form
new shapes, now, and when I want them
to stay close, they stick to me like glue.
Longing is the middle ground, when you have
distant connections. It's such a hard place to be in.
The waiting and the hoping for a time
when you won't any longer then feeling guilty
for that. Then, it all runs together
in rhythm, like dirty rivers, seeking a new mouth.

The Graphics of Home

Were broken by the Great
Depression, the textile mills,
and the golf ball factories.
We came from The Azores
and the mainland and Canada,
settling in Hawaii and New Bedford
and San Pedro, the original
Navigators. No one was documented.
Here was what I learned at home
thru the lifecycle of a shirt.
It arrived from Sears, in the mail,
sent as a hand-me-down
from Fall River, carefully washed
and ironed and pressed,
on a tomato box that had been
repurposed and wrapped in brown
paper and smelling of stale
cigarettes. That shirt was worn
and washed and used many times,
as if it had been new. When they
frayed, the elbows were mended,
and torn pockets were reconnected
with thick carpet-makers thread.
When the sleeves were too worn
to restore, they were scissored
off to make short sleeves and then
the new ends were folded and hemmed
until no more and then there was the time
when the sleeves were cut off
entirely, to create a summer top
or costume for play time, sleeveless,
perhaps a vest for a pirate.
When outgrown and too worn
for even that, the buttons were removed,

in one straight hard cut along the shirt
front, through and through.
The buttons were removed by hand,
for storage in an old cookie tin,
the cloth cut into small usable pieces
for mending, for doll clothes, for
whatever was left over. The rest, torn
into jagged rags for cleaning and, if the fabric was soft,
used for Saturday's dusting of the good furniture
in the den. Whatever was left, was sold
by the pound, wrapped and rolled into
giant cloth balls, sold to the rag man
who made his rounds in the neighborhood
all oily and urgent and smiling as if
his soul were a miracle of naturalized
birth.

POETRY & FICTION   Millicent Borges Accardi

And, at last, God Returns
from a line by José Tolentino Mendonça

Sordid and sallow, a harsh
disappointment
to the prepared flock awaiting
for salvation or the next thing
coming, the judgement call
or all judgement calls.
The reckoning or the vanishing.
The end of the narrative.
What is it they call it? The
Rapture, and not in a sexual
way, when the faithful are
suddenly taken above, under
the dove wing of god, leaving
behind only the sinners, the
men and women who walk
the blind earth, able-bodied
and kind, perhaps they do not
know or are yet have lived their
delicious lives yet un-indoctrinated
into the secret work of Christ or
deliverance or hatred. The
salvation, a sweetness, alone,'
like a small boy
who cannot find the last puzzle
piece to the lake with the swans
on the family table and is punished for it
forever and ever.

MILLICENT BORGES ACCARDI HAS received awards from the National Endowment for the Arts, CantoMundo, Fulbright, the Corporation of Yaddo, FLAD, and California Arts Council. Her most recent poetry collection is *Only More So*. Find her @TopangaHippie

ANTÓNIO LADEIRA

The Teacher

Translated by Christopher Larkosh, Andrea Arruda, Jonathan Matos, Mackenzie Benjamin, Carlos Ribeiro, and Quinn Pittman

I am 13 years old and want to be a writer. It was the teacher who explained to me what it means to be a writer.

I was 10 years old when I met this teacher. I did not like him when I met him. He was an ugly and old man, that looked at us as if we had done something that deserved punishment. The teacher's gaze hurt when it was sudden. The teacher's look was almost always fixed. He wore dark glasses that lightened when he came in the classroom. Behind those glasses two little eyes were hiding that you could hardly see. The skin of his hands and arms had brown stains and was very thin, almost transparent, with thick veins. I thought that the teacher was about to die, that he would die after class ended. The teacher coughed a lot, and at times, when he coughed like this, I swear that I saw little tears popping out from behind those half-darkened lenses.

I was outraged when my parents asked me to participate in a pilot program with the teacher. This meant that I wasn't able to go to my motocross classes. Besides that, I didn't know what a "pilot program" was. My mom explained to me that a pilot program was a special scientific experiment, "a pedagogical experiment," she said. There was a teacher in the city that had strange ideas about the ways of basic and higher education teaching. The teacher was looking for students to test these strange ideas.

My mom insisted and I agreed so that she would stop insisting.

On the night before the first day, I could not sleep. They said many things about the teacher and the pilot program. For example, they said that the teacher would ask that all of the students use paper and pencil. I have never used a pencil. Nor paper. I have seen a pencil. My mom has one saved deep in a drawer, but does not let me or my brothers play with it. Not even my dad is allowed to use it. My mom said that it was a keepsake, an antique, that belonged to her grandmother, that they don't sell pencils in the stores anymore, that you won't see them anywhere, and for this reason, no one was allowed to use the pencil in that house. Much less sharpen the pencil. (At the time I didn't know what it meant to "sharpen a pencil." Now I know.)

I was also inexperienced with paper. One time I saw a sheet of paper fly through the air, in a movie. The sheet was big and thick. The size of a boy my age. It happened to be a boy my age that caught the flying sheet. It jumped, he grabbed it in the air, folded it, saved it in a backpack, and started walking down the street, all smiles.

My friend Jaime didn't have just one sheet of paper, but a whole notebook, hidden in the attic of his house. My friend Jaime would say that writing on paper was "forever." Because of this, caution was needed. It was needed of us to think well in what we wanted to write before writing words that would stay on paper "forever." I didn't believe in everything that my friend Jaime said. I didn't believe, for example, that what you wrote stayed written "forever." One day Jaime took back what he had said. He said that he had exaggerated: "forever" was a long time, in the end it wasn't "forever." But he also said that if we wrote a word with pencil, on paper, we could press all of the keys we wish to imagine (paper doesn't have actual keys, it only has the keys we want to imagine) that the words would not be erased. We could shake the paper as much as we wanted, or even stomp on the paper, that the words would not disappear. My friend Jaime would also say, half-kidding, half-serious, that we could go years without charging the paper's battery, because it did not get charged. "But why?" Jaime would ask, starting to crack a smile. "Because paper does not need a battery!" My friend Jaime would laugh a lot after saying these things. What I enjoyed hearing Jaime say the most- although I didn't believe in everything he said- was this: we could keep a paper in a drawer that, ten years later, you could still read what was written on it. Ten years later! That we could bury a paper in the ground and that if we dug it out fifteen years later, or twenty years later, the words would still be there. This I believed. And since that day I went on really wanting to learn to write on paper. With a pencil.

There were four students in the class. They had not gotten more volunteers for the pilot-program. I don't know if the teacher was disappointed; he didn't appear disappointed. The first thing he did was ask us our names. With a fine, white cylinder stick (called "chalk") he drew lines on a black wall (which was called a "blackboard") and the traces stayed completely still on the board, without twinkling, without disappearing, without transforming or multiplying into other lines, smaller or larger. The traces didn't respond to any buttons or keys that we would have pressed, because there were no such buttons nor keys. There were no cursors. No batteries. Nobody told me this, nor did I tell anyone, but I came to the following conclusion: if, for some reason, no one erased the letters written on the board—in twenty, thirty years- the traces drawn by the teacher would still be there.

I kept thinking about this.

One day the teacher said that the moment had arrived for us to write on a sheet of paper. (Now in each desk there were a pencil and some sheets of paper). Writing on paper with a pencil is not easy. It's like drawing letters with a stylus made of carbon (or what the teacher called "graphite"). In the beginning it's difficult, but after we get used to it. A lot of practice is needed. You have to sharpen the pencils frequently, yet be careful as to not over sharpen with too much force and break the tip.

The teacher also let us take some paper books home since we promised that we would try to read a few pages. It was not easy to read paper books. It was necessary to turn them page by page. "Turning the page" meant holding the corner of the sheet between your index finger and thumb, very carefully, and transfer each page from the right stack to the stack that is forming on the left. I tore a few pages, but the teacher did not protest. It is easier to read e-books because the stories are there "temporarily," or "on loan," and for that reason, reading has only the importance of stories that exist "temporarily" or "on loan." In e-books the stories change. They change from day to day. From hour to hour. From minute to minute. Sometimes even from reading to reading, or while they are being read. Stories change because "the circumstances" change, said the teacher. Technology itself changes. "The products that have just come out" change. The news changes, the current topics that are fashionable change, the interests of boys my age change. And the books should reflect "the rapidly changing world" or "the rapid change of the world," I no longer remember exactly how the teacher said it. On the other hand, it is easier to read books on paper because the paper book does not tell me that it took me too long to read a word. Or that I skipped words. It does not ask why I like certain words, or why I do not like certain words. Nor does it tell me that a candy made from strawberry extract, but without a strawberry flavor (with a raspberry flavor …), has just been invented and we can order it from the link below. It does not even tell me that I'm already late for school (for the "other" school, not for the pilot program) and that, because I'm late, "it would be convenient to resume reading another time."

One day the teacher looked at the time sheet where the letters of our names were drawn, saw the letters of our cities and states, and said that all names and cities and states were spelled correctly. The teacher must have been satisfied because he was not so angry that day. And if we continued this way, one day we could do two things that few people knew or could do: read the paperbacks in library museums and write more of the paperbacks that exist in library museums. And he said that on paper we could write whatever we wanted, and not just what the computer screens would let us write. This was important, said the teacher. At the time, I did not quite understand what the teacher meant. Now I get it.

The teacher must have been really happy that day because he shook hands with everyone at the end of class and said, "See you tomorrow."

The next day, in addition to the teacher, there was a school inspector in the room. Right in the middle of the room. The teacher was sitting at his desk, his eyes lowered, as if he did not know there was a school inspector in the middle of the room. The school inspector was a big man. He seemed even larger when he opened his arms and spoke loudly. And when he spoke – the inspector spoke very loudly – he pointed at the students, at the blackboard, at the big paper posters with their painted letters and, finally, at the sheets of paper and at the pencils on top of the desks. The school inspector had never seen anything like it. He said that, with these materials, the students will never learn to use "the adequate pedagogical tools" for the age in which we lived. The "adequate pedagogical tools" for the age in which we lived, said the inspector, were the digital materials. And to not learn how to use these materials was "harmful" to the students (the inspector pronounced each syllable of the word "harmful" very carefully). He said that using paper was terrible for the environment, that it decimates the trees, that the chalk dust isn't good for the lungs, that the students were going to get sick, if they weren't all sick already. The inspector had an enormous coughing fit when he said "all sick," and he went on to say that "our learning capacity" would be "seriously," maybe even "irreversibly" stunted. (I could even swear that the teacher, who coughed so habitually, made a great effort not to cough in that moment, as to not give that satisfaction to the inspector).

The school inspector said these things with arms raised, turning his body in our direction, in the direction of the board, in the direction of the posters, in the direction of the professor, who continued to look downward as if there wasn't a school inspector in the middle of the room. The inspector seemed like a priest who frightened the faithful instead of consoling them. He also seemed like a dancer who holds his hands wide open and waves his arms a lot; that has more energy than one can spend if one started to run with all their might and only stopped after ten kilometers. The school inspector said further that, with the method of the teacher, there wouldn't be time to complete "primary school," "secondary school," "a bachelor's degree," "a masters degree," "a doctorate," and "a post-doctorate" before we were thirty-five. It was necessary to complete these courses – the inspector called these "steps of life" -- before the age of thirty-five, at the maximum. That afterwards there would be time to live "the rest of one's life" in "peace, harmony and wisdom." The school inspector said that we shouldn't waste time, that it was necessary to respect time, that time was "a limited resource."

The school inspector stopped turning around and shrugging his shoulders and shaking his arms. He stopped looking at us, at the board, at the posters, at the teacher. He took a few steps towards he desk – where the teacher continued to sit as if he didn't know that there was an inspector in the middle of the room – and said that he felt sorry for us. So very sorry. Then the teacher looked the inspector in the eyes while sharpening a pencil, with his legs crossed, while the shavings fell on the floor.

When the inspector left, the teacher said that there wouldn't be lessons the next day, nor the day after, nor ever again. The students were silent, without knowing what to say. I was silent, without knowing what to say. The teacher said that he needed to return the key to the room – "tomorrow afternoon." I raised my hand and asked if I could come back the next day to learn to be a writer. It was just that—as I had announced to the class—I wanted to be a writer.

The teacher said that I still could not be a writer. The school inspector had interrupted the school year before teaching the lesson on how to be a writer. And this lesson could not be given "out of order," that is, "out of the sequence of lessons" which prepared students for such a lesson that taught them to be writers. The teacher approached my desk, bent over, and instead of telling me that he was very sorry, he whispered something different in my ear.

The next day, I was in class at the usual time. There were not any students, just the teacher and I. The teacher seemed happy, or maybe less angry than usual. He asked me if I knew what it was to be a writer. I said that I did not know well, but even so nothing would make me give up being a writer. The teacher explained that to be a writer, one must not like to write. "Not like to write?" I asked. "You actually like to write?" he asked. I answered yes. The teacher stood quiet for a few seconds, and then said: "You want to be a writer because you don't know what it is to be a writer."

The teacher said that being a writer is to access the pages of the publishers on the internet and engage in "complicated negotiations" - I did not know what he meant by "complicated negotiations" with "writer assistance programs." "Do you know what a "writer assistance program is?" he asked. I did not know but the teacher opened his computer and showed me. We visited a publisher for writers my age. I signed up, putting my personal information in the spaces and I began to write a story: "I visited my grandmother for Christmas". The program asked the following questions: "How old is the grandmother?" "What funny things does the grandmother say?" "Is she kind like all grandmothers?" "Smiling like grandmothers should be?" "Does she have wrinkles like grandmothers should have?" "Does she have warts like grandmothers should have?" And so on. The program would not let me write another word if I did not answer the questions. If the given answers were not those recommended by the program one of the two would happen: one could not continue to write the sentence - or the paragraph, or the story, or the book; or two, one would have to convince the automatic editor of the "validity of my options," or "the relevance of my arguments." (At the time I did not know what "validity of options" or "relevance of arguments" meant. Now I know).

The automatic editor "recognized the difficulties in the career of a young writer" and even apologized for causing that inconvenience. It also reminded young aspiring writers that writing was difficult. Very difficult. Difficult because it was necessary to "grab" the readers, "seduce" the readers and, above all, "keep the readers seduced." The automatic editor said that readers were not a "given." (I did not know what was a "given" but I did not dare to ask). The automatic editor added that one should not have the "arrogance" to think otherwise than he had written. It also insisted that readers like funny grandmothers, smiley with many wrinkles and warts. They have more wit, more interest, and more mystery.

The teacher said that he had already been a writer and that he hadn't liked it. Now I understand that what he had been in reality was not "a writer." The teacher said that he had once written the following: "A boy hit his head against a wall and it split into two equal halves, like two halves of an orange." The program didn't accept that. The teacher justified the sentence as best he could, but the program continued to stop the sentence from staying written that way. The teacher decided to "engage all the necessary mechanisms to defend what he had written," and requested an interview with a more sophisticated automatic editor. He was lucky; instead of a more sophisticated automatic editor, the publishing house allowed him to speak with a real live flesh-and-blood editor. That flesh-and-blood editor rejected the sentence even more quickly than the automatic programs had. The teacher was not discouraged and decided to submit the same sentence to the automatic programs of other publishing houses. The publishers of realist literature rejected it, without any explanation. The publishers of children's literature said it wasn't appropriate for children. Those that published horror literature said it wasn't horrific enough. Those for fantastic literature said it wasn't fantastic enough. Those for serious literature said it wasn't serious enough. And those for comical and absurd books said it was neither comical not absurd enough. One of them—a publishing house with problems, one that urgently needed authors—recommended "The boy hit his head." Why not say what you intended to, simply and concisely? Why complicate things? Indeed, why complicate things when the world was already complicated enough?

These programs—the teacher said, without ever taking his severe gaze off of me—were "too logical, sensitive and useful." So "logical, sensitive and useful" that they were unbearable. The teacher put his hand on my shoulder. His hand had never rested on my shoulder for so long and had never felt so heavy. He took my pencil and sheets of paper from his desk and gave them to me. They were mine. I could keep them "forever," he said, half joking, half serious. The teacher told me whatever letters I wrote on those sheets of paper, with that pencil, would last at least as long as I would last. Maybe more. Maybe quite a bit more. And that I could write whatever I wanted. Anything I wanted. Complicated or simple things. Intelligent or stupid. Terrifying or comforting. Harmful or uplifting. Funny, or not funny at all. Sentences that were illogical, insensitive or useless. Or—why not?—ones that were logical, sensitive and extremely useful. Or even, and at this point he got more serious, sentences that were all those things at the same time, or that were combinations of all these things according to my own desired proportions.

He said that I could address my words to whomever I wanted. To specialists and to the ignorant. To the tormented and the happy. To the insane and the lucid. Or else, if I preferred, not to address them to anyone. I could write to a reader who did not exist. One who was yet to be born. And that was what being a writer was. That's what the teacher said.

ANTÓNIO LADEIRA is an Associate Professor of Portuguese (and Director of the Portuguese Program) at Texas Tech University. He has a 'Licenciatura' in Portuguese Studies by Universidade Nova de Lisboa and a PhD in Hispanic Languages and Literatures by the University of California in Santa Barbara. His research interests include Portuguese-American literature, masculinity in contemporary Lusophone literatures, contemporary poetry, literature and ethics, etc. He has published five books of his own poetry. In 2018 he published a duology of short stories in Portugal about technology, ethics and authoritarian/totalitarian regimes: Os Monociclistas e outras histórias do ano 2045 (Lisboa: On y va, 2018) and Seis Drones: novas histórias do ano 2045 (Lisboa: On y va, 2018).

IRENE MARQUES

Five Poems

Small words

I told myself last night that I would, from now on,
Write short poems, ephemeral words here and there
Where life or the hint of its intractable sense could be figured out
Incanted in small doses to find body and house

I told myself this promise
Write small words, senseless lists that my intrinsic Lusitanian taste
Bred on the other side of the Atlantic, with lush, emotional, visceral sentences
Naturally rejects
Avid that it is to spew ink through nothingness and appease the fear
And loneliness of life—that *fado* that we cannot escape

Go against that inclination, be the other of yourself
And in that process find the twin that walks in you
And makes sense of you
You are, after all, a citizen of the world
And adaptation and growth is your ontological destiny

The kitchen

The kitchen where she stands is bound to nothingness
In the middle there is the table
The bread and the olive oil, and in special days, a note of rosemary
Singing its perfume amidst the stale air of condiments
Suspending the hard labour that the mistress of the house endures

If I stare at the table enough time, I see all the people she has fed
Over the centuries, in aprons of colours entangled in grease stops
All marks of life, days and nights come and still your place remains
The same corner is your corner

Dreams, you say,
Dreams are made of incense smells that I conjure in this small corner
Where I live
Dreams are built from inside out

Perhaps she is right,
And I am only intruding in her perfection

Notions of God

There are truly beautiful people in the world. And when they are truly beautiful, they remind you of God. They are God. And then you want to go on living in the world. In this world. Forever.

She dreamed of a Pegasus: a sturdy, gentle white horse with wings that would cross her from here to the end of the world, that would dance her into a round interminable whirl when she could finally be whole, nothing missing, accompanied by all. Feel the exact point. That would be her voyage to God. That would be God.

Between the point of her chest, where purple gulfs of life are executed impeccably by jinn from regions in superior Abyssinia, and the lower back of her spine, where marrow meets bone, she could spend whole days, immersed into things, true, full things, and feel as if all that ever was or would be, had joined her for a solemn session of precise collective understanding. Between those points and in those correct days, she sworn in frank and sincere faith that her meeting had been with God.

Sometimes the valleys and the hills merged, and she could only know the world through encrypted notes, sounds that only people who don't speak any language know to be of very high value. It happened on special days when she chose to crisscross time without the thick sheet separating all the geometric figures that mark up the world, when she meandered between hopes and the ropes of minimal possibility, laying down her body fully on the earth. It was a darling pleasant game brought about by the deep nobility that drove her ontological desire, that inescapable fever always boiling in her blood. The red crimson lust of the voice that never left her, incessantly calling her to enter a better house: that coveted sleep into the dome of darkness or the castle of blind insight, depending on the alphabet you choose to name your prophet.

The Gemini in me

I am a Gemini. Full of selves: well, two selves at least—my father and my mother. From my father I possess a poetic undertone: I inherited his love for proverbs, those wise words told to him by his father who heard it from his grand-mother in a line that never ends. Words and words travelling down, from the very beginning, when humans started to think about how to express their love for one another through clean syllables—likely because they felt lonely and the other was the way to the self. He, my father, also gave me another genetic inheritance: the capacity to feel, very deeply, the earth in my bones: the astonishing and vibrant power of the spring, the warm darkness of the winter and the milder feelings of the other two seasons, each entering every fiber of my body so that I can fully feel like a being of the land. My mother is another story: mama of ten children she had to think complicated thoughts to explain the complication that her life came to be. The dialectics of her oppression got enmeshed in the Hegelian twisted philosophical ideology of the one who slaves and the one who masters and all the ensuing confrontations that arise from such disagreeable dichotomies. She passed this hindrance to me making me more intellectual than I in fact wish to be, for in being more intellectual, I lose my natural ways of life: to love just because one loves, to be just because one is fundamentally a being who fundamentally is. I wish I could only follow my father's inheritance and feel like a true daughter of this earth, speak that language that emerged at the beginning as a way to tell the other the love we feel. This does not mean that I can renounce my mother. I cannot for I am truly her daughter.

I sit here

I sit here and I wait for death. Sometimes I go out and love the world, every person in it, every bit of it, but then I return to my destiny and I wait again. My bones bend up and down, I do all the chores that life demands: discuss philosophy in my classes, the anxiety of our human responsibility or the anxiety of knowing that we will never know everything and control in fact very little: despite the microscope, the telescope, the cell phone, the great wide web—or the tall beautiful body dressed in a masculine suit that turns eyes. I sit here and I wait for death: I get excited sometimes, stare in wonder and awe at a magnificent letter that composes a magnificent word because once upon a time, our ancestors, moved by the same fear invented symbols to interpret the unnameable. I read the fluid Clarice and her Água Viva and I melt under a beautiful illusion that I am in sync with everything, that God is in my bones, that I am God, soul and matter joined in a communion superior to the consubstantiation that happens at mass on Sundays when Padre Lévito raises his white ring-less hand with the round and pristine wafer before he gently breaks it in his mouth barely moving his teeth, careful not to bite into the sacred and disturb the spell. Last week, under an act of love and fundamental need, I read Clarice to my class, my class on ethics and rhetoric, full of young eager students who want to find their divine on their Apple terminal to get rid of the lack, because, being novices of life, they still believe that can be done. I ask them: "Is Clarice psychotic?" They smile at me, their eyes not saying what they feel, holding on to the rational grip they have been taught to keep since they entered grade one and their magic was broken by the unkind ruler of the teacher who herself was a victim of a system that breaks us all. One of them, though, is brave and says: "There is a sadness, a longing in her writing, but also a joy." My eyes rose to splendour when I heard her because I no longer felt alone. I said: "Yes, you got it." And then I said it again. I sit here and I wait for death and on good days I go out to perform the duties of life and I am lucky like that. Lucky like that.

IRENE MARQUES is a bilingual writer (English and Portuguese) and Contract Lecturer at the University of Toronto, Ryerson University and York University (Toronto, Canada). She holds a PhD in Comparative Literature, Masters in French Literature and Comparative Literature and a BA (Hon.) in French Language and Literature all from the University of Toronto, in addition to a Bachelor of Social Work from Ryerson University (Canada). Marques's academic publications include, among others, *Transnational Discourses on Class, Gender and Cultural Identity* (Purdue University Press, 2011) and numerous articles in international journals or scholarly collections. Her creative writing publications include the poetry collections *Wearing Glasses of Water* (2007, Mawenzi House), *The Perfect Unravelling of the Spirit* (2012, Mawenzi House) and *The Circular Incantation: An Exercise in Loss and Findings* (2013, Guernica Editions), the Portuguese language short story collection *Habitando na Metáfora do Tempo: Crónicas Desejadas* (2009, Edium Editores) and the novel *My House is a Mansion* (2015, Leaping Lion Books/York University). Her English language novel *Daria, Tales of a Woman and Other Idealists* (Inanna Publications) is scheduled for publication in 2020.

ANGELA FERREIRA

An Imagined Encounter

I'm out of makeup. Well, mascara. And eyeliner. And blush. I have a wedding later today – the Portuguese kind – and I can't be seen au naturel. Immediately, a future conversation with my tia pops up; she will say: what happened to your face? I will respond with: nothing, Tia, it's just my face. My aunt will then say: but in the photos, on the machine, you look so nice. I say: I didn't have time to look at my face.

I suddenly realize I've given away too much information. My tia says: You don't have time? And she launches into a monologue about how young people only want to hang out, and go to restaurants, and not make their beds. It goes on for about five minutes. I say goodbye and run away, missing the wedding festivities.

Every Portuguese girl plays out conversations with various matriarchs in order to avoid scrutiny, or at least to minimize it. This policing of behavior is still a remnant of the Salazar regime, when secret spies populated even the smallest of towns. I'd bet money that Portuguese aunts invented the kind of surveillance Michel Foucault talks about – the kind that turns everyone into policing each other's behavior.

The paradox here is that my aunt still thinks that Portugal has remained the same since she left in the 1950s. My tia upholds behaviors from over 50 years ago, and expects that Luso-Canadians maintain Salazar's ideals and policies. This was precisely Salazar's aim – to keep people incapable of seeing the power structures controlling them so as to instead observe their own family, friends, and neighbors. Keep them looking sideways. It's not all bad though, gathering information through surveillance is kind of like the predecessor to a neighborhood block watch.

My plan today, on my cousin's wedding day, though, is to avoid being compared with all the nice Portuguese girls, women with successful careers like Nelly Furtado, Mariza, and Cristina Ferreira (no relation to me – I swear). I decide that, instead of this, I'll arm myself with makeup. My glamorized face will perhaps distract my Tia.

I walk to the pharmacy in my neighborhood, Commercial Drive. I was born in Vancouver, Canada and this neighborhood epitomizes my experiences - I know so many people here that I constantly run into someone I know, especially in East Vancouver. It has taken some time for the world to notice Vancouver, as it is the furthest west inland in Canada and just near the American border.

The city is also located on the Pacific Rim, which connects Vancouver to Asia through the Pacific Ocean; for me, this is a meaningful connection because this ocean was named by Ferdinand Magellan, due to the water's *pacifico* quality, in comparison to the Atlantic Ocean. This unique geographical confluence has perhaps led to Vancouver's diversity. Even before Vancouver landed on the most-livable-list, accompanied by its expensive housing, the city has been a sought-after place to live, due to, in part, its role as the pacific gateway.

Two other large-scale cultural events also impacted the global attention Vancouver has received. The first was Expo '86; I was a child then. I explored the ceramic bicycle sculptures with my big Portuguese family, and asked for an Expo Ernie mascot doll, which I didn't get – I got a keychain instead. The Expo Line Skytrain was built as result of this event, and a new cycling culture slowly emerged.

The second event was the Vancouver 2010 Olympics, which was met with some resistance. This event significantly impacted the city, because various infrastructures were built during this time, such as the Canada Line (YVR to downtown), the Richmond Oval, and Hillcrest Community Centre.

The event itself provided the city with unforgettable memories. My family laughed alongside Canada when Jon Montgomery drank beer out of a pitcher after winning a gold medal on live TV. And, after the Men's Hockey gold medal win, my family and I took the Skytrain downtown to celebrate; the entire train, including my immigrant family, sang "O Canada" on repeat until Granville Station.

We watched the Opening Ceremonies and wondered if any Portuguese people would participate, and we felt a bit bad watching just one Portuguese Olympian walk the flag through BC Place. The ceremony's performances included KD Lang, who sang Leonard Cohen's "Hallelujah" barefoot; Shane Koyczan performed "We Are More." Nelly Furtado and Bryan Adams sang "Bang the Drum," which celebrated the Indigenous people who existed here before, well, everyone else. And, Wayne Gretzky, with the Olympic Torch, made his way into downtown on a pick-up truck. A chef passerby spotted Gretzky, abandoned his restaurant duties by tossing his apron aside, and ran after the torch. So Canadian.

During the ceremony, Nelly Furtado, a Luso-Canadian from Victoria, my province's capital city, performed for the world – for Portuguese-Canadians, but even more for me this was a big deal. We saw a representation of ourselves on a world stage – this was affirming to our Luso-Canadian identity, especially as the Portuguese community in Vancouver keeps shrinking.

I rush by a few side streets, to get the pharmacy, remembering the families who lived here. They used to pick up bread and olives, just after church. Their doctors and dentists were here. They would renew their driver's license and then go to the travel agent next door to book their trip to Portugal. All of this, on The Drive. Most of this, just a memory. There are still remnants of the Portuguese immigrants who once had businesses here, but many families have moved outside the city. Many of my young relatives and close friends no longer live in Vancouver because of the city's high living costs. Now, there is a total of one Portuguese restaurant and two coffee shops on Commercial Drive: the Portuguese Club of Vancouver, Joe's Café, and Café Algarve. Further South, there is Casa Verde, Serra Bar, and Metro Coffee, but most Portuguese businesses nowadays are found in Burnaby and beyond.

Many people complain that "The Drive," like much of Vancouver, has become gentrified. In the city, development is rampant, with new projects around every corner. Unlike my Tia, who still acts like the neighborhood police, not realizing that the Portugal she left behind has changed, the entire Drive neighborhood is in constant flux. Vancouver does not have equivalents to Little Portugal in Toronto or Height-Ashbury in San Francisco, but The Drive is a big mash up of all these things on one long street that runs only a dozen blocks. It is the perfect place for people watching. Here, the culinary options are almost endless; on a rainy day I go for pho, and on a sunny day I head to a patio debating whether I want to eat Cuban, Jamaican, or Italian food.

But I return to my task for the day: make-up shopping at the pharmacy. The usual types are inside; the person about to go on vacation, the one who needs to quickly color their hair, and the person embarrassed to buy something embarrassing. Then there's me, the person who almost never wears makeup – only on occasions to deflect deprecating comments. I briskly walk through the cosmetics.

Ah! So many colors, things, options. What do I buy? I don't want to ask anyone...so I look around. It's just a wall filled with products, half of which I don't even know how to use.

Finally, I find a mascara; my sister wears this brand. I see blush next to it. I don't have a brush to blend it with, so I guess I'll use my fingers. Who's going to notice an unblended cheek? So I grab it. Now eyeliner. I'm out of eyeliner, because I've never owned it. Not in high school, and definitely not now. So I browse the products, horizontally, and finally land upon a Katy Perry product. *Katy Perry has makeup?* I mean, she wears it for concerts and on American Idol, but I can't buy a Katy Perry product. Seems childish. But, but…she's Portuguese… well, some form of Portuguese. Pereira. Katy Pereira. Katherine Pereira. Just doesn't sound LA glam. Katy Perry is much better. More American. Getting rid of the immigrant trace, I say to myself. Look, I don't have time to get into an intercultural and political debate on immigration. It's the *wedding day*. It's about *fun*. Not about the depressing facts of life.

So, with courage, I reach out and get a black and a white eyeliner. I must support Portuguese businesses…even though she's not waving the flag…I feel a sense of obligation to buy this. No one will know. I run to the checkout. I say to the woman: a lotto ticket as well. Lotto Max, with the extra. This woman who has clearly worked here for at least a decade, turns to me. She's got heavy mascara, a smoker's cough, and hard-earned wrinkles to scare off any unwanted trouble. Her employee name tag reads LINDA in capital letters. She turns to me and says: ID please. I look around. Linda can't possibly mean me. She stares at me. *Really lady?* Just because I'm buying Katy Perry makeup does *not* mean I'm living a teenage dream. Linda says: anyone under the age of 30, or at least anyone we think is under 30 has to show ID. I flash her my card, giddy with joy. I'm well over 30, pushing 40. It must be my good Portuguese genes, and the Mediterranean diet. Well, technically my childhood diet was hotdogs and grilled cheese sandwiches, but whatever.

I exit the store, makeup in hand, and look for the closest establishment that I know has a washroom. I'm on The Drive, so there's plenty to choose from. I feel like eating something though; maybe it's a craving for some chouriço and caldo verde? Why am I craving this before a huge meal? Today I don't question it.

I run over to the PCOV. It's that place that looks like you shouldn't enter, because of the gates and dark atmosphere. In reality it looks that way because it used to be a private club, for members only, but now anyone can enter and order a meal. I walk in and there's a soccer game on. Cristiano Ronaldo is on the big screen. Of course. He's playing with his new team.

Everyone's focused on the screen. I dash by the people watching the game, and yell to the waitress: Tenho que ir à casa de banho. *I have to go to the washroom.* She nods. I'm a regular on Sundays. It's a Saturday, though. I'm thrown off. I walk up to her and say: I'll have a bica, and a pastel de nata. Maria says: you sure? Isn't there a wedding in a few hours? I nod. There are no secrets in the Portuguese community, only enlarged versions of truth. Maria says: How about I give you a papo seco? I say: and butter? Maria: claro que sim, menina. She turns towards the counter and disappears.

I run to the washroom. As I'm fumbling with my Katy Perry mascara, Nelly Furtado comes out of the stall. Looking fabulous. I've heard that she used to hang out as a teenager on The Drive, but this is now.

She's right in front of me. Right now. Nelly Furtado. And me. In the washroom of the PCOV. She washes her hands, takes a paper towel, and dries her hands. I start thinking of all the things I could say to her. I think, acoustic or electric guitar, or Portuguese guitarra? Toronto or Vancouver? *Bica* or *galão*? Gold or silver hoops? I then think, *Powerless (Say What You Want)* from your album *Folklore* inspired me to be a proud Luso-Canadian; the folklore dancing in that video was something I never thought I'd ever see. I think: are the Portuguese people an easy or hard sell for your records? I want to tell her I loved her concert; I went by myself – front row. I want to tell her that I admire how she is taking time to learn how to sew, to make her daughter outfits. I want to say a thousand more things.

What comes out is: uh. Help. Nelly turns to me and sees I am struggling. Nelly takes both eyeliner pencils, and begins to color in my eyes. From left to right. Right to left. My eyes are closed. I don't know which color she picked. It doesn't matter. I feel free, like a bird, feeling seen for the very first time. No judgment. Two Luso-Canadians understanding the struggle. A tear drops from my face. I hear the cap placed onto the eyeliner, and onto the counter. I stand there for a moment. I'm overwhelmed by my stillness.

I feel a rush of air go by me, and I know that Nelly's gone. I open my eyes. It's just me, and my tears. I recall her song, "All Good Things (Come to an End)." I look in the mirror. My eyes are softer, my lips less pursed, my cheekbones relaxed: my face is transformed. There's a smile greeting me in the mirror. My eyes look vibrant and unafraid to express all that's inside of me. I look at the Katy Perry eyeliner, and feel confident – dare I say happy. I'm energized. I tuck the eyeliner in my purse, and walk out of the washroom, ready for tonight's celebration.

ANGELA FERREIRA IS Luso-Canadian and a Ph.D. Performance Studies student at the University of Alberta with a focus on post-dictatorship Portuguese theater and female representation on stage. She holds a B.A. (Theatre/French) from the University of British Columbia and M.F.A. (Interdisciplinary Studies) from Simon Fraser University. Angela has presented papers in Canada, U.S.A., and Europe; she is a theater director, playwright, and co-founder of the theater company Theatre Elsewhere.

Forum

CHRISTOPHER LARKOSH

Descolonizando os Estudos Luso-Afro-Brasileiros: Uns passos concretos

Em outubro de 2017 o Centro de Estudos Portugueses e Cultura convidou duas pesquisadoras para a Universidade de Massachusetts em Dartmouth para organizar uma série de diálogos, tanto para professores quanto para alunos, sobre o papel de intervenções acadêmicas ao contribuir a descolonizar as nossas disciplinas e assim, as nossas universidades. As professoras Damares Barbosa e Patrícia Schor participaram de aulas, lições e conversas com alunos e professores, dando palestras sobre diversos temas (literatura luso-africana, afro-brasileira, goesa e timorense, teoria queer e pós-colonial, feminismo). O evento culminante da semana foi um fórum com o tema "Enfrentando o Racismo Anti-Negro na Pesquisa Acadêmica e no Ativismo," com a participação por teleconferência de ativistas europeus, inclusive o ativista português afro-descendente Mamadou Ba.

Uma segunda visita em abril de 2018 acrescentou mais uma voz a esta discussão: a da Post-Doctoral Fellow da Columbia University Selina Makana, convidada pelo Departamento de Português. Participou de uma conversa com alunos na Frederick Douglass Unity House sobre o papel do aluno na vida intelectual da universidade pública, e deu uma palestra sobre mulheres na literatura lusófona africana contemporânea. Todos os eventos tinham como objetivo o de criar mais espaço para pessoas de cor negra em termos reais nos programas acadêmicos universitários, e realçar o perfil de temas relacionados com as populações de cor negra no material pesquisado e ensinado no nosso currículo.

Os textos adjuntos servem como testemunho e documento concreto desta série de eventos, que poderiam proporcionar um modelo diferente para o estudo da língua portuguesa e os estudos literários e culturais associados com ela no Século XXI, um momento epocal no qual esta lingúa é já falada na sua maioria por pessoas de cor negra.

DAMARES BARBOSA

Realidade dos alunos negros na universidade brasileira

Nesse texto, serão apresentadas questões relativas aos negros, na Universidade, e também às políticas positivas implantadas no Brasil, para ensinar e propagar o combate ao racismo. Assim, o texto pretende abordar e elucidar ações que dão resultado positivo e, consequentemente, apontar o que fazer para construir uma identidade positiva do negro, para a conscientização da população em geral. Assim, essas ações positivas no Brasil e no Mundo surgiram para combater o racismo na literatura, na mídia e em outros campos.

Nas universidades brasileiras, mesmo com modificações no cenário atual, encontramos um número de negros, que não corresponde ao percentual populacional de negros na Nação. Mesmo os órgão oficiais demográficos, como o IBGE, e os órgãos educacionais, como o MEC, apresentam dados preocupantes sobre os negros nas universidades, pois os números apontados são ainda pequenos.

Então, vejamos: a população brasileira, formada por cinquenta por cento negros e pardos, e em seus quadros universitários tem apenas dez por cento de negros, em sua totalidade. Essa divergência se dá por diversos fatores e um deles é a questão da construção da identidade do negro. Assim, como a identidade étnica deve ser construída, desde a infância, ao longo dos anos, o racismo é implantado em larga escala na educação básica, e de forma inversamente proporcional se dá o acesso dos negros à universidade, ao ensino superior.

Os ensinamentos sobre questões raciais começam dentro de casa e, já em âmbito acadêmico, na educação infantil, vide os livros indicados para a leitura na primeira infância, bem como a postura dos alunos e professores em sala de aula. Conforme a educação recebida em ambiente doméstico e a postura dos dirigentes escolares, perante questões de cunho racial, assim se dará o aprendizado da criança, que passa a respeitar ou não seus colegas de etnia diferenciada. Para tanto, já num segundo momento, com a educação básica há a adoção dos livros que abordam o assunto.

Os livros, via de regra, não incentivam a boa formação e formação de identidade para o aluno negro. À parte os livros históricos, que naturalmente retratam a história do Brasil com o hediondo episódio da escravidão, os livros paradidáticos raramente apresentam personagens negros ou tais livros raramente são adotados pelas escolas.

Outros fatores que contribuem para uma a não construção da identidade negra, na infância, são os pressupostos e estereótipos usados ao longo de décadas, para retratar o negro. Assim, em alguns ambientes, o negro é apresentado sem qualidades, em contraposição à apresentação da imagem eurocêntrica como padrão de beleza, sucesso, força e inteligência. Isso contribui para o baixa autoestima do aluno negro, já nas bases escolares, o que culmina com o sentimento de inadequação no ambiente escolar e resulta na baixa porcentagem de alunos nas classes de nível superior e quiçá nos quadros de pós-graduação, por evasão escolar.

Ainda, relembrando questões histórias, após a abolição da escravatura, não houve uma política no sentido de integrar à sociedade o negro libertado. O negro, antes escravizado, ao ser libertado ficava sem trabalho ou um trabalho com remuneração muito baixa. Era a política do governo, para que o negro se sentisse excluído da sociedade. Assim, os governantes queriam mostrar que a proposta de abolição não havia dado certo, como vemos a seguir:

" O insucesso econômico, real ou imaginado, dos processos abolicionistas, as revoltas que às vezes lhe sucederam, o fato de os africanos não terem correspondido às expectativas de quem achava que lhes tinha doado a liberdade, de não se terem convertido em trabalhadores disciplinados e em fiáveis cumpridores dos contratos de trabalho para eles pensados, permitiram que a mentalidade colonia europeia reforçasse a imagem de indolentes e só trabalhavam se fossem direta ou indiretamente forçados. Tal imagem encontrou sua 'confirmação' científica nas teorias racistas que ganharam terreno a partir dos finais do século XIX, provavelmente ajudadas pela conjuntura pós-abolicionista." (Silva 24)

Com essa postura, seguiu a mentalidade e o pensamento da população branca sobre os africanos escravizados, com base também em doutrinas que apontavam os brancos como superiores. Isso perdurou durante muito tempo.

Na literatura, também no Brasil, após décadas, quando o negro começa a ser retratado nos livros, aparece em posições inferiores, subalternas e com o propósito de ser castigado. Isso, em literatura, justifica e reforça o pensamento anterior, já relatado no texto. Mesmo o negro já sendo liberto, continua o estigma e o estereótipo de escravizado, nos textos literários.

Da mesma forma, assim são ensinados, indiscriminadamente, nos bancos escolares, alunos negros e brancos, sem haver a preocupação de formar a identidade positiva do negro, apenas relatando a descrição dos textos literários, que retratavam o negro como escravizado. Nas escolas, os livros relatam os castigos aplicados aos negros escravizados e como eram tratados à semelhança dos objetos, para os brancos que os compravam.

De fato, nas classes do ensino básico, tal leitura aliada aos comentários domésticos, à margem da lei contra o racismo, já indica a formação que dá ensejo ao preconceito racial, por tornar a leitura escolar algo a legitimar a ofensa aos negros. Leitura dos textos, que tratam os negros escravizados como objetos, remontam à fase degradante vivida pelos escravizados, encorajando a não exaltação do negro e, consequentemente, formam uma identidade deficitária, imbuída de preconceitos.

E daí, seguem os métodos utilizados que, na normalidade da época, eram descritos e aceitos pela população, que via nos negros escravizados objetos de tortura e servidão:

> "A descrição de instrumentos de controle e tortura dos escravos – revelando o funcionamento de alguns dos aparatos físicos e ideologicos empregados pelo 'senhores' contra seus escravos – é detalhada com precisão naturalista. Um exemplo contundente é o ferro ao pescoço, descrito no conto como 'uma coleira grossa, com a haste grossa também à direita ou à esquerda, até ao alto da cabeçoa e fechada atrás com chave'. Ironicamente, essa coleira menos castigo do que estigma de reincidência." (Scarpelli 357)

Naturalmente, resta dizer que, com a influência das leituras e ações racistas em ambiente doméstico e escolar, o racismo evoluiu com rapidez e facilidade. Décadas transcorreram e, ao longo dos anos, ações afirmativas foram necessárias para tentar diminuir o abismo existente para os negros, nos bancos escolares. Para criar mais oportunidades aos alunos negros, política de cotas e leis especializadas foram instituídas para equalizar e dirimir as diferenças entre negros e brancos.

A legislação facilitou o acesso e permanência dos negros nas escolas, desde o ensino básico até pós-graduação:

> "(...) vivemos em um país que apresenta uma enorme disparidade social, a qual determina os espaços e acessos das pessoas à materialidade de que todos são iguais. Assim, hoje a educação formal, tanto a básica como a

superior, faz com que sujeitos de diferentes classe sociais estejam na sala de aula (...)." (Costa 3)

Ainda assim, com todas as ações instituídas, o número de negros nos bancos escolares, sobretudo em nível superior e pós-graduação, é extremamente diminuto. Os negros não são estimulados a concluir seus estudos em nível de graduação e, na justa medida, o pior ainda acontece em termos de pós-graduação, sobretudo nos cursos strictu sensu, mestrado e doutorado.

A referência para o número diminuto de negros, ainda na área de Estudos Afro-Luso-Brasileiros, é um reflexo do que acontece nos quadros universitários, quando são apresentados os docentes. Sem falar em causa ou consequência, a questão realísticamente apresentada, os números têm crescido, ano após ano, sem contudo apresentar resultado satisfatório. O número de docentes e discentes negros, nas universidades, deveria ser bem maior.

A questão do colonialismo ainda está presente, mesmo que de modo tácito, também nos bancos escolares. Ao aluno negro é necessário transpôr barreiras que um aluno branco desconhece. E, infelizmente, muitas vezes o aluno negro se depara com quem não está familiarizado ou não aceita o acesso do negro ao nível superior, conforme acontece em algumas instituições acadêmicas. A supremacia ainda é usada como moeda de troca, em determinados ambientes. E, assim, é determinado quem tem voz e a voz de quem é ouvida.

Questões de raça e gênero devem ser cuidadosamente tratadas, em ambiente escolar, desde a educação básica, para que não haja evasão das minorias e, consequentemente, novas oportunidades sejam criadas, diante do novo cenário mundial.

Ao longo das últimas décadas, questões de raça e gênero têm sido discutidas e tratadas, de tal maneira, a fim de dar voz àqueles que antes sentiam prejuízo, ao receber tratamento inadequado. Isso ocorre em todas as áreas escolares, também nos Estudos Afro-Luso-Brasileiros. Mesmo mediante ações afirmativas, os livros que adotam temas sobre raça, políticas anti-racistas e igualdade apresentam pouca circulação, quando são publicados. Sem dúvida, a militância dos movimentos de raça e gênero tem um papel fundamental para fomentar tal discussão. Porém, quando o número populacional é considerado, é nítido perceber que ainda são poucos os negros que chegam ao curso de pós-graduação e menos ainda os que podem publicar seus estudos.

As ações positivas para combater o racismo têm seu ponto de partida quando a população pensa a respeito do preconceito e passa a agir de maneira diferente, ao perguntar: "como fazer para deter o racismo no Mundo". Cada um encontrará a resposta, quando começar a combater o preconceito racial com suas atitudes.

O ponto de partida é olhar para os negros que estão em posição confortável e privilegiada, e não olhar para os negros que estão em situação ruim; pensar nos negros de forma positiva, para combater o pensamento negativo associado aos negros, por imposição cultural.

No Brasil e no Mundo, para mudar a mente das pessoas sobre racismo, as pessoas devem olhar para os negros e focalizar a beleza, a inteligência e o nível de capacidade.

Paralelamente, a formação dos professores é fundamental para a aplicação efetiva das leis que contemplam as ações afirmativas em prol dos negros, para que os livros adequados sejam adotados, conforme preceituam as referidas leis. Não basta existir apenas a lei, quando não há um esforço por parte dos educadores e da sociedade para combater de vez o racismo nas escolas e dentro de suas próprias casas.

OBRAS CITADAS

Costa, Rosilene (2017). *Literatura e formação de professores*. Revista Grupo de Estudos em Literatura Brasileira Contemporânea.

Machado de Assis (1974). *Conto e teatro*. In: Obras Completas. Rio de Janeiro: Nova Aguillar, 3v. O caso da vara. Mariana. Pai contra mãe.

Pena, Martins (1997). *O noviço. O juiz de paz na roça*. Publifolha, São Paulo.

Scarpelli, Marli (2006), *Machado de Assis: literatura e emancipação*. In Marcas da diferença, as literaturas africanas de língua portuguesa. Alameda Editorial, São Paulo.

Silva, Cristina N. (2013), in *África, Brasileiros e Portugueses*. "Estatutos incertos: ser português e ser cidadão em territórios americanos, africanos e asiáticos do Império Português (séculos XIX-XX)." Mauad Editora Ltda. Rio de Janeiro.

Taylor, Charles et alii (1994), *Multiculturalismo*. Instituto Piaget, Divisão Editorial, Porto Alegre, RS.

DR. DAMARES BARBOSA, pesquisadora do grupo Timor-Leste: Literatura, Cultura e Sociedade (CNPq) e LIA - Laboratório de Interlocuções com a Ásia (USP), possui graduação em Letras pela Universidade de São Paulo (2002), mestrado em Letras (Letras Clássicas) pela Universidade de São Paulo (2008) e doutorado em Estudos Comparados de Literaturas de Língua Portuguesa.

PATRICIA SCHOR

Racismo: Incitação ao Discurso e Economia do Conhecimento em Certas Geografias da Diáspora Africana

Coloco aqui breves observações sobre a presença e o lugar designado a sujeitos diaspóricos africanos, neste amálgama desigual denominado Estudos Luso-Afro-Brasileiros, onde o status do *Afro* é invariavelmente precário. São observações feitas a partir da Europa, entre a academia e outros lugares de (outros) saberes.

Inicio apontando para a necessidade fundamental da análise crítica da construção da autoridade acadêmica centrada no sujeito normativo – aquele que Sylvia Wynter denomina *Man* (a versão hegemônica branca ocidental do humano).[1] As tecnologias do poder tem sua expressão nos *corpos nos espaços*: quem pode estar aonde. A colonialidade (Aníbal Quijano)[2] e a sobrevida da escravatura (Saidiya Hartman)[3] são irrefutáveis quando se depara com a ausência marcada de mulheres negras nos Estudos Luso-Afro-Brasileiros. Em recente entrevista à Joana Gorjão Henriques, Inocência Mata afirma sobre a academia em Portugal:

> Mesmo que existam pessoas com um óptimo trabalho sobre questões de racismo na sociedade portuguesa, por exemplo, não vêem a falta de representatividade étnico-racial como um problema de justiça social como no caso da desigualdade de géneros. ... A presença de negros na academia é nula. Isto é um grande problema, mais grave porque acontece na academia.[4]

Não só há uma discrepância exorbitante entre a auto-imagem progressista das ciências humanas e sua prática, o problema é grave porque a academia, como sabemos, (re)produz relações e discursos de poder, e manufatura sujeitos de autoridade, assim como sujeitos desprovidos de fala autorizada; produz sujeitos ausentes. A economia e política do campo acadêmico relega sujeitos que carregam o fardo de uma colonialidade insistente a uma existência fantasmagórica ou precária.

Essa ausência históricamente (re)produzida é condição familiar às diásporas africanas em suas várias geografias do pós-império. Assim os negros seguem sendo *corpos estranhos* nos corredores e cargos universitários. Gloria Wekker, durante décadas a única professora negra no Departamento de Humanas da Universidade de Utrecht,[5] conta, em seu último livro, seu encontro com estudantes brancos:

> Para a maioria dos alunos, esta é a primeira vez que são confrontados com uma professora negra: "uma mulher negra em uma posição intelectual, oficialmente poderosa aparece como uma contradição em termos para eles," (Habel 2012, 109) provocando toda uma série de efeitos contraditórios: a descrença, sou vista como uma impostora, como estando *fora de lugar*.[6] (ênfase minha)

A acadêmica revela a genealogia colonial deste corpo em lugar indevido:

> Ser preto, no masculino ou feminino, e instruído são, aparentemente, irreconciliáveis; eles se excluem. Ser negro é associado a ser atlético, à baixa escolaridade, à estupidez, a ser divertido, um animador e, naturalmente, àquele que ocupa um lugar nos degraus mais baixos da escada social. Existe uma longa tradição acadêmica no racismo científico que criou, invocou e defendeu essa ordem natural. Essas imagens circulam amplamente, elas nos cercam. Nós, tanto negros quanto brancos, somos construídos por elas como inferiores e superiores. As representações da raça que eram comuns no século XIX também foram preservadas na academia, esse *bastião do conhecimento objetivo*, e na mídia. (ênfase minha)[7]

Mata conta episódios recorrentes e semelhantes a Wekker a partir da academia em Portugal, "[u]m país que se orgulha da sua "experiência africana": "Uma vez ia a entrar para uma sala onde haveria uma reunião e ouvi uma colega, que não me tinha visto, dizer: "não sei o que é que esta preta veio para aqui fazer"."[8] Esses são momentos reveladores de um problema endêmico porém sistematicamente negado e forçosamente silenciado.

A cena acadêmica brasileira não é diferente, com o notável exemplo da Universidade de São Paulo, examinado pela investigadora Viviane Angélica. Angélica colocou a questão: sendo a USP "a universidade que mais tem trabalhos sobre a questão racial no país, então porque não tem docentes negros?" Levando-se em conta que o Brasil tem mais que metade da população de "pretos e pardos," a situação é gritante. Segundo dados (de 2015) da própria USP, 1,53% do corpo docente é pardo, 0,3% é negro. Em sua investigação, Angélica indica a branquitude da Universidade não somente na composição da sua população mas também no projeto higienista que a fundou, assim como na resistência ao confronto às desigualdades no processo de entrada à docência. Dessa forma, a universidade se mantém um reduto branco, onde "o processo de ingresso também funciona como uma forma de herança."[9]

Recentemente questionei duas mulheres negras ativas na luta contra o racismo anti-negro na Europa, sobre como vêem o papel da universidade. Marlyn Mimi Mau-Asam, fundadora do movimento holandês *Mothers of (an) African Descent* afirmou: "Eu acho que a universidade deve começar a considerar-se como parte de todo o sistema educacional. Todo o sistema contribui para um círculo contínuo. Deve haver mais consciência de como se é parte desse círculo, ao invés de se considerar somente como destino final."[10]

O trabalho de Melissa Weiner sobre os livros de história lecionados nas escolas primárias holandesas evidencia como o racismo se inscreve no currículo. A investigadora conclui que os livros didáticos de história para ensino fundamental "apresentam metanarrativas eurocêntricas de europeização racial no contexto único da sociedade holandesa." E explica:

> Esses livros perpetuam o esquecimento social, pelos holandeses, da escravidão e do colonialismo científico, justificam intervenções históricas e contemporâneas na África, essencializam e problematizam os imigrantes e suas culturas, destacam a superioridade holandesa e facilitam a ideia de um "fardo holandês", que encontra a Holanda auxiliando, com relutância, minorias dentro e fora de suas fronteiras.[11]

Esse trabalho se alinha com a investigação de Marta Araújo e Silvia Rodríguez Maeso sobre os livros didáticos de história contemporâneos portugueses. As autoras apontam que este material "mostr[a] como, nos debates sobre a história e, mais concretamente, sobre o ensino do colonialismo e da escravatura, se tem esvaziado a sua relevância política e evadido o racial para compreender a chamada escravatura Atlântica dos séculos XV ao XIX."[12] Essa historização do colonialismo português é também uma prática efetiva de esquecimento histórico.

Tais epistemologias tem uma vida violenta no quotidiano das crianças racializadas. A investigadora Nina Vigon Manso denunciou e fez queixa em Portugal (até o momento sem resultado) contra o racismo nos manuais escolares, a partir do alerta da própria filha. Em entrevista a Joana Gorjão Henriques, conta dos artifícios utilizados nos manuais a partir dos quais "a criança deduz que as pessoas pretas não são de confiança." Nota ainda nos mesmos materiais que: "A pessoa central é sempre a criança branca que está a mostrar o seu mundo." Pergunta então: "Quando é que vai começar a acontecer serem as outras crianças a falar?" Finalmente indica que: "As crianças não-brancas continuam a ser tratadas como estrangeiras e não portuguesas." A jornalista narra o *encontro* de Vigon com o material: "quando se chega à parte das profissões, nem uma das pessoas representadas é não-branca." E Vigon questiona: "Com que direito é que se apagam as crianças não-brancas dos manuais, o direito a existir no seu próprio país?"[13]

Esta doutrinação para o racismo marca a escolarização das crianças negras e não negras através dos livros e manuais que lêem, pintam e manuseiam, assim como se faz sentir nas práticas da sala de aula. A partir da análise de uma escola primária em Amsterdã, Melissa Weiner explica:

> Tanto na Europa como nos EUA, os estudantes de minorias raciais e étnicas experimentam discriminação em mãos de professores que afetam negativamente seu desempenho acadêmico. Nos EUA, pesquisadores documentaram como o corpo docente predominantemente branco educa os estudantes não brancos através de práticas disciplinatórias [punitivas] e de baixas expectativas, o que afeta o desempenho educacional. Mas na Europa, a negação da existência [do racismo] dificulta a pesquisa sobre questões estruturais que explicam a desigualdade educacional das minorias, e muitas vezes a baixa escolaridade é justificada em função de diferenças culturais. Examinando as práticas da sala de aula em uma escola primária diversa de Amsterdã, document[ei] mecanismos de racialização manifestados no desprezo, disciplinação e silenciamento de estudantes de populações minoritárias. Além disso, [notei que] muitos estudantes eram menos recomendados para faixas de ensino médio de nível superior.[14]

Este relato/retrato, atualiza a necessidade de se refletir sobre as considerações de Mau-Assam sobre a universidade – onde os negros não chegam- como parte de um *círculo (racializado) do sistema educacional*, e não somente como estação final de uma herança.

Mau-Asam afirmou peremptoriamente que "a academia é parte do problema e não da solução," e criticou o *hábito* acadêmico de não prestar contas às populações estudadas. Notou que poucas pessoas de descendência africana completam os estudos universitários – negros que chegam, mas não ficam- e que "a questão é de raça e classe," sendo a universidade um lugar da/para a elite. Retoricamente, pergunta: "A quem a universidade está servindo?" Por outro lado, afirma, "toda sociedade precisa de acadêmicos."[15]

Jamie Schearer, co-fundadora e coordenadora da *European Network of People of African Descent* e membro da *Initiative of Black People in Germany* diz, de modo similar, que a universidade é ou pode ser parte do problema assim como da solução, dependendo de "quem é a universidade e quem lá tem agência." A universidade poderá contribuir à luta anti-racismo na medida do seu "olhar crítico ao racismo e às estruturas que modelam a sociedade. Como algumas instituições ainda acreditam na neutralidade da academia e na produção do conhecimento, este conhecimento pode reforçar os estereótipos em torno da resistência. Se a produção do conhecimento tem uma lente crítica ao racismo e um compromisso de desconstruir o colonialismo, colocando em evidência como essa história continua nos afetando hoje, acredito que as universidades podem fazer parte da inventarização da resistência e da sua inscrição na produção do conhecimento." Sobretudo, Schearer insiste em um caminho de duas vias: "Eu também acredito que um envolvimento mais forte, através do qual o conhecimento seja levado de volta às comunidades, pode ser útil para a análise do estado atual e para informar estratégias [de luta]."[16]

Para tal, é imperativo que a academia abra as portas históricamente cerradas àqueles sujeitos de existência fantasmagórica. Recentemente, nos mídias sociais, Mamadou Ba, dirigente do *SOS Racismo* – Portugal, atacou essa dinâmica:

> Uma sugestão à academia que se tem dedicado a estudar e bem o racismo: criem espaços para os sujeitos racializados na produção de saberes. Do tanto dinheiro destinado a estudar a situação do racismo, algum podia ser canalizado para atribuir bolsas de estudo e/ou investigação a sujeitos racializados.[17]

Os comentários da curadora Diane Lima sobre a inclusão de símbolos "afrografados" – da produção simbólica afrodescendente - nas "investidas e experiências contemporâneas brasileiras" se alinham a esse processo exclusionário encoberto pelo discurso mitológico da democracia racial: "um mito oportunista e excludente onde se fala sobre, ao invés de falar com. Um jogo de aparências onde a visibilidade da cultura se faz na invisibilidade das presenças."[18] Essa crítica se aplica também à produção acadêmica.

Aspecto fundamental da colonialidade do campo acadêmico que se crê não racializado, é a distância que este estabelece com relação aos movimentos sociais e articulações espontâneas de dissidência e/ou expressões que fujam do controle institucional. Sujeitos racializados estão nestes espaços e são recorrentemente diminuídos, suas vozes silenciadas, suas expressões apropriadas e canibalizadas. Por via de regra a academia não interrompe mas reforça esse processo de descredibilização do *outro*.

Há, neste momento, renovada visibilidade à denúncia e crítica ao racismo na sociedade portuguesa, através da mídia progressista. Ao mesmo tempo que leio sucessivos artigos com júbilo, observo também que este *incitamento ao discurso* (Michel Foucault),[19] representa uma renovada tecnologia voltada a disciplinar, regulamentar e controlar o campo discursivo *sobre* o racismo. Assim, o racismo *estrutura o campo*. Diariamente *aprendemos* quem são os sujeitos que falam com propriedade sobre a temática, e definitivamente quem não são, como devemos falar e/ou nos silenciar, com quem, em que circunstâncias, entre tantas outras prescrições. Essa dinâmica, bem conhecida por ativistas, intitula-se *política de respeitabilidade*. Através dela ganham materialidade velhos fantasmas coloniais como a imagética das/dos negras/os raivosas/os, e em particular da *angry Black woman*, um sujeito *excessivo* (de excesso civilizacional), supostamente despido de capacidade intelectual, que não argumenta, mas vocifera (lembremo-nos que *o africano* foi construído como sujeito colonial a ser civilizado também porque não possuía língua). Esta herança ganha vida no *framing* que os mídias (sociais) fazem das/os negras/os que, corajosamente, denunciam o racismo. Há algo de lusófono nesta dinâmica, nomeadamente daquela longa tradição da cordialidade reservada aos pares nos espaços de sociabilidade fraccionada (*cada um em seu lugar*). Porém esta dinâmica tipifica ao racismo anti-negro em sua expressão mais abrangente, transatlântica.

Nos últimos sete anos vivemos similar proliferação de discursos *sobre* o racismo nos Países Baixos. A *questão do racismo* entrou no âmbito (antes inpenetrável) das instituições e dos mídias hegemônicos, através dos mídias sociais e alternativos, após marcar presença nas ruas, na militância. Palestras, debates, mesas redondas, cadernos especiais, livros e matérias de jornais, grupos de pesquisa acadêmica, novos cargos e salários. Pouco surpreendentemente, o maior beneficiário desta prolífica economia é o sujeito normativo (nomeadamente branco ocidental). A/O negra/a (dissidente) carrega o peso fenomenal do *bashing* generalizado dos mídia, é descreditado/a publicamente, e as portas das instituições se mantém fechadas - aos sujeitos que "vociferam" a crítica ao colonialismo do *aqui e agora*, à colonialidade.

Há que se adotar atitude de vigilância frente a essa abundância discursiva *sobre* o racismo em *nosso lugar*. É fundamental interromper o curso das questões proeminentes neste *debate*, nomeadamente: qual é a entonação que a/o dissidente negra/o deve adotar ao endereçar o questionamento e a denúncia ao sujeito hegemônico?; qual timbre de voz ao falar da violência? As questão subjacentes devem ser des-cobertas, notadamente: qual é o tom da pele de quem *pode* falar *como se deve?*; quem pode entrar nesse *nosso lugar* de autoridade? Cabe a nós a intervenção na economia associada a esse incitamento ao discurso, e a transformação da geografia racializada que ele informa e refaz.

NOTES

1. Wynter, Sylvia. "Unsettling the Coloniality of being/Power/Truth/Freedom: Towards the Human, After Man, its Overrepresentation - An Argument,"." CR: *The New Centennial Review*, vol. 3, no. 3, 2003, pp. 257-337.

2. Quijano, Anibal. "Colonialidad y Modernidad/Racionalidad." *Perú Indígena*, vol. 13, no. 29, 1992, pp. 11-20.

3. Hartman, Saidiya V. *Lose Your Mother: A Journey Along the Atlantic Slave Route*. New York, Farrar, Straus and Giroux, 2007. Todas as traduções de termos e trechos de artigos e livros são de minha autoria.

4. Henriques, Joanna G. "A Presença de Negros na Academia é Nula." *Público*, 9 Sept. 2017, www.publico.pt/2017/09/09/sociedade/noticia/a-presenca-de-negros-na-academia-e-nula-1784760.

5. No município de Utrecht, 22% da população não é branca (Dados do Município de Utrecht para 2017). Estou traduzindo o termo "inwoners van niet-westerse herkomst" (literalmente "habitantes de proveniência não ocidental") como "não-brancos," sendo que este é o significado desta expressão no contexto holandês. Fonte de dados: "Etniciteit Utrecht %," Gemeente Utrecht, acesso 1 de outubro, 2017, https://utrecht.buurtmonitor.nl//jive?presel_code=p635804133201299301.

6. Gloria Wekker, *White Innocence: Paradoxes of Colonialism and Race* (Durham: Duke University Press, 2016), p. 73.

7. Id., p. 74.

8. Henriques, Joana Gorjão."A Presença De Negros Na Academia É Nula."

9. Martins, Leandra R. "Perfil Racial dos Docentes da USP Analisa Baixo Índice de Professores Negros." AUN – *Agência Universitária De Notícias* – USP, 23 Mar. 2017, paineira.usp.br/aun/index.php/2017/03/23/perfil-racial-dos-docentes-da-usp-analisa-baixo-indice-de-professores-negros/.

10. Entrevista concedida em 22 de abril de 2017, pela qual agradeço sinceramente.

11. Weiner, Melissa F. "O Fardo Holandês: Escravidão, África e Imigrantes nos Livros de História da Escola Primária na Holanda." *Sociologias*, vol. 17, no. 40, Dec. 2015, pp. 212-54.

12. Araujo, Marta, and Silvia R. Maeso. "A presença Ausente do Racial: Discursos Políticos e Pedagógicos sobre História, 'Portugal' e (Pós-)Colonialismo." *Educar Em Revista*, no. 47, Mar. 2013, pp. 145-71.

13. Henriques, Joanna G. "Com Que Direito Se Apagam as Crianças Não-Brancas Dos Manuais?" *Público*, 9 Sept. 2017, www.publico.pt/2017/09/09/ sociedade/noticia/com-que-direito-se-apagam-as-criancas-naobrancas-dos-manuais- 1784746.

14. Weiner, Melissa F. "Racialized Classroom Practices in a Diverse Amsterdam Primary School: The Silencing, Disparagement, and Discipline of Students of Color." *Race Ethnicity and Education*, vol. 19, no. 6, 2016, pp. 1351-67.

15. Entrevista concedida em 22 de abril de 2017.

16. Entrevista concedida em 1 de maio de 2017, pela qual agradeço sinceramente.

17. Ba, Mamadou. Facebook - Post, 19 de setembro, 2017.

18. Lima, Diane. "Agora Somos Todxs Negrxs?" Revista Bravo!, 18 Aug. 2017, medium.com/revista-bravo/agora-somos-todxs-negrxs-2673f09ba940.

19. Foucault, Michel. *The History of Sexuality, Volume 1: An Introduction*. Translated by Robert Hurley, Harmondsworth, Penguin Books, 1990.

PATRICIA SCHOR é Professora no Amsterdam University College (University of Amsterdam & Free University Amsterdam). Possui graduação pela Fundação Getúlio Vargas – São Paulo, mestrado pelo International Institute of Social Studies (Erasmus University Rotterdam) e doutorado pela Utrecht University em Estudos Pós-Coloniais, com a tese "Disencounters with Africa in the Portuguese language: Postcolonial literature and theory in the Portuguese postempire". Algumas de suas (co-)publicações de interesse são: "White Order, Corporate Capital and Control of Mobility in the Netherlands" na colectânea Smash the Pillars: Decoloniality and the Imaginary of Color in the Dutch Kingdom (2018, Lexington Books), "Language as Art Object. Africa in the Representations of the Portuguese Language - Brazil & Portugal" (2016, Luso-Brazilian Review), e o número temático "Brazilian Postcolonialities" (2012, P.: Portuguese Cultural Studies) que co-editou.

Afro-descendência, nova categoria politica e novo espaço do activismo anti-racista negro?

No Portugal contemporâneo, a marginalização social, económica e política a que está vetada a comunidade negra e de ascendência africana inscreve-se numa continuidade histórica, fazendo dela a vítima privilegiada do racismo no país.

Esta continuidade histórica, que remonta à Escravatura e ao Colonialismo, também se traduz em subalternidade nas dinâmicas de luta social pela emancipação e na gestão política da agenda da igualdade.

Nem o fim do Colonialismo nem o do Fascismo representaram uma rutura ideológica nas políticas de igualdade que garantisse um avanço significativo na melhoria das condições de vida destas comunidades em Portugal.

Nem mesmo a adesão à União Europeia, que acelerou substancialmente o desenvolvimento do país através da sua infraestruturação económica e logística, com as grandes obras públicas, contribuiu para superar as desigualdades que fustigam estas comunidades.

No geral, a comunidade africana e de ascendência africana, que foi a principal mão-de-obra das grandes obras públicas que transformaram económica e socialmente o país e o puseram na rota da coesão com o resto da União Europeia em termos de desenvolvimento económico e social, não beneficiou de melhoria da condição e da qualidade de vida.

Na verdade, esta circunstância tem a ver com uma escolha política que assentou na relegação desta comunidade para a condição de estrangeira, porque a sociedade portuguesa olhou e, culturalmente, continua a olhar para ela como não fazendo parte integral do tecido nacional, apesar de ter substancialmente alterado o mosaico da composição étnico-racial do país.

Aliás, os filhos dos imigrantes africanos nascidos em território nacional, seja por convenção jurídica ou por perceção social e política, foram sempre remetidos para a categoria de estrangeiros no país onde nasceram por causa da filiação originária dos seus pais.

Esta circunstância restringiu imenso a sua possibilidade de almejar a condição de cidadania de pleno direito. A situação de subalternidade cidadã alimentou-se das ditas políticas de igualdade que, na arquitetura jurídico-administrativa e na gestão politica da diversidade étnico-racial, produziram uma barreira real e simbólica contra a afirmação da chamada "segunda geração de imigrantes" enquanto cidadãos nacionais.

A manutenção, por exemplo, do ius sanguinis em detrimento do ius soli no acesso à nacionalidade portuguesa faz das crianças nascidas em Portugal estrangeiras no seu próprio país.

A segregação escolar, a guetização habitacional, o encarceramento desproporcional, a precariedade laboral, a violência policial e o racismo sistemático que a população negra enfrenta foram e continuam a ser o motor das diversas formas de organização e mobilização social e política das comunidades negras em Portugal.

A chamada "segunda geração de imigrantes" partiu desta circunstância para dar um passo em frente na forma de organização e mobilização em relação às formas tradicionais de organização das comunidades africanas em Portugal. Decidiu não apenas sair do carcão político e jurídico de imigrante para reivindicar uma nova categoria política, a de portugueses Negros e afrodescendentes.

A assunção desta identidade política é obviamente herdeira de um longo património de lutas das comunidades negras, com vários momentos, espaços e formas de mobilização política que sempre esbarraram nas dificuldades de reconhecimento e de identificação por parte da sociedade e das suas instituições.

Na década de 90, através da cultura suburbana, nomeadamente do Hip-hop, Rap Funk e Punk e, no início deste milénio, através de convergências com o movimento social português - que sempre os remeteu para um espaço lacunar -, os jovens negros afrodescendentes procuraram reivindicar o seu lugar na sociedade portuguesa através de várias formas de mobilização.

Ainda assim e, apesar destas tentativas de conquistar o seu lugar na sociedade e nas disputas políticas, as dificuldades de reconhecimento e de aceitação continuaram a crescer. Daí que, de há 10 anos para cá, tenham surgido outros espaços e formas de luta exclusivamente protagonizadas por jovens negros afrodescendentes, completamente autónomos das lógicas tradicionais de organização do movimento social imigrante e nacional.

Estes espaços e formas de luta tentaram não apenas superar os limites das reivindicações minimalistas do movimento social imigrante, inscrevendo-se numa dinâmica de rutura e de elevação dos níveis de confronto político e ideológico sobre o privilégio branco, mas também, ampliar o alcance das suas propostas reivindicativas no jogo político.

A diferença substancial entre as formas tradicionais de organização do movimento social imigrante das primeiras gerações e a dos jovens negros afrodescendentes reside, essencialmente, na transversalidade, formulação, diversidade e a abrangência dos seus objetivos e domínios de luta.

Enquanto o movimento social imigrante tradicional foi condicionado a lutar por direitos mínimos e sectoriais, os afrodescendentes assumem uma agenda ambiciosa que pretende abarcar todas as áreas de intervenção política e social.

O desafio da Afro-descendência, esta nova categoria política na movimentação social e política que se situa entre a identidade e a condição social, assumindo com frontalidade a sua identidade negra na sociedade portuguesa, é o de disputar um novo espaço de ativismo capaz de desafiar os atavismos de uma portugalidade que teima em não reconhecer a sua diversidade.

Da década de 90 até a metade da primeira década deste milénio, a luta antirracista estava confinada no espaço político da extrema-esquerda e um pouco na esquerda tradicional e na social-democracia, sobretudo através das primeiras associações de imigrantes. Os intérpretes maiores deste período foram, sem dúvida, o SOS Racismo, a primeira e a maior organização antirracista, e algumas organizações comunitárias como a Aguinenso, o Moinho da Juventude, a Associação Caboverdiana, a Casa de Angola, a Casa de Moçambique, o Olho Vivo e, mais tarde, a Solidariedade Imigrante.

Nos inícios de 2000, surgem várias organizações de jovens negros nos bairros periféricos das áreas metropolitanas, com maior destaque para a Khapaz, Associação Espaço Jovem, Associação Unida e Cultural da Quinta do Mocho, Associação Cavaleiros de S. Brás, KUTUCA-Associação Juvenil Do Bairro das Faceiras, Centro Cultural Africano de Setúbal e Plataforma Gueto.

Mas a segunda década deste milénio viu surgir ainda mais organizações negras que, com um espectro diversificado de áreas intervenção, vão desde a economia solidária, a produção cultural, passando pela criação artística diversa e heterogénea, pelas questões de identidade, de género e de orientação sexual, até à mobilização política. Pode-se destacar apenas algumas com relevância no espaço público, dentro e e fora das comunidades negras, como a Afrolis, GTO LX – Grupo de Teatro do Oprimido de Lisboa, Djass–Associação de Afrodescendentes, a Femafro-Associação de Mulheres Negras, Africanas e Afrodescendentes em Portugal, Lisboa Griot- Associação Cultural, Movimento Crespas e Cacheadas de Portugal, I Love Carapinha, Roda das Pretas, Queering Style, Movimento Simentis de África, Muvimento Nu Sta Djuntu - Estamos

Juntos, Coletivo Consciência Negra, Tabacaria Tropical, Teatro IBISCO, etc, sem falar dos vários núcleos de estudantes africanos em várias faculdades. O dinamismo deste ativismo negro ultrapassa a tradicional mobilização em torno do racismo e reflecte-se em todo o debate politico sobre as desigualdades no país.

É neste contexto que o debate, tanto a nível político como académico, ganhou uma maior visibilidade. Porém, o debate actual sobre a disputa da memória da Escravatura e suas consequências na vida de sujeitos racializados, especialmente negros, permanece marcada por uma relação de poder bastante desfavorável à militância antirracista. Em Portugal, salvo raras e honrosas exceções, o lusotropicalismo canibalizou a debate sobre o racismo anti-Negro e conseguiu impor uma hegemonia cultural e doutrinal sobre o alegado excepcionalismo do colonialismo e do imperialismo português. No entanto, a capacidade de articulação do movimento negro português com outros movimentos a nível nacional e internacional contribuiu grandemente para o alargamento desta articulação e a sua potencialidade de desenclausurar a mobilização em torno da luta contra o racismo. Também na academia ainda existem muitos problemas derivados da quase ausência de negros nos espaços académicos, mas também, da falta de centralidade da questão racial na disputa epistemológica em Portugal.

Entre identidade e condição sociopolítica desafia o Movimento Negro a consolidar o seu espaço na disputa pela reconfiguração da luta política e social. Este desafio passará, entre outros, por:

- Afirmar e consolidar a categoria politica de afrodescendente na cena da disputa política e social;
- Denunciar a continuidade histórica da branquitude e as suas consequências no presente;
- Conquistar legitimidade política junto do poder político e do movimento social tradicional, constituindo-se como força de pressão política capaz de influenciar o debate político, ou seja, "tornar-se na sua própria força" e sem tutoria nem procuração política;
- Garantir reconhecimento popular junto das comunidades negras afrodescendentes e saber traduzir este reconhecimento popular na capacidade de mobilização da comunidade negra afrodescendente;
- Afirmar uma agenda transversal que seja capaz de fazer a síntese do património de lutas das comunidades e federar as várias sensibilidades de afirmação da afro-descendência, construindo um movimento negro amplo e forte em Portugal;

- Contribuir para a construção de uma cultura diaspórica que a coloque como interlocutor privilegiado na construção de redes de solidariedade nacional e transnacional entre as comunidades africanas e afrodescendentes.

Da década de 90 até agora, a luta antirracista em Portugal lavrou no erro de confundir antifascismo e antirracismo. Enquanto, academicamente, o lusotropicalismo se foi reciclando, ideologicamente as forças políticas teimam em não assumir a raça como categoria política. Perante este complexo quadro, onde a possibilidade de uma mudança de paradigma se revela ainda muito difícil, o movimento negro tem muito caminho por percorrer. Começou a fazer o mais impor ter peso nas disputas políticas.

MAMADOU BA é Dirigente do SOS Racismo Portugal. Ativista e militante anti-racista, dedica-se à luta pelos direitos humanos dos migrantes e das *"minorias étnicas"*. É licenciado em Língua e Cultura Portuguesa pela Universidade Cheikh Anta Diop de Dakar (Senegal).

SELINA MAKANA

Precarity in and through Black Bodies:
A Response from a Transnational Perspective

Across the African diaspora, both the individuality and sociality of the lives of black people have always been politicized by the violent intrusions of race as a regime of social order and control.[1] The essays in this volume of PLCS 32 take several important steps forward in thinking through what I would call "Precarity in and through black bodies." The contributors, feminist scholars, Patricia Schor, Damares Barbosa, and anti-racist activist, Mamadou Ba, grapple with and reflect on the meaning of black life in Europe and Brazil in the present moment. Concerned with how black bodies are marked as "the privileged victims of racism" (Mamadou Ba), the ways that black subjects, especially black women, in European academic spaces are considered to be "bodies out of place" (Patricia Schor), and question of race in Brazilian universities, these contributors underscore the illegibility and "foreignness" of blackness and black politics in Portugal, the Netherlands, and Brazil. By focusing on anti-blackness within and outside academic and political spaces, these contributors argue that the hegemonic ideology of white supremacy has historically and still continues to construct the black body as a space of absolute Othering. Or as literary theorist Darieck Scott cogently observes, "blackness is produced through humiliation and degradation."[2]

This idea of the process of "humiliation and degradation" speaks very strongly to the fact that blackness as a category cannot be delinked from the notion of precariousness. Precariousness, thus, becomes a shared condition that connects people African descent wherever they may be. In my use of precarity, I draw from Judith Butler's framing of precarity as an acknowledgement of dependency, needs, exposure, and vulnerability.[3] Precarity, therefore, is understood here as a social positioning of insecurity and is linked to processes of racial Othering. It is, indeed, well known that due to the violent institution of slavery, the barbarity of colonialism, and the economic anxieties in the global South as a result of structural adjustment programs, the identity of black people transnationally has always been that of a people-at-risk. In fact, the decolonization era in Africa and the Civil Rights Act in the U.S did not put an end to this vulnerability. This condition of precarity has continued, unabated, in the age of neoliberalism with the ever-expanding penal and policing systems acting as the vehicles for the denial of basic rights to black people in the U.S and elsewhere in the African diaspora.

To this end, given that the "fact of blackness"—to borrow a Fanonian phrase—also means living a precarious life, anti-blackness can then be seen as an instrument of governmentality that confiscates the body and lifeworld of blacks and distorts it for the purposes of capitalist accumulation and exploitation.[4] For instance, current global trends in the policing deaths and anti-policing protests of blacks: from the recent assassination of Brazilian scholar-activist, Marielle Franco, on March 23, 2018, the killing of African immigrants in Italy, the forced deportation of African immigrants living in camps in Israel, to the numerous black deaths in the U.S at the hands of the security state; serve as clear reminders of the various quotidian dangers of living as a racialized Other in a world that renders black bodies as killable, disposable, and deportable.

Legal scholar Tayyab Mahmud notes that while precarity is an unavoidable historical and structural feature of capitalism, neoliberalism has resulted in the "hyper-precarious" status of a population whose labor pool is "large, flexible, super-controlled and super-exploited."[5] Precarity in the neoliberal capitalist world, especially in the present moment of tougher immigrations laws and hyper militarized border control, is therefore worth addressing. Mamadou Ba does an excellent job in his essay by reminding us that in the ongoing European debates over immigration reform the situation of African immigrants in Portugal remains precarious as most of them are not counted citizens or the are seen as a threat to the nation-state. African diaspora theorist, Carole Davies Boyce has rightfully pointed out that deportation as a result of one being considered to be "out of place"/"foreign" and incarceration have historically been connected to regimes of dispossession used to punish, control, criminalize, and render stateless "alien" dissidents.[6] The above cases and many more highlight not only the precarity of black lives but also of the ways that contemporary forms of state racial violence in Western capitalist and liberal democratic polities continue to subordinate and repress disruptive and radical forms of black protest.

The question of the "whitening" academic spaces, disciplines, and national histories in Portugal, the Netherlands, and in Brazil, as the contributors have shown, leads to another equally important point about precarity in and through black bodies. Using examples from institutions of higher learning in Portugal and the Netherlands, Schor demonstrates how academic institutions actively participate in deciding which population of workers is allowed in these spaces and which is not. In Brazil, Barbosa's reflection reveals the challenges that black students and teaching staff go through in various institutions of learning. She highlights the lower rates of graduation of black students in different levels of schooling, a problem that is compounded by the fact fewer black students are admitted in universities. The marginalization, and in some cases near absence, of black faculty members in many of these academic institutions is a manifestation of these universities' interest in maintaining a racial hierarchy by securing the interests of white academics even when it means the exclusion, dispossession, and precarization of the racialized Others. As bodies that are deemed "out of place", black academics in predominantly white disciplines have to contend with the difficulties they face in reconciling their personal experiences, identities, values, and perspectives with those that dominate academia, or what Black feminist scholar Patricia Hill Collins refers to as the "outsider within" position.[7] I, therefore, argue that paying attention to the precarity of black bodies within the academia can also be revealing of the ways that these neoliberal and democratic spaces of higher learning become sites that reproduce and rigidify racial and class hierarchies through punitive and exclusionary processes.

What then is the way forward? Taking a cue from Anibal Quijano who explicitly linked coloniality of power—that is the ways that coloniality as a concept opens up the possibility of reconstructing silenced and repressed histories—with the coloniality of knowledge,[8] Patricia Schor, Damares Barbosa, and Mamadou Ba push us to take seriously the marginal place of blacks in the academia in Europe and Brazil, and their precarious conditions of work in order to critically engage with the project of decolonizing knowledge. Decolonizing knowledge, pedagogies, and various institutions of learning is not a trivial issue. Achille Mbembe rightfully reminds us that the project of decolonizing spaces is a democratic process and it is not about "tinkering with the margins."[9] By putting the question of race at the center, rather than on the periphery of their analyses, the essays in this issue accomplish much necessary and overdue work.

These essays necessarily respond to two crucial demands: first, what is the most productive way to address the question of race and racism in the neoliberal era when the racial inequalities in socioeconomic, political, education, and other outcomes persist?; second, given that the Black Lives Matter movement continues to resonate with racially minoritized groups transnationally, how do we create alternative avenues for productive, meaningful, radical approaches to global anti-racist activism? These are both legitimate and essential projects that are worth pursuing, even though they produce inevitable ongoing tensions in black politics transnationally.

SELINA MAKANA is a Postdoctoral Research Scholar at the Institute for Research on Women, Gender, and Sexuality at Columbia University. She holds a PhD from the University of California-Berkeley in African Diaspora Studies, and Gender and Women's Studies. Her recent publication, "Motherhood as Activism in Angola's People's War, 1961-1975" (2017) has appeared in *Meridians: Feminism, Race, and Transnationalism*. Her research and teaching interests include contemporary African women's social history, transnational feminisms, war and militarism, and African diaspora theory.

NOTES

1. Since as Alexander Weheliye (2014) points out that "blackness designates a changing system of unequal power structures that apportion and delimit which humans can lay claim to full human status and which humans cannot," I use "Black" and "People of African descent" synonymously.

2. Scott, Darieck. *Extravagant Abjection: Blackness, Power and Sexuality in African American Literary Imagination*, NYU Press, 2010. pp. 108.

3. Butler, Judith. *Precarious Life: The Power of Mourning and Violence*. Verso, 2014.

4. For a detailed analysis of anti-blackness, see: Burden-Stelly, Charisse. "Constructing Deportable Subjectivity: Anti-foreignness, Antiradicalism, and Antiblackness during the McCarthyist Structure of Feeling." *Souls*, vol. 19 no. 3, 2017, pp. 342-358.

5. Mahmud Tayyab. "Precarious Existence and Capitalism: A Permanent State of Exception." *Southwestern University Law Review* vol. 44, 2015, pp. 699–726.

6. Davies, Carole Boyce. "Deportable Subjects: U.S. Immigration Laws and the Criminalization of Communism," *The South Atlantic Quarterly* vol. 100, 2001, pp. 949-966.

7. Collins, Patricia H. "Learning from the Outsider Within: The Sociological Significance of Black Feminist Thought," *Social Problems* vol. 33, no. 6, 1986 pp. 14-32.

8. Quijano, Anibal. "Colonialidad y modernidad/racionalidad." 1989. Reprinted in *Los conquistados. 1492 y la población indígena de las Américas*.

9. Mbembe, Achille. "Decolonizing the university: New directions." *Arts and Humanities in Higher Education*, vol 15, no. 1, 2016, pp. 29-45.

Review

MAGGIE L. N. FELISBERTO

Kale Soup and the Portuguese-American Soul: The Work of Millicent Borges Accardi

Millicent Borges Accardi, a Portuguese-American poet from California, has dedicated much of her art and her time as a fundraiser and event coordinator to advancing Portuguese culture in American literature. As a poet, Accardi's writing is soft around the edges, full of whispers and intrigue, mimicking the sounds of spoken Portuguese through primarily English words. While she writes on a wide array of themes and topics, her lyrical sensibility belies her cultural background and enhances her "non-Portuguese" poems. This deep connection to her cultural background spurred Accardi to establish the *Kale Soup for the Soul* reading series.

When talking about Accardi, it is impossible not to speak about *Kale Soup for the Soul*. The traveling reading series, which was founded in 2011 and began in earnest in 2012 with their first event in Chicago during the AWP conference, has grown over the years to become a key component of Portuguese-American literature. *Kale Soup* events have taken place at conferences, universities and Portuguese clubs around the country, each time presenting a rotating cast of poets and prose writers whose writing is connected through the themes of food and family, and through the shared cultural experience of Luso-America.

This reading series, the first of its kind for the Portuguese-American writing community, has found success in its ability to attract a diverse crowd, both in terms of readers and audience members. At a 2015 AWP panel on fundraising, Accardi spoke about the effect that *Kale Soup* has on potential funders, saying that "once someone gets a picture of what we do, they start trying to figure out how they can plug this into their environment. Like Tom Sawyer painting a fence, our enthusiasm about Portuguese culture has an addictive affect." This addictive affect extends to the writers and the audience as well.

Over thirty different writers have read as part of *Kale Soup*, myself included, and the type of audience is completely different each time. Some *Kale Soup* events take place on college campuses, funded in part by the universities, and those audiences are larger and include many high school and undergraduate students of creative writing. A *Kale Soup* event affiliated with a conference like AWP will see

MFA students and established authors sipping wine and sampling Portuguese refreshments—kale soup, if it can be found; other petiscos if not.

Some *Kale Soup* events take place at Portuguese clubs, which bring in the Portuguese audience. This is where *Kale Soup for the Soul* shines the brightest. *Kale Soup* was born out of a desire to "connect with Portuguese communities in the US by sharing stories and writing workshops," a goal which became part of the official mission statement. At readings with primarily Portuguese and Portuguese-American audiences, the atmosphere is electric with a heavy sense of community. As *Kale Soup* writer Carlo Matos says, "I thought I was the only person exploring the Portuguese-American experience. What a relief it was to find others who were in the exact same boat I was."

"Branding is everything," Accardi went on to say in that 2015 panel. "We could have been called the Portuguese Writers Association or the Luso-American Academic Snobby Club, but no, we called it something else. We reached out to a sense of community, to a familiar touchstone, to a place where food acts as an entry point to so much more. Everyone who has a Portuguese heritage recognizes kale soup as comfort food, as something they remember from childhood, and once you taste it, you want more."

Accardi's poetry is like that kale soup—once you taste it, you want more. In her fourth book, *Only More So*, Accardi achieves a balance of flavors from childhood to California to feminism, from Portuguese-American life to World War II. For a collection of poems, having so many different topics and angles could cause the book as a whole to feel disjointed, but *Only More So* carries itself throughout, and while only a few poems in the book specifically make reference to Portuguese-American life, where they are placed is careful and deliberate. The result is a book of poems that is distinctly Portuguese, despite not having much luso content. The pieces that do focus on Portuguese and Portuguese-American culture grapple with them unabashedly.

In "The Last Borges," the speaker wrestles with her desire to have had training in Portuguese from her father, who instead chose to raise her as solely English speaking. The frustration of a stolen language and the sorrow of perhaps never getting it back drips on every line. In the fifth stanza, when she says, "I would catch you: sitting at/ Rudy the barber's chair/ I would sneak up behind to hear/ foreign words," the speaker is reaching for the language, and by extension the culture, while simultaneously sneaking, as if to speak Portuguese were a transgression. Just a couple stanzas down, she adds that "After a while it seemed/

that someone else/ had heard a grandmother's/ lullabies at night." This disconnection from her own experience is iconic of the immigrant child, and particularly to Accardi's generation and the generation before of Portuguese-Americans whose parents were so concerned with adapting to the English-speaking US that their children never had the opportunity to learn their parents' native tongue.

This pain and frustration reaches its sharp apex in the final stanza, when the speaker confesses that "the only Portuguese words/ you ever gave me do not stand for love./ Que queres, que queres/ What do you want, what do you want." In Portuguese, this phrase can come off as curt and affronted, whereas in English the same phrase is imploring and nearly desperate when paired with the Portuguese. What do you want? There is a simple answer, based on the body of the poem, that the speaker wants to be able to communicate in Portuguese. But there is a more complex answer, wrapped up in the reaching for a world that could have been hers, reaching for a father who could have been more present if only a language had changed between them. This experience is emblematic of Portuguese-American life.

Another poem that grapples, though in a very different way, with Portuguese-American life is "Breaking with the Old," a poem about New Bedford, MA. At the heart of the largest Portuguese-American community, New Bedford is inescapable. Accardi herself was born in New Bedford and lived there as a child until her family relocated to California, and her relationship with the city is just as complex as the poem. Written partially by glossing the Urban Dictionary entry on New Bedford, "Breaking with the Old" is a poem of dissatisfaction, befitting the once dying city in Southeast Massachusetts. In the act of leaving, the speaker recalls "the city on the south coast where you can eat linguisa/ and Jag. A place where you know to stay away from/ The Front after dark" without fondness. The festas that are iconic of Portuguese culture are treated with a dismissive flippancy: "you know that Sassaquin Pizzao/ isn't really New Beige, but then you get dressed up/ to go to the Madeira feast, or the Holy Ghost./ And even you can prove the Dartmouth refs get paid off." The second half of the poem builds into a list of aka's, each one more violent than the last. It begins as "New Bedford/ Mass, I say, aka 20 aka the secret city" before moving into "aka the new war zone/ Aka the new Baghdad aka the druggy capital of the world." This violent imagery transitions to an ending which, like "The Last Borges," emphasizes the things unsaid. In "The Last Borges," what is unsaid is intimate, the love between father and daughter. Here, however, that silence is city wide: "And here's the bit most people don't know/ this but it's called *the secret city because there is no snitching/ in New Bedford.* No one ever tells. New Beige, a place where half/ of the hell of this city don't even speak."

Her most Portuguese-centric poem in the book, "How to Shake off the Policidade Segurança Publica Circa 1970" is another poem that deals in secrets and things unsaid. In this poem, the speaker follows a man as he walks home through Lisbon, putting forth his best effort to appear non-threatening to the regime. The speaker advises him to "Carry an ordinary/ briefcase. Dress in shades of brown,/ as if you could fold/ up and turn back/ into dirt if you needed to." The figure ducks into crowded establishments and hides in upstairs rooms where he doesn't belong, hoping to evade an ill-fate at the hands of the regime. In a way, all Portuguese writing post-Salazar must be in communication with the effects of the Estado Novo, and Portuguese-American writing is no different.

This poem is different from Accardi's other offerings directly related to the Portuguese-American experience, but in the book it is placed after a run of four poems written about World War II and the Holocaust. This placement is essential for all five poems in helping them each carry the weight they deserve, and is well-thought for an audience that may not be familiar with modern Portuguese history. By tying the PSP to WWII and the Nazis, Accardi challenges our historical narrative and forces us to reexamine Portugal, which as a nation remained neutral throughout WWII. By reexamining Portugal, we as Portuguese-Americans grow in our culture and in our connection to our roots. That desire present in "The Last Borges" is fulfilled, though in a way much more somber than anticipated. However, to be somber is also something that comes naturally to the Portuguese.

MAGGIE L. N. FELISBERTO is a Ph.D. student at UMass Dartmouth in Luso-Afro-Brazilian Studies and Theory and the editor of *Pre-existing Poems*, an online poetry journal dedicated to work about healthcare and medical conditions. She holds an MFA in Creative Writing from the University of Tampa in fiction. She was a 2014 FLAD/Disquiet Luso-American Scholarship recipient. Her work has appeared in the Portuguese-American Review and Behind the Stars, More Stars. Her family lives primarily in the Setúbal region, between Azeitão and Sesimbra.